FROM SMOLLETT

TO JAMES / Studies in the

Novel and Other Essays

Presented to

Edgar Johnson

FROM SMOLLETT TO JAMES / Studies in the Novel and Other Essays Presented to Edgar Johnson

---

EDITED BY Samuel I. Mintz

Alice Chandler and Christopher Mulvey

UNIVERSITY PRESS OF VIRGINIA

CHARLOTTESVILLE

THE UNIVERSITY PRESS OF VIRGINIA
Copyright © 1981 by the Rector and Visitors
of the University of Virginia
Chapter 1 copyright © 1981 by Leon Edel
Chapter 2 copyright © 1981 by David Daiches
Chapter 11 copyright © 1981 by J. Hillis Miller

First published 1981

Library of Congress Cataloging in Publication Data
Main entry under title:

From Smollett to James.

"Checklist of the printed works of Edgar Johnson"; p. 289
Includes index.
CONTENTS: Chandler, A. Edgar Johnson.—Edel, L. Principia biographica.—Daiches, D. Smollett reconsidered.—Raleigh, J. H. Scott and Pushkin.—Hart, F. R. The regency novel of fashion. [etc.]
 1. English fiction—19th century—History and criticism—Addresses, essays, lectures. 2. Fiction—Addresses, essays, lectures. 3. Biography (as a literary form)—Addresses, essays, lectures. 4. Johnson, Edgar. I. Johnson, Edgar. II. Mintz, Samuel I. III. Chandler, Alice. IV. Mulvey, Christopher.
PR863.F7   823'.03   7925865
ISBN 0-8139-0663-6

Printed in the United States of America

CONTENTS

PREFACE			vii
Alice Chandler		EDGAR JOHNSON / An Appreciation	ix
Leon Edel	1	PRINCIPIA BIOGRAPHICA Notes for a Preface	1
David Daiches	2	Smollett Reconsidered	11
John Henry Raleigh	3	Scott and Pushkin	48
Frances Russell Hart	4	The Regency Novel of Fashion	84
Lionel Stevenson	5	Thackeray's Dramatic Monologues	134
Philip Collins	6	Special Correspondent to Posterity / How Dickens's Contemporaries Saw His Fictional World	157

George H. Ford	7 |	Light in Darkness / Gas, Oil, and Tallow in Dickens's *Bleak House* 183
Jerome H. Buckley	8 |	George Eliot's Double Life / *The Mill on the Floss* as a Bildungsroman 211
D. A. Robertson, Jr.	9 |	Weave a Circle / Baron Kirkup and His Greatest Friends 237
Gordon S. Haight	10 |	Strether's Chad Newsome / A Reading of James's *The Ambassadors* 261
J. Hillis Miller	11 |	Character in the Novel / A "Real Illusion" 277

Checklist of the Printed Works of Edgar Johnson   289

Contributors   295

Index   297

PREFACE

The essays in this volume were solicited by its editors from among colleagues and friends of Edgar Johnson. They were asked to write on subjects relating to the British novel—chiefly though not exclusively of the nineteenth century—or on subjects that are related to Edgar Johnson's profound interest in biography. To the latter category belong the essays by Leon Edel and David Robertson. The remainder of the essays, constituting the bulk of the volume, are on the novel considered in its broadest aspects, whether from the standpoint of literary history and criticism, cultural history, comparative literature, or the theory of fiction.

This book would have seen the light of day sooner than it has were it not for the financial crisis into which the city of New York (and hence also the City College) were plunged. Publication was assisted by a grant from the Research Fund of the English Department of City College. Other financial assistance was rendered by individual members, past and present, of the college, as well as by friends in the larger scholarly community. We are grateful for encouragement and other help given by Theodore Gross, Samuel Middlebrook, Edward Quinn, Gordon Ray, John D. Rosenberg, Irving Rosenthal, the late James L. Clifford, and the late Lionel Trilling.

Samuel I. Mintz
The City College
The City University
of New York

EDGAR JOHNSON / *An Appreciation*

Alice Chandler

In his preface to a new edition of one of his books, Edgar Johnson comments on the difference between his younger and older selves, saying that he is in many ways "the grandson, almost the great-grandson" of the man who wrote the book. A career in letters that spans more than half a century gives ample opportunity for the development of a series of selves. It is characteristic of Edgar Johnson's sequence of selves that they are all literary, revealing the man of letters as scholar, biographer, teacher, critic, editor, poet, novelist, and voluminous reviewer of books.

Born in Brooklyn in 1901, Johnson entered Columbia College at the end of World War I, majoring omnivorously in English. After graduation in 1922, he taught at Columbia for two years before a brief teaching stint at Washington University, where he prevailed upon the editor of The *St. Louis Post-Dispatch* to let him write book reviews. In 1927 he joined the faculty of City College as a tutor, again managing to involve himself, even as a very junior faculty member, in active book reviewing for the lively New York newspaper world of the 1920s.

As a teacher Johnson favored the lecture method. His students, some of whom are among the most distinguished graduates of the college, remember him as one of their most stimulating teachers. They recall the clarity of his mind, his wit, his use of lively anecdote and apposite quotation, and the astonishing flow of periodic sentences always grateful to the ear. He achieved through the lecture method something of the eminence that his colleague Morris Raphael Cohen gained through the use of the Socratic method, and like Cohen he served as a model for aspiring writers and scholars. Johnson is also warmly remembered for his fifteen-year chairmanship of the English Department. His five terms were marked by the doubling of the full- and part-time faculty to more than 130 members, the expansion of honors work, and the development of graduate programs in English at the City College and at the Graduate Center of the City University. In 1972 City College awarded Edgar Johnson the degree of Doctor of Letters, *honoris causa*. He is now Distinguished Professor Emeritus.

Recipient of both Fulbright and Guggenheim fellowships, Johnson served as a visiting professor at a number of noted institutions; appeared on radio and television programs; and was on the editorial boards of Dell Publishing, *Nineteenth-Century Fiction*, and Funk and Wagnall's *New Standard Dictionary*. He was also President of the American Center of P.E.N. and has been active in the Dickens Fellowship and other professional and literary associations both in America and abroad.

Johnson's first published book, *Unweave a Rainbow: A Sentimental Fantasy* (1931), strikes the keynote for much that follows. Its hero, an aspiring writer, pursues the life of the idealizing imagination, as symbolized by his love for the timelessly beautiful Cynthia, who endows even the most ordinary and unlikely objects "with wonder and beauty." She serves as a foil to hard-boiled materialism, on the one hand, and to science and technology, on the other. If the hero's intellectual progress involves the repudiation of the mechanistic view of life, it also involves the painful realization that the mind is not free from the mutations of time and that his visionary Cynthia, transcendent in her immutable perfection, is only a figment of his imagination. The novel closes with the realization that "only in things, and in the beauty of things, was there refuge." For it is only "the form and the perfume and loveliness of things" that are real.

The somewhat melodramatic *The Praying Mantis* (1937)

is an inverted mystery novel in which the true subject is not "who done it?" but "why was it done?" It represents something of a digression from Johnson's major themes. *One Mighty Torrent: The Drama of Biography,* also published in 1937, is very much in the mainstream. Biography represents to Johnson the "living sense of personality" without which the "abstractions of history are only half-truths." In his characteristically visual and cadenced prose, he epitomizes the contrast between history and biography by comparing the abstraction we name Queen Anne with the "stout lady richly dressed," who touched Samuel Johnson for scrofula and walked with her steep-periwigged courtiers and statesmen among the topiary work and rose-flushed brick parterres of Hampton Court. For Johnson, the grand themes of biography are the "great interests and activities of humanity . . . money, ambition, religion, truth-seeking, happiness, love." He tends to see the great curve of history as revealing the ascendance of democracy and a benevolent science, although his view is well tempered by realism. Biography is a hybrid muse for him, "inspired by the power of imagination, but ever held, too, within the limits of what has actually been attained among all the range of the possible." As in *Unweave a Rainbow,* the book concludes by celebrating the plenitude of human existence. Its last words are a quotation from Ruskin: "There is no wealth but life."

The significance of literature as a criticism of society is the theme of Johnson's lengthy introduction to *A Treasury of Satire* (1945). Much broadened and deepened, the relationship between literature, especially humor, and society permeates *Charles Dickens: His Tragedy and Triumph* (1952). The work of many years, the book was both critically and popularly acclaimed as the definitive biography of Dickens for this century, praised for its massive research, psychological acumen, critical insight, and eminent readability. In this book, Johnson again shows his novelistic flair both in his vivid narration of Dickens's personal drama and by his evocative rendering of the novels and tales. Aware of the darker elements in Dickens's imagination that lie below the surface everywhere, from the intercalary tales in *Pickwick* to the nightmarelike subsurface of *Our Mutual Friend,* Johnson focuses primarily on Dickens as a social critic. He states that "on every level, everywhere, Dickens shows the money ethic of an acquisitive society, crippling human nature and blighting the flowering of humane values." The restoration of values, however, lies not so much in a restructuring of society as in a reordering of the self. As Johnson states in his discussion of *Our Mutual Friend,* "in the individual, learning control for generous ends, in the love of the human heart, lies the hope that can conquer the dust-heap and bring fruitful bloom back to the waste land."

Like his Dickens study, *Sir Walter Scott: The Great Unknown* (1970) is the definitive biography for the century. Indeed, after Lockhart and Johnson, it is unlikely that any future biographer will again attempt on the same scale to assault that sheer mountain of detail, particularly the financial transactions, that Johnson has so lucidly and objectively portrayed. His vivid and detailed analyses of the poems and novels, though criticized by some reviewers as too generous, will also be difficult to supercede.

Johnson's study of biography as a genre equips him to recognize the role that history plays in the Waverley Novels. He sees Scott as the great novelist of history, aware of the interplay between the individual and a shaping society and fully conscious of the high drama that is eternally played out by those mighty contraries, past and present. Like Lukács, Johnson sees Scott as recognizing that the great transformations of history are really the transformations of popular life—an awareness borne in on him by both his wide reading and his deeply ingrained familiarity with his own Scottish background. In the current critical tradition, Johnson argues against the superficial interpretation of Scott that sees him as a romantic because he wrote about romantic topics. Far more important to Johnson is Scott's immersion in eighteenth-century rationalism and common sense, which he believes guided both Scott's literary and personal development.

In many ways Johnson's study of Scott reflects the more

realistic side of his own hybrid muse. Using a leaner prose style, he concentrates more on the external details of Scott's life and surroundings than he did in the more internalized portrait of Dickens. The nature of the subject, and perhaps Johnson's own intellectual evolution, lead him to concentrate on Scott's judgment and balance quite as much as on his fecund imagination. The major theme is the same one that has always attracted Johnson, the struggle between "the life-denying and the life-fulfilling." But the artist himself is the protagonist. As Johnson sees the drama of Scott's existence, the whole world vibrated "with his bravery, his stoic control, his noble love of the noble, his undismayed contemplation of impersonal fortune and the struggle of mankind."

Edgar Johnson's extraordinary verbal felicity, his confirmed belief that literature is the only true subject of conversation, his unquenchable love of reading, his prolific output of books and other writing, and his lifetime of activity in literary and scholarly circles, all proclaim him quintessentially the man of letters. In a literary career that has spanned more than half a century, he has remained wonderfully unperturbed by the currents of critical style; Marxist interpretation, the New Criticism, Freudianism, structuralism, psychobiography, have all passed him by. It is no accident that he has written the definitive studies of the two nineteenth-century giants of the English novel who most completely captured the imagination of their day, for his is the synthesizing intellect that can absorb and interpret their largeness. Not every critic can or should be an Edgar Johnson. But those who do share his gifts for utter absorption in his subject, for long years of patient study and research, for breadth of understanding, for psychological and literary sensitivity, and for vivid and evocative prose will be among the most valuable critics of an era, not just for other scholars but for the more general reader as well. Accompanied and aided in all his endeavors by his wife Eleanor, Edgar Johnson serves as an example of that perennial figure, the scholar-humanist, whose achievement is honored in this book.

FROM SMOLLETT

TO JAMES / Studies in the

Novel and Other Essays

Presented to

Edgar Johnson

1 | PRINCIPIA BIOGRAPHICA

Notes for a Preface

Leon Edel

Je veux faire parler les silences de l'histoire. To make history's silences speak: this was Michelet's wish. But ours is that they should not say too much. An historian of human lives, endowed with a rage of curiosity, does not want to be drowned in a roar of voices. An interminable chronicle of the hours, days, years is no longer needed. The gaps modern biography must bridge are those Virginia Woolf called "moments of being." And what survives can have its own measured eloquence. I once knew an old French scholar who, in his youth and passion for English poetry, went on a walking tour through Italy. He sought every landscape, every town, every house mentioned by the Romantics. On the Grand Canal he met a grizzled gondolier who described the way in which Byron threw open his casement every morning and flung gold coins on the stones of Venice—shaking with laughter at the scramble of penury and greed. I once met a man who sat in the same box at a play with Henry James. What had he noticed? Few had had a chance to be as close to the distancing Master. My informant said "he had one of those faces—a kind of transparent whiteness of the skin—that made him seem blue-shaven." This tiny bit of visual information seemed as credible as the glimpse of an insolent young English poet scattering largesse out of a Venetian window. Tiny moments surface in the great silences. The color of James's blue-shave, the gestures of Byron—moments of existence, moments of things seen and heard, out of which we write some part of the poetry of human lives.

Biography is a noble and adventurous art, as noble as the making of painted portraits, poems, statues. We know how a painter can give voices to an entire wall; and a sculptor, with skill of chisel and eye, can bring durable life to clay. So a biographer fashions a man or woman out of documents, words. Poetry talks in icons and symbols. A novelist, in his omniscience, knows the measure of his characters, out of his passion for all sorts and conditions of human life. The biographer however begins with certain limiting little facts. "How," exclaimed Virginia Woolf when she sat down to write the life of her friend Roger Fry—"how can one make a life out of six cardboard boxes full of tailors' bills, love letters and old picture postcards?" How indeed? Yet Virginia Woolf was able to construct a singular life by using such facts as she possessed and bridging the silences with the poetry of her observing and constructing imagination. Her biographer friend Lytton Strachey spoke of his art as "the most delicate and humane of all the branches of the art of writing." No more delicate, I am sure, than verse, or certain forms of drama. Biography, however, has a particular kind of delicacy. It seeks to evoke life out of inert materials—in a shoebox or an attic—records of endeavor and imagination, cupidity and terror, kindness and love. Strachey called the writing of lives humane, I believe, because it is a refining and civilizing process: it deals after all with strange, volatile, delicately orchestrated beings. The ambiguous records are packed with the contradictions of life itself. A biography (as I have had occasion to say) is a record in words of something that is as mercurial and as flowing, as compact of temperament and spirit, as the entire human being. Perhaps this is what Yeats implied when he wrote "we may come to think that nothing exists but a stream of souls, that all knowledge is biography." Is it not true that all that we know, all that we discover, all that we feel, comes from this stream of souls, and from our own soul or inwardness—human stuff and human sagacity? Every step forward or backward in civilization has been a human step. Behind every mask (Yeats again) there has always been a human face.

Not all artists or historians have such an exalted notion of biography. Some feel it to be a prying, peeping, and even predatory process. Biography has been called "a disease of English literature" (George Eliot); professional biographers have been called "hyenas" (Edward Sackville-West). They have also been called "psycho-plagiarists" (Nabokov), and biography has been said to be "always superfluous" and "usually in bad taste" (Auden). Nabokov and Auden felt strongly that lives of individuals who were writers cannot and should not be written. The works writers create—the traced imaginations—suffice; I think they would argue no personal gloss is required. The New Criticism certainly held to this view: the "biographical fallacy" was critical dogma. It is the work, not the life, they said, that counts. In using the word "psycho-plagiarist," Nabokov suggests that biographers are individuals who somehow complete their own lives by writing the lives of others. Such identifications might indeed be called a form of plagiarism; the biographer totally immerses his Self in the Self of his subject. According to Nabokov, he seeks to fortify or reconstruct his own ego by using someone else's. Proust said as much of critics: they were incomplete men, he said, who complete themselves with the work of another. Nevertheless, in biography—whatever the biographer's motivations—a work takes its form, for better or worse. And if the work counts, it is like the breath of the human body, and that body counts as well. A writer writes out of his whole physical, as well as mental, being. I am not sure the work and the life can be dissociated. As Sainte-Beuve reminded us, *tel arbre tel fruit*.

Written lives engender strong feelings. Yet the biographer works within the unavoidable limitations and restraints of which Virginia Woolf spoke. Biography, we must remind ourselves, is a nascent art even though hundreds of lives are written every year. And it is vulnerable. The antibiography of Nabokov and Auden reflects artistic reticences. Auden's repeated assertion that biography is "superfluous" may indeed have been more than fear of revelations or even a belief in the sufficiency of his own works. He kept few secrets from his readers. There wasn't much to reveal: his homosexuality was known. Perhaps he felt no further dredging was required. Certainly he had read a great many incompetent biographies. Perhaps he was frightened—enough bad lives are published to frighten any great man. And Auden, moreover, was not alone. William Makepeace Thackeray died commanding that there be "no biography." Matthew Arnold did the same. And in our time, T. S. Eliot. But Eliot also admitted that "the line between curiosity which is legitimate and that which is merely harmless, and between that which is merely harmless and that which is vulgarly impertinent, can never be precisely drawn." Henry James went much further. He called down Shakespeare's curse on anyone who might try to stir his bones. Let us add that Arnold and Thackeray almost succeeded. Their heirs obediently lowered a curtain: they shut all the doors. When the lives were ultimately written, in a later generation, there had been so great a lapse of time that the biographers worked in considerable detachment and distance. To this day we have had no satisfactory life of Matthew Arnold, and Gordon Ray's pioneer life of Thackeray became possible only after he created a monumental edition of Thackeray's letters. T. S. Eliot, as I write, is being loyally defended by his widow. In spite of her efforts, certain "vulgarly impertinent" biographies have appeared. Henry James was defended by his nephew and executor. He had also taken personal precautions. He burned his papers in a great bonfire in his garden at Lamb House. Like Dickens, who lit a similar fire at Gad's Hill (as Edgar Johnson tells us), he could not burn letters which had reached other's hands. When his nephew died, James's own epistolary genius, like Thackeray's, betrayed him. His life was made possible because thousands of letters had been treasured and saved. We may note that Auden's request in his will beseeching his friends to burn his letters is not being scrupulously heeded. To some of them it would seem like burning Auden himself.

The novel, still hardy and in late middle age, seems to have run its course as a form. One wonders whether there is much more to be learned about the craft of fiction, after the experiments of James, Proust, Joyce, Kafka, and the *nouveau roman*. In its three centuries, fiction galloped from the epistolary-picaresque to the high-dramatic, through phases we label "romantic-realism" and "naturalism-symbolism." From dealing with the outwardness of things, the novel tried to describe "the stream of consciousness"—indulging in angles of vision, simultaneities, and spatial form, as if the novel were a camera. But if fiction has, it seems, exhausted experiment, there remains much to be learned about biography. It cannot claim narrative sophistications. It is backward enough still to invoke Boswell as a supreme model, forgetting that not all biographers can know their subjects as a living presence. Nor has life-writing developed a freedom of form and structure approximating the novelist's freedoms: even as it has not articulated a "methodology." There is a book called *The Craft of Fiction*, but no such book exists for biography. By its very nature, biography has been wedded always—and always will be—to the document, to fact and anecdote, and certainly to gossip; and it will have to reckon increasingly with the portentous libraries heaped around modern figures. Also, in opposition to the novel, it may not invent conversation. The world does a great deal of talking—but rarely in biographies. This is biography's greatest limitation. One of the reasons for the enduring charm and force of Boswell is that he recorded Johnson's words and wit—one suspects, accurately—because Boswell himself could not have invented such talk. The tape recorder will be an increasingly useful instrument in providing "oral history" for biographers; but the essential character of the art remains unchanged. As I had occasion to say in *Literary*

Biography (1957), "the biographer may be as imaginative as he pleases—the more imaginative the better—in the way in which he brings together his materials." "But," I added, "the biographer *must not imagine his materials.*" Here lies the heart of our problem. A biographer's narrative imagination is fettered by the very nature of his enterprise. He may be judged therefore by the resourcefulness with which he works—within prescribed conditions. Biographers must be neat, orderly, logical, detached, perhaps even finicky in their tidiness—and yet in this very process they must arrive at the elusive flamelike human spirit which delights in defying order and neatness and logic—and endures so many hours and days doing quite ordinary things, the kitchen work of life.

We have reached a moment in literary history when time and circumstance summon biography to declare itself and its principles. Can it take its place as a primary art form? I would like to think so; and it should summon poets and novelists to attempt the form instead of leaving it (in Strachey's phrase) to "journeymen of letters." Biography has been the wayward child of individual talents; it has suffered, through three centuries, from a lack of definition, a laxity of method. The biographical feeling inherent in man which gave us the vignettes and stories of the Old Testament and the lives of Christ, which guided Plutarch to write his fabled narratives making us party to the passions of the ancient world, has culminated in singularly few masterpieces. Buried within the unexplored narrative forms of biography is an urge to charter a human odyssey. The fabulous and the magical, the tales of man as a creative enigma, give way now to the exactitudes of science. And caught up in a technological society, man tends to feel himself increasingly dehumanized; thus he once more reaches for the lives of others to assure himself of the commonalities of existence. Biography, when it dealt with ancient times, could allow itself freedoms of conjecture: the material was thin; much of it was folktale and the biographer had to make his peace with Michelet's silences—the royal grant of wine acorded Chaucer, Shakespeare's second-best bed. The historian of human lives, in his saturation, could allow himself, at best, an "educated" guess. Like the architect, he might extrapolate columns from fragments. Still, biography has lacked the courage to discover bolder ways of human reconstruction. Our times certainly provide wider latitudes.

What gives strength to biographers is the science of anthropology, the observations of the social sciences, above all the explorations of the individual psyche opened up by Freud. The new "science of man" offers biography a new role in literature and in history. It tells biography that it has for too long grasped the "empirical" and has smothered itself too much in externals. There have been too many graveyard lives, the panegyrics Strachey mocked. The celebration of worthies is still considered sufficient—at a moment when there has opened for us new horizons which enable us to use both technology and art in capturing extinct lives. The best counsel Lytton Strachey could give to practitioners was that biography should possess a "becoming brevity": that we should emulate French writers of memoirs and lives, like Fontenelle and Condorcet. These compressed "into a few shining pages the manifold existences of men." Strachey's advice relates principally to craft; yet it implies a great deal of insight into the nature of men *within* their manifold existences. Virginia Woolf wrote more than a dozen brilliant essays on biography. In essence, they talked of the struggle between the "granite" of fact and the "rainbow" of fiction. She also wrote a fable for biographers in *Orlando;* and a history of the scent of things, when (in her highly imaginative way) she adumbrated a life for Elizabeth Barrett Browning's dog. Having written two imagined biographies, one of an androgynous protean human who takes varied shapes through the centuries and the other of a canine, she finally wrote the life of the art critic Roger Fry. Her diaries reveal how she felt harnessed to "fact" while her mind struggled for the freedom of her fancy. If we go back two centuries, we find Boswell, the architect of one kind of modern biography, secure in his intimate knowledge of Dr Johnson, whom he had observed closely for two decades. He boasted that he would not melt down his materials. He wanted the voice of his subject to be constantly heard. "I cannot conceive," said Boswell, "a more perfect mode of writing any man's life than . . . interweaving what he privately wrote, and said, and thought." Splendid, indeed, when one has access to the subject in the flesh! What would Boswell have done with a modern tape recorder? Let us imagine him confronting, at the end of twenty years, a house filled with tapes; he would have been forced to melt down his materials or be choked by them. Boswell was, in any event, being ingenuous; his "oral history" had the benefit of condensations from the first. It was imposed by the labor of the tracing pen in the remarkable minutes he kept of Dr Johnson's aggressive and pungent manner of conversation. No other instrument was available to him. In the very process of writing these minutes (he did not use shorthand), he selected and even at times "melted down" his data. Yet in spite of this, one reviewer complained that Boswell's gold had not been "ingotted."

His doctrine, or the workshop observations of the moderns, hardly constitute a *principia biographica*. Such a *principia*, less formal and scientific than those of mathematics and philosophy, or the anatomies of criticism of our time, might now be set down in a modest way. Let us recognize that the explorations of Sigmund Freud and his successors have created a new province for biographical adventure and knowledge, and a new audience eager to study particular kinds of human nature and the motivations of human achievement. We might even enunciate certain principles for those increasingly attracted to the recording and telling of human lives. One would be that the writings and utterances of any subject contain more secrets of character and personality than we have hitherto allowed. A life-myth is hidden within every poet's work, and in the gestures of a politician, the canvases and statues of art and the "lifestyles" of charismatic characters. Whole "case histories" could be compiled out of revealed experience, out of what human beings "express." In this way we can draw larger conclusions about an inner life, of which the "outer" life is constant expression. Some such principles come to us from the new psychology.

In recognition that biography is accorded at present a secondary place in literary studies, we may note the continuing vogue of what some critics have called "an age of criticism." Biography deals with so much human stuff that the interest of both the critical and the lay reader has resided in the materials and not in their form or their manner of presentation. When the media speak of the "Nixon story" or "the Patton story," it sounds as if there were only one story to be told. The New Criticism would not listen when the new biography argued that the poet is his poem, the novelist his novel. Criticism, singularly self-centered, refused to understand that a critic is constantly involved not only in his own process, which he regards with such self-absorption and often self-indulgence, but in a biographical process as well. The winds of change can be seen in the curious theorems of critics like Harold Bloom, who uses Freudian generalizations, and splashes about in biography. In this indirect way, such a critic is announcing the belated wedding of biography and criticism; but also of biography and psychology—or to put it another way, he announces the gradual awakening of criticism to the fact of an inexorable and undivorceable marriage. Is it not strange that many critics who attempted to write lives floundered in the archives? They thought of biography only in Boswellian terms; they felt as if the recital of the classic laundry lists was what biography really is. The critical ego often is so deeply concerned with critical ideas and their justification, that it is incapable of empathy with the vicissitudes of lived lives. So we are now in the process of putting the poet back into his poem after trying to remove him or to drown him in floods of critical explication. We are beginning to understand—what historians knew always—that literary history is a record of what happens from the moment an imaginative writer puts pen to paper, or speaks words into an electronic device, or applies his fingers to a typewriter keyboard. The world's curiosity asks more insistently than ever for the humanity of the lived life. It wants to know how poems or stories, paintings or music, politicians or soldiers, came into being. Strange indeed the ways in which poets themselves in popular readings of their words, facing enraptured audiences, have found it expedient to talk of their art, their thoughts, their divorces, their children. The impersonal poet and his impersonal poem disappear. A whole new land of biography has been opened by "confessional poetry." Biography seems to be at a threshold. Individuals in our society proclaim their lives from the rooftops. Our greatest problem is to find artists equal to the task of setting them down.

2 | SMOLLETT RECONSIDERED

David Daiches

Smollett is something of an odd man out in the history of our literature. In spite of the significant influence he had on both Scott and Dickens, he has not come in for modern revaluation as one of the pioneers of the English novel, as have Defoe, Richardson, and Fielding. He is not discussed, except for an occasional casual aside, in Ian Watt's influential study *The Rise of the Novel;* indeed, Watt specifically excludes Smollett, observing that he "has many merits as a social reporter and as a humorist, but the manifest flaws in the central situations and the general structure of all his novels except *Humphrey Clinker* . . . prevent him from playing a very important role in the main tradition of the novel." He is of course wholly excluded from F. R. Leavis's "great tradition" of English fiction, and he is not given separate mention in the index to the twenty volumes of *Scrutiny,* though he is briefly alluded to in a review of a book on Dickens as being one of the sources of Dickens's brand of humor, with the additional comment: "Smollett had no subtlety; he is coarse and crude in a way that Fielding never is, and this element, toned down to Victorian requirements, is very obvious in Dickens." The Americans have concentrated either on his biography and personal relationships, as in the work of Lewis Knapp, or on constructing hypotheses concerning the influence on his handling of character and action of eighteenth-century Scottish philosophers, as in Morris Golden's interesting but doctrinaire *Smollett and the Scottish School*. Few seem concerned with a critical reappraisal of Smollett's work.

Students of English literature read *Humphrey Clinker*, his last and undoubtedly his best novel, but as a rule know of *Roderick Random* and *Peregrine Pickle* only by repute as robust picaresque novels of adventure which hold no special attractions for the modern reader. His third novel, *Ferdinand Count Fathom*, is unknown to most modern university students of English even by name, and in any case the history of an out-and-out rogue who undergoes a sudden and puzzling conversion to virtue at the end of the book can hardly be expected to compete for students' attention either with the genuine rogue literature of the Elizabethans or with Fielding's gravely ironical *Jonathan Wild the Great* or Thackeray's *Barry Lyndon*. Smollett's fourth and penultimate novel, *Sir Launcelot Greaves*, is pretty well universally dismissed by critics, when they concern themselves with it at all, as a feeble attempt to produce an eighteenth-century *Don Quixote*.

Yet I think that it is with *Sir Launcelot Greaves* that a reappraisal of Smollett might well begin. For preposterous though the idea is of an eighteenth-century knight in armor riding round the English countryside to redress wrongs, and absurd, melodramatic, contrived, and coincidental as the course of action in the novel is, *Sir Launcelot Greaves* is the novel in which Smollett exposes most directly the moral center which lies at the heart of all his fiction and gives it proportion and meaning. Smollett is not generally presented as a moralist. His own deep sense of personal grievance, his crotchetiness, his masochistic descriptions of motiveless violence and cruelty, his belligerent coarseness in writing of smells and excretions—all this, combined with the apparently episodic nature of his plots, which seem to have no other function than to entertain the reader until the author is too fatigued to carry on, suggests the amoral if not immoral writer whose only object is to amuse and shock simultaneously. Nevertheless, Smollett was essentially a moralist and a man of feeling, deeply moved by human suffering, especially if it was caused by deliberate injustice or wanton cruelty. All his novels contain scenes in which a good man is brought into personal contact with some terrible example of injustice and suffering and is enabled to undo the injustice and to punish the perpetrator of it. Sometimes these scenes take on the dimensions almost of a harrowing of Hell and a deliverance of the innocent who are held captive there. A notable example of this, and a virtually archetypal scene in Smollett, is provided in Chapters 11 and 12 of *Sir Launcelot Greaves*. Sir Launcelot, in the course of his questing around the country in search of occasions to perform good deeds, finds himself in the jail of an unnamed market town as a result of the ignorance and malice of a certain Justice Gobble. In the jail he meets various other victims of Justice Gobble's cruelty and malevolence. ". . . a crew of naked wretches crowded around him, and, like a congregation of rooks, opened their throats all at once, in accusation of Justice Gobble. The knight was moved at this scene, which he could not help comparing, in his own mind, to what would appear upon a much more awful occasion, when the cries of the widow and the orphan, the injured and oppressed, would be uttered at the tribunal of an unerring Judge, against the villanous and insolent authors of their calamity." He learns that Justice Gobble was the son of a tailor who, by cunning and marrying his master's widow, had worked his way up from a journeyman hosier to a position of wealth and power in this country neighborhood. Once settled in the country and having acquired a commission as justice of the peace through the influence of a peer who owed him money, Gobble proceeded to ruin certain shopkeepers in the country town who had voted contrary to his interests. By various devices he drove these individuals to financial ruin and a debtors' prison. Among his victims in the jail was a woman who had been driven half mad by her terrible misfortunes, deliberately inflicted on her by Gobble: a gentlewoman born, she had married a wealthy farmer, and on his death had determined to manage the farm herself with the help of her hopeful son, who was engaged to a daughter of a prosperous farmer in the neighborhood. But because Mrs. Gobble once fancied herself insulted by the young man's fiancée, she and the justice together conspired to take revenge: the young man was pressed for a soldier, to be killed in action soon afterwards, and his forlorn fiancée "wept and pined until she fell into a consumption." The widow, consumed by grief and without the help of her son, was unable to manage the farm and lost both her goods and her reason. "Then [in Smollett's words] the landlord seized for his rent, and she was arrested at the suit of Justice Gobble, who had bought up one of her debts in order to distress her, and now pretended that her madness was feigned." When he learns the details of the unhappy woman's story (from one of her fellow prisoners) Sir Launcelot discovers that she is his own former nurse, "the very woman who watched over my infancy, and even nourished me with her milk!" On his realizing this, "a tear stole softly down each cheek." Eventually, because of his rank and wealth, Sir Launcelot is able to intimidate Justice Gobble and to find means of proving his total corruption. He forces Gobble to make amends to those whom he had persecuted. Everyone is discharged from prison, their debts canceled or paid. The widow, Mrs. Oakley, recovers her reason—and her son, for it turns out that the report of his death had been false, and he returns home just after Sir Launcelot has completed his mission of restoring justice all round. Mother and son meet again in a "tender scene" which Smollett refuses to elaborate on: "let it suffice to say, their mutual happiness was unspeakable." Suky, the young man's fiancée, "though very weak, and greatly emaciated," is found still alive, and of course recovers quickly on the return of her sweetheart. And the chapter ends thus:

> This adventure of our knight was crowned with every happy circumstance that could give pleasure to a generous mind. The prisoners were released, and reinstated in their former occupations. The justice performed his articles from fear, and afterwards turned over a new leaf from remorse. Young Oakley was married to Suky, with whom he received a considerable portion. The new-married couple found a farm ready stocked for them on the knight's estate; and the mother enjoyed a happy retreat

in the character of housekeeper at Greavesbury-hall [Sir Launcelot's country house.]

It is interesting that here, as in similar scenes throughout Smollett, we find retributive justice, the redressing of wrongs, sensibility, and the restoration of order. Smollett believed in order; he believed in people acting decently and humanely in the particular rank of life to which they were called. He also had an ideal of rustic felicity and accepted that modified Horatian ideal of contented country living which so many eighteenth-century writers found attractive. "The new-married couple found a farm ready stocked for them on the knight's estate": it is a characteristic Smollett happy ending. Towards the end of *Humphrey Clinker*—a novel which is organized so as to point steadily to the superiority of a peaceful, ordered country life over anything the bustling and wicked city can provide—Mr. Dennison describes to Matthew Bramble (who is in many respects Smollett himself) how he "became enamoured of a country life" and how in consequence he established himself in the country: this description provides one of the moral centers of the novel. "I drained bogs," Dennison tells Bramble, "burned heath, grubbed up furze and fern; I planted copse and willows where nothing else would grow; I gradually inclosed all my farms, and made such improvements that my estate now yields me clear twelve hundred pounds a year—All this time my wife and I have enjoyed uninterrupted health, and a regular flow of spirits, except on a very few occasions, when our cheerfulness was invaded by such accidents as are inseparable from the condition of life." The combination of healthy rural activity, financial prosperity, and personal content marred only by the inevitable misfortunes to which human life is subject, sums up Smollett's ideal of the good life—an ideal he conspicuously failed to realize in his own checkered career.

Again and again we find in Smollett that the ultimate in human felicity is to land up with a country estate, loved and esteemed by one's tenants and the surrounding rustics. *Sir Launcelot Greaves,* which is the morally simplest of his novels and sets out his principles in almost allegorical terms, has a conclusion in which the knight and his newly married wife (who is of course the beautiful and sensitive girl from whom he had long been parted by the unscrupulous machinations of a wicked relative) return to Greavesbury-hall in a scene of ritual celebration. Sir Launcelot

> was met by about five thousand persons of both sexes and every age, dressed out in their gayest apparel, . . . and the rector from the knight's own parish. They were preceded by music of different kinds, ranged under a great variety of flags and ensigns; and the women, as well as the men, bedizened with fancy-knots and marriage favours. At the end of the avenue, a select bevy of comely virgins arrayed in white, and a separate band of choice youths, distinguished by garlands of laurel and holly interweaved, fell into the procession, and sung in chorus a rustic epithalamium composed by the curate.

The solemn ritual note here is almost reminiscent of Milton's account of Lycidas's reception into heaven, where he

> hears the unexpressive nuptial song,
> In the blest kingdoms meek of joy and love.
> There entertain him all the saints above,
> In solemn troops and sweet societies . . .

It is indeed a symbolic and exemplary conclusion, as the next paragraph makes clear: "The perfect and uninterrupted felicity of the knight and his endearing consort diffused itself through the whole adjacent country as far as their example and influence could extend. They were admired, esteemed, and applauded, by every person of taste, sentiment, and benevolence; at the same time beloved, revered, and almost adored, by the common people, among whom they suffered not the merciless hand of indigence or misery to seize one single sacrifice."

The relation between Smollett's realism and his moral sensibility—his sentimentality if you like—is a central question in all his work. All his novels are punctuated by scenes of moral edification in which virtue triumphs to the accompaniment of tears of sensibility on the part of the virtuous; these scenes provide, at a deliberately different level of realism from the bulk of the narrative, directions to the reader on how to interpret the author's intentions and moral standards. Professor A. A. Parker, in his illuminating study of the picaresque novel entitled *Literature and the Delinquent,* emphasizes that the picaresque novel in Spain arose "out of [a] climate of a social satire born of the urge to religious reform." If we change the phrase "religious reform" to "moral reform," this statement applies exactly to Smollett's novels. The incidents of high moral sensibility which Smollett interpolates amid his scenes of violence, comic coarseness, and brutal realism, and which operate at a different level of probability from these scenes, are analogous to the moralizing digressions in Mateo Alemán's *Guzmán de Alfarache,* the novel which Parker calls "the first fully-developed picaresque novel and the first full-length realistic novel in European literature." Guzmán, as Parker reminds us, "has been persistently criticized for attempting to cover up in hypocritical moralizing a relish for unsavoury delinquency." A similar charge has been made against Daniel Defoe's *Moll Flanders* and other of his novels, and it could be made too against Smollett, though in Smollett's case it is not so much hypocrisy as a radical difference in style and feeling between the vividly realistic passages and the highly stylized scenes of moral edification that may disturb the reader. But these stylized scenes are crucial: they provide the moral justification for the vivid exhibition of the wickedness of the world. The motiveless malignity of individuals—and it is worth noting how many of Smollett's villains, from Captain Oakum and Doctor Mackshane in *Roderick Random* to Justice Gobble in *Sir Launcelot Greaves,* seem to act out of impersonal malice—can drive morally neutral people to crime in order to make a living, and in both *Roderick Random* and *Peregrine Pickle* projects the hero into a life of adventuring and fortune hunting which often strains the reader's belief in him as an acceptable hero. But so long as he remains open to the assault of sensibility, he is redeemable, and Smollett sees to it that all his heroes—even, at the end, the atrocious villain Ferdinand Count Fathom—do remain open to such an assault. As a result, the hero is *educable* by experience. Roderick Random, having been united with his long-lost father by one of those positively stunning coincidences in which Smollett's novels abound, and which always serve a moral purpose, tells his father about the life he has led:

I recounted the most material circumstances of my fortune, to which he listened with wonder and attention, manifesting from time to time those different emotions which my different situations may have raised in a parent's breast, and, when my detail was ended, blessed God for the adversity I had undergone, which, he said, enlarged the understanding, improved the heart, steeled the constitution, and qualified a young man for all the duties and enjoyments of life, much better than any education which affluence could bestow.

Roderick Random is thus a Bildungsroman, as in some degree are all Smollett's novels. The significant phrase in the passage I have just quoted is "improved the heart." The culture of the heart was, of course, a theme that much exercised eighteenth-century philosophers, especially those in Scotland. Ten years after Smollett's death, Henry Home, Lord Kames, published a book with this very title, *The Culture of the Heart,* in which he argued that "the culture of the heart during childhood, is the chief branch of education." And it was in the year of Smollett's death that Henry Mackenzie published *The Man of Feeling,* generally regarded as the prime document in the history of the cult of sensibility in Britain. But Smollett had been there before him. Matthew Bramble in *Humphry Clinker* is as much a Man of Feeling as Mackenzie's Harley. Both are given to weeping tears of sensibility. Bramble, however, usually covers his sensibility in public with an appearance of gruff irascibility. The reason is given quite explicitly by his nephew, Jeremy Melford. "He is as tender as a man without a skin," Melford writes to his friend Sir Watkin Phillips, "who cannot bear the slightest touch without flinching. What tickles another would give him torment; ... " Bramble's bad-temperedly vivid descriptions of everything that offends the senses when people are gathered together in public places in Bath or London are done with a kind of masochistic relish which represents the other side of his sensibility. When he is faced with one of those ritually presented symbolic situations which occur in all Smollett's novels, his reaction is one of pure sensibility:

As we stood at the window of an inn that fronted the public prison, a person arrived on horseback, genteelly, tho' plainly, dressed in a blue frock, with his own hair cut short, and a gold-laced hat upon his head:—Alighting, and giving his horse to the landlord, he advanced to an old man who was at work in paving the street, and accosted him in these words: "This is hard work for such an old man as you."—So saying, he took the instrument out of his hand, and began to thump the pavement.—After a few strokes, "Have you never had a son (said he) to ease you of this labour?" "Yes, an please your honour (replied the senior), I have three hopeful lads, but, at present, they are out of the way." "Honour not me (cried the stranger); but more becomes me to honour your grey hairs.—Where are these sons you talk of?" The ancient paviour said, his eldest son was a captain in the East Indies; and the youngest had lately inlisted as a soldier, in hopes of prospering like his brother. The gentleman desiring to know what was become of the second, he wiped his eyes, and owned, he had taken upon him his old father's debts, for which he was now in the prison hard by.

The traveller made three quick steps towards the jail, then turning short, "Tell me (said he), has that unnatural captain sent you nothing to relieve your distress?" "Call him not unnatural (replied the other); I made a bad use of it; I lost it by being security for a gentleman that was my landlord, and was stript of all I had in the world besides." At that instant a young man, thrusting out his head and neck between two iron bars in the prison-window, exclaimed, "Father! father! if my brother William is in life, that's he!" "I am!—I am!—(cried the stranger, clasping the old man in his arms, and shedding a flood of tears)—I am your son Willy, sure enough!" Before the father, who was quite confounded, could make any return to this tenderness, a decent old woman bolting out from the door of a poor habitation, cried, "Where is my bairn? where is my dear

Willy?"—The captain no sooner beheld her, than he quitted his father, and ran into her embrace.

I can assure you, my uncle [i.e., Matthew Bramble: the story is being told by Melford in a letter to a friend], who saw and heard every thing that passed, was as much moved as any one of the parties concerned in this pathetic recognition—He sobbed, and wept, and clapped his hands, and hollowed, and finally ran down into the street. By this time, the captain had retired with his parents, and all the inhabitants of the place were assembled at the door.—Mr. Bramble, nevertheless, pressed thro' the crowd, and entering the house, "Captain (said he), I beg the favour of your acquaintance—I would have travelled a hundred miles to see this affecting scene; and I shall think myself happy if you and your parents will dine with me at the public house."

In the end "the whole family retired to the inn with my uncle, attended by the crowd, the individuals of which shook their townsman by the hand, while he returned their caresses without the least sign of pride or affectation."

Now this is not one of the scenes in *Humphry Clinker* that admirers of the novel are likely to quote. They understandably, and up to a point justly, prefer the racy humour in the self-characterisation of Bramble and of his sister Tabitha in their letters, the unconsciously suggestive malapropisms of Jenkins, the absurd yet convincing—and in its way moving—character of Lieutenant Lismahago, and the progressive mellowing of Bramble's character as he moves northwards to Smollett's native Scotland. They enjoy picking out the didactic threads, identifying the moral satire, showing how Smollett mediates between the extremes of primitive barbarity and corrupting luxury in developing his ideal of the good country life, and pointing to the vitality and humor of the novel. They pass over the preposterous coincidences, such as Humphry Clinker, a casually discovered young pauper, turning out to be Bramble's illegitimate son or the actor Wilson, with whom Bramble's niece has been having a clandestine love affair, turning out to be the son of Bramble's worthy friend Dennison and the very person Bramble wants his niece to marry. Up to a point they are right to do so, for the life of the novel resides elsewhere. Yet what we might call the scenes of stylized sentiment provide a sort of emblematic acting out of the moral pattern on which the whole novel is based. One cannot help being struck, in the scene from which I have quoted, by its almost primitive allegorical quality—an old man mending a road, a stranger on horseback accosting him, the brother putting his head out of the prison window to recognize the stranger. It is like a primitive book illustration, a sixteenth-century woodcut illustrating a moral tale. Everybody in the story is simultaneously visible. The prison happens to be right beside the place where the old man is working; the mother emerges from a house equally near; and the whole scene is looked down on by Bramble from the window of his inn, which is, as it were, another panel of the same woodcut. This is typical of Smollett's moral vignettes. They operate on a different level of probability from the main narrative of his novels, just as the preposterous coincidences—long-lost friends meeting in the most improbable places, people believed dead on the strongest evidence turning out to be alive, transformations of identity which turn A into the much-lamented or long-sought B, and so on—are contrivances to force moral crises. For Smollett's actual narrative art is episodic—at its best, vividly and brilliantly episodic. It cannot by itself shape the episodes into a moral pattern, or indeed into any sort of pattern. To achieve the moral pattern, he needs the coincidence and the stylized moral vignette.

I began by taking *Sir Launcelot Greaves* as not the best but the most central of Smollett's novels. It is the novel in which his seething indignation in the face of injustice found its "objective correlative" in an actual knight-errant who went about the country redressing wrongs. But of course that is a very unsophisticated technique for an eighteenth-century novelist who wanted to attack the vices of contemporary society. And in endeavoring to give it some plausibility, he had to invent melodramatically sentimental reasons for his knight's becoming sufficiently touched in the head so as to embark on his venture. He is not really crazy of course, and it is interesting to see how cagily Smollett keeps bringing in touches of essential sanity after Sir Launcelot's initial introduction as a latter-day Don Quixote. The discovery that his lady love had never really betrayed him, as he had been led to believe, restores him to sanity completely. The fact is that Smollett shows considerable uneasiness about the whole business, and it is this uneasiness that hastens the book (the shortest of his novels) to its rapid conclusion. The reader today will turn to it for help in understanding Smollett, but having got that help, it is not likely that he will return.

Sir Launcelot is a wholly good man from the beginning; but what about Roderick Random and Peregrine Pickle, who after a long period of pretty dubious adventuring are rewarded with wealth, social position, and the hand of the beautiful girl they have long loved? The Bildungsroman is not necessarily a success story: to be educated by life is not necessarily to get everything you want in the end (and while you are still young enough to enjoy it); but this is evidently how Smollett sees it. The happy endings here can hardly be regarded as stylized moral vignettes, like the ending of *Sir Launcelot Greaves,* for they concentrate quite specifically on matters of finance and personal vindication. "Fortune seems determined to make ample amends for her former cruelty," writes Roderick Random at the end of the novel he tells in the first person; "for my proctor writes, that notwithstanding the clause in my father-in-law's will, on which the squire founds his claim, I shall certainly recover my wife's fortune, in consequence of a codicil annexed, which explains that clause, and limits her restriction to the age of nineteen, after which she was at her own disposal." As for Peregrine Pickle (whose story is told in the third person): "Many persons of consequence, who had dropped the acquaintance of Peregrine in the beginning of his decline, now made open efforts to cultivate his friendship anew; but he discouraged all these advances with the most mortifying disdain; and one day, when the nobleman whom he had formerly obliged [and who had behaved ungratefully] came up to him in the drawing-room, with the salutation of—'your servant, Mr. Pickle,' he eyed him with a look of ineffable contempt, saying,—'I suppose your lordship is mistaken in your man,' and turned his head another way, in presence of the whole court."

Of course part of the reason for the happy endings here is that they had become—as they were long to remain—a convention of the novel. Readers expected and wanted them. Another reason—at least as far as *Roderick Random* is concerned, for, in its early part at least, this novel has considerable autobiographical elements—is that the happy ending represents a degree of wish fulfillment. Further, a happy ending provides a way in which the author can thumb his nose at the spite and malice of those who hinder a young man's getting on in the world. In this connection, it is worth looking at what Smollett says in his preface to *Roderick Random:* "I have attempted to represent modest merit struggling with every difficulty to which a friendless orphan is exposed from his own want of experience, as well as from the selfishness, envy, malice, and base indifference of mankind. To secure a favourable prepossession, I have allowed him the advantage of birth and education, which, in the series of his misfortunes, will, I hope, engage the ingenuous more warmly in his behalf. . . ."

Roderick is a young man of "modest merit"—reasonably moral, but with plenty of weaknesses. His sufferings are wholly the result of "the selfishness, envy, malice, and base indifference" of others. It is therefore particularly satisfying to see the forces of selfishness, envy, and malice deliberately affronted by the hero's final success. It is true that there are parts of the novel in which Roderick acts as a shameless fortune hunter, trying to maintain himself in wealth and reputation by sheer imposture, but even this is shown as the product of desperate necessity, not of malice. His behavior to the faithful and humble Strap is far from admirable. Yet weakness, vanity, inexperience, and credulity, rather than any cruelty of disposition (which he conspicuously lacks), account for his bad behavior. And if he is forced into trickery to maintain himself, the fault is clearly shown to be in society, which does not reward honesty, industry, openness, or kindness, but estimates people entirely by the degree of persuasiveness with which they can act the part of the wealthy and well-connected person of influence. We see this even more clearly in *Peregrine Pickle*. Peregrine is far more the shameless adventurer than Roderick and is a far from attractive character. But from the beginning he is persecuted by the motiveless malice of his mother (a character treated by Smollett with an obsessive savagery); vanity and unbridled passion are his chief vices, and these are no more the gravest vices for Smollett than they were for Fielding. It is society that forces him to be a fortune hunter, not, as with Ferdinand Count Fathom, an evil disposition.

So the happy ending in *Roderick Random* and *Peregrine Pickle* can be explained partly as a convention of the novel, partly as wish fulfillment, partly as nose-thumbing at the spiteful and the malicious people whom Smollett believed to have been responsible for his own lack of success in a variety of fields. But there is something more than this. The happy ending is an expression of what in the last analysis was a moral optimism on Smollett's part. This may sound an outrageous observation to anyone who knows Smollett's life and character. Was he not peevish, irascible, proud, thin-skinned, with a constant chip on his shoulder? Yes he was; yet he was optimistic in the sense that he believed that moral problems could be solved by the good heart, by moral sensibility, and that the combination of a basically good heart and abundant fortune could in the end anchor a young man in a life of exemplary virtue. If, in his assumption that people not innately vicious can be forced into a life of tricky fortune hunting by the way society judges its members and the way it treats them, Smollett reminds us of the Thackeray of *Vanity Fair* (and Becky Sharp is more of a Smollett heroine than has been generally recognized), then in his bringing of his heroes to a haven of wealth and regenerated moral feeling he reminds us of Defoe. Of the final prosperity and religious conversion of Defoe's Moll Flanders and Colonel Jack, Parker has this to say: "Conversion, which had been so real and important an element in the picaresque tradition, is now merely a literary and social convention—the adjunct to a respectable life, which has come to mean a prosperous one. Respectability had been attained by Guzmán on the torture-rack, by Simplicissimus [the hero of Jacob Christoffel von Grimmelshausen's picaresque novel set during the Thirty Years War] in the cavern on the uninhabited island." It is not fair to apply this to Smollett, for neither Roderick nor Peregrine are "converted" to virtue as a result of acquiring prosperity, while Ferdinand Count Fathom, the villain who really *is* converted at the end, is converted by his misery, by seeing that vice doesn't pay. But it is true to say that, for Smollett, vice—though ubiquitous—is unnatural, and virtue results from the natural and easy promptings of the good heart. The good heart manifests itself in acts of benevolence, and acts of benevolence can best be performed by men of wealth. Virtue is not the forgiving of your torturers while you are suffering on the rack. True, in Smollett a poor man can give his last penny to a friend or to someone worse off than himself (consider how Strap helps Roderick Random), and in a debtor's prison, a place we see so often in Smollett, the less desperately off can help the desperate. But for Smollett the *model* act of virtue is exercised by benevolent wealth through good feeling. If you are to harrow Hell and redeem the innocent that lie there, you must have the physical means to enable you to do it, as well as the good heart to prompt the action. Ideal virtue is effortless, and with a rich estate, a good and beautiful wife, loyal and affectionate retainers, and a good heart, a man is in a position to yield to the moral promptings of his heart and to be effortlessly virtuous. This is the position in which we see Roderick Random, Peregrine Pickle, and Sir Launcelot Greaves at the end of the novels of which they are respectively the heroes. Dickens, who learned so much from Smollett, had a more complex moral vision. Even in the early *Pickwick Papers* the benevolent and prosperous Mr. Pickwick's period in prison is less a harrowing of Hell (though there is an element of this about it, derived from

Smollett) than a part of his own education. And in *Great Expectations* (that mature Bildungsroman), gentlemanliness, wealth, and virtue are seen to be, if not inevitably incompatible, at least in a very disturbing and problematical relationship.

All this is very abstract, it might well be objected. We don't read Smollett (when we do read him) for the moral ideas underlying the novels, however, but for the texture of the narrative, the violence, color, vitality, physical reality, of the sights, sounds, smells, actions he so vividly presents. There can be no doubt that we do find these qualities in Smollett. *Roderick Random* provides an amazing list of strong adventures.

"Blood and wounds!" cried Weazel, "d'ye question the honour of my wife, Madam? Hell and damnation! no man in England durst say so much. I would flea him—carbonado him! Fury and destruction! I would have his liver for my supper." So saying, he drew his sword, and flourished with it, to the great terror of Strap; while Miss Jenny, snapping her fingers, told him she did not value his resentment a louse. In the midst of this quarrel, the master of the waggon alighted, who, understanding the cause of the disturbance, and fearing the captain and his lady would take umbrage, and leave his carriage, was at great pains to have everything made up, which he at last accomplished, and we sat down to supper together. At bed-time we were shown to our apartments: the old usurer, Strap, and I, to one room; the captain, his wife, and Miss Jenny, to another. About midnight, my companion's bowels being disordered, he got up, in order to go backward; but, in his return, mistaking one door for another, entered Weazel's chamber, and without any hesitation, went to bed to his wife, who was fast asleep; the captain being at the other end of the room, groping for some empty vessel, in lieu of his own chamber pot, which was leaky. As he did not perceive Strap coming in, he went towards his own bed, after having found a convenience; but no sooner did he feel a rough head, covered with a cotton night-cap, than it came into his mind, that he had mistaken Miss Jenny's bed instead of his own, and that the head he felt was that of some gallant, with whom she had made an assignation. Full of this conjecture, and scandalized at the prostitution of his apartment, he snatched up the vessel he had just before filled, and emptied it at once on the astonished barber and his own wife, who, waking on that instant, broke forth into lamentable cries, which not only alarmed the husband beyond measure, but frightened poor Strap almost out of his senses; for he verily believed himself bewitched; especially when the incensed captain seized him by the throat, with a volley of oaths, asking him how he durst have the presumption to attempt the chastity of his wife. Poor Strap was so amazed and confounded, that he could say nothing but—"I take God to witness, she's a virgin for me." Mrs Weazel, enraged to find herself in such a pickle, through the precipitation of her husband, arose in her shift, and, with the heel of her shoe, which she found by the bed-side, belaboured the captain's bald pate, till he roared—"Murder." "I'll teach you to empty your stink-pots on me," cried she, "you pitiful hop-o'-my-thumb coxcomb. What! I warrant you're jealous, you man of lath. Was it for this I condescended to take you to my bed, you poor withered sapless twig?" The noise occasioned by this adventure had brought the master of the waggon and me to the door, where we overheard all that passed with great satisfaction. In the mean time, we were alarmed with the cry of—"Rape! murder! rape!" which Miss Jenny pronounced with great vociferation. "O! you vile abominable old villain!" said she, "would you rob me of my virtue? but I'll be revenged of you, you old goat! help!" Some servants of the inn, hearing this cry, came running up stairs with lights, and such weapons as chance afforded, when we beheld a very diverting scene. In one corner stood the poor captain shivering in his shirt, which was all torn to rags, with a woeful visage scratched all over by his wife, who had by this time wrapped the counterpane about her, and sat sobbing on the side of her bed. In the other end lay the old usurer, sprawling on Miss Jenny's bed, with his flannel jacket over his shirt, and his tawny meagre limbs exposed to the air; while she held him fast by the two ears, and loaded him with execrations.

We can leave this "very diverting scene" while it is still going full blast, observing only that there are literally hundreds more of the same kind in this novel. It is like an expansion of a quintessential medieval fabliau. It is all there—entering the wrong room or bed in the dark; the emptying of the chamber pot; the screams and accusations and counteraccusations; the grotesque figures, scantily clad, sprawling with their limbs in the air; the misunderstandings; the insults. This is presented as comedy, and there can be no doubt at all that a relish for this kind of simpleminded comedy coexisted in Smollett with the overriding moral sensibility I have already discussed. It would be a very naive view of human nature indeed that would dismiss them as incompatible. (Incidentally, it is interesting that this kind of nighttime misadventure recurs several times, derived from Smollett, in Dickens's *Pickwick Papers,* but suitably purged of frank sex talk and chamber pots.) Altogether darker in tone are the scenes set on board the *Thunder.* Here Smollett drew on his own experiences on board the *Cumberland,* where he served as surgeon's mate during the ill-fated Carthagena expedition of 1740–41. The appalling brutality of life on board an eighteenth-century man-of-war, where most of the crew were found by the press-gang, is presented with a vividness that makes one positively wince. Yet, though much in these chapters is documentary, the scenes as a whole are far from simple documentaries. The brutal actions are described as acts of calculated malice on the part of individuals of evil character. In some characters Smollett puts all the evil characteristics he can think of: Mackshane, for example, the new ship's surgeon, "was grossly ignorant, and intolerably assuming, false, vindictive, and unforgiving; a merciless tyrant to his inferiors, an abject sycophant to those above him." And this description is borne out by numbers of particular incidents. The Captain, too, is a monster and acts accordingly. Life is made possible for Roderick by the kindness of other individuals, particularly by the friendship of the first mate, the proud and eccentric Mr. Morgan, a stage Welshman whose speech contains distinct echoes of Shakespeare's Fluellen and Sir Hugh Evans, yet who remains a vivid and persuasive character (though scarcely three-dimensional) who brings much needed comic relief into these grim scenes.

Chapter 33 gives an account of the actual attack on Carthagena, which Smollett later developed in a separate pamphlet. He almost steps out of Roderick's character in giving his ironical explanation of the stupid behavior of the admiral: this is clearly Smollett speaking. First he tells the reader that there were those who "taxed this commander with want of honesty, as well as sense; and alleged that he ought to have sacrificed private pique to the interest of his country; that where the lives of so many brave fellow-citizens were concerned, he ought to have concurred with the general, without being solicited, or even desired, towards their preservation and advantage." He then lists other accusations made by some against the admiral, before concluding: "But all these suggestions surely proceeded from ignorance and malevolence, or else the admiral would not have found it such an easy matter, at his return to England, to justify his conduct to a ministry at once so upright and so discerning." This, of course, is political satire, and the discursive, episodic form of the novel enables Smollett to inject political and social satire at many points, often paying back personal scores, as in his account in chapter sixty-two of the poet Melopoyn and his scurvy treatment by theatrical managers and other influential people when he tried vainly over a long period to have his tragedy put on the stage. Smollett himself had left Scotland for London in 1739, at the age of nineteen, with a tragedy, *The Regicide, or, James the First of Scotland,* which, much to his indignation, he could persuade no one to put on. The account of his vain struggle to have it accepted which he gives in the preface to the published edition of the play shows how autobiographical the Melopoyn episode is: in this episode he tried to *pay back* those who—out of deliberate malice as he believed—kept his play off the stage. (It never occurred to him that it was a bad play: it is in fact a highly rhetorical performance in imitation-Shakespearean blank verse, and though of very little merit, it is no worse than many plays that were successful on the eighteenth-century stage.) Though Smollett believed in the good heart, he was always a great one for paying back: as I have suggested, his happy endings are a way of paying back his heroes' and so his own enemies.

The account of Roderick's adventures loses something of its brutal vividness after he leaves his ship. His encounter with Narcissa, whom at the end of the book he marries, is described, as are all Smollett's accounts of the heroes' meetings with their future wives, with a studied elegance of romantic feeling that is in sharp contrast with other parts of the narrative: the object is to show the hero possessed of genuine sensibility, which is brought out by the ideal woman. Indeed, the tough adventurism which Roderick has hitherto displayed and which has enabled him to survive great physical hardships now gives way to the soft languishing of a lover, which he expresses in an ode.

> Thy fatal shafts unerring move,
> I bow before thine altar, Love.
> I feel thy soft resistless flame
> Glide swift through all my vital frame!
>
> For while I gaze, my bosom glows,
> My blood in tides impetuous flows;
> Hope, Fear, and Joy, alternate roll,
> And floods of transports 'whelm my soul!

This is a far cry from the world of broken heads and emptied chamber pots of which we have hitherto seen so much. But again it must be emphasized that for Smollett the world of sensibility coexisted with the world of violence and provided the moral standard by which we recognized the world of violence as undesirable, even though it might be interesting and entertaining. In *Humphry Clinker* a similar modulation into the verse of sensibility occurs when Matthew Bramble reaches Smollett's own native part of Scotland. In a letter to his friend Dr. Lewis, Bramble waxes enthusiastic over Loch Lomond and the Water of Leven, an area which he calls "the Arcadia of Scotland." To express his enthusiasm, he encloses in his letter a "copy of a little ode to this river, by Dr Smollett, who was born in the banks of it"—by this device disclaiming responsibility for Bramble's authorship of the poem, though, as we know that Bramble is in many respects Smollett, the device is pretty transparent. But what a remarkable poem it is for the outwardly satirical and misanthropic Bramble to admire!

> Pure stream! in whose transparent wave
> My youthful limbs I wont to lave;
> No torrents stain thy limpid source;
> No rocks impede thy dimpling course,
> That sweetly warbles o'er its bed,
> With white, round polish'd pebbles spread.

We cannot help asking, Is this really Smollett? Isn't it Henry Vaughan, who wrote similar lines in his poem "The Waterfall" a hundred years earlier?

> Dear stream! dear bank, where often I
> Have sate, and pleas'd my pensive eye, . . .

The resemblance must be a coincidence, but it is significant nonetheless. Though Vaughan uses the beauty and clarity of the stream to symbolize the fountain of life and the mystical truths of religion, while Smollett is led on to describe an ideal community of happy pastoral workers, both attitudes stem from a sensibility that represents a variety of the Renaissance development of the *beatus ille* tradition. That tradition—of seeking happiness in a garden, in rural retirement, in meditation in the midst of nature, in country content—has been studied in all its varieties by Maren-Sofie Røstvig in her two-volume work entitled *The Happy Man: Studies in the Metamorphoses of a Classical Ideal*. It would take me too far afield to examine the ways in which this tradition reached Smollett, but the fact that it is possible to refer to this tradition at all in discussing Smollett is itself significant.

But to return to Roderick. Having lost all his money at the gaming table, he is imprisoned for debt in the Marshalsea. This is the first of the many prison scenes in Smollett; in this underworld microcosm he is able to make points about the nature of society both through direct satire and through the presentation of symbolic situations. Both Scott and Dickens learned from Smollett here. When, in *The*

Fortunes of Nigel, the desperate hero takes refuge in Whitefriars, "then well-known by the cant name of Alsatia," Scott gives us a picture of an underworld society in which "bankrupt citizens, ruined gamesters, irreclaimable prodigals, desperate duellists, bravoes, homicides, and debauched profligates of every description, all leagued together to maintain the immunities of their asylum." Dickens knew and admired Scott's picture of life in Alsatia, although of course he had direct access to Smollett as well. The underground world—realistically and symbolically treated at the same time—is an important tradition in the nineteenth-century novel, and it owes much more to Smollett than to earlier picaresque and rogue literature.

Roderick is rescued from prison by his benevolent uncle, Lieutenant Bowling, the first of the series of naval characters in Smollett's novels, and after that the novel proceeds fairly rapidly to its happy ending. Before leaving *Roderick Random,* I must mention another of its features—the inset "history of Miss Williams." Such inset histories were, of course, common in eighteenth-century fiction—one thinks at once of the history of the Man of the Hill in Fielding's *Tom Jones*—and Smollett introduces them in most of his novels. But the point I want to make about Miss Williams's story is that it is the story of a good woman of respectable birth who is driven by betrayal and misfortune to prostitution. She tells the story of her life in a style of conscious elegance, as does, to an even greater degree, the "Lady of Quality" who tells the extremely long story of *her* life in *Peregrine Pickle.* The good prostitute, the prostitute of sensibility, who in the end is redeemed (and in this novel marries Roderick's faithful retainer Strap), has traditionally been an interest of the Man of Feeling. This is another tradition that stems from Smollett.

Lieutenant Bowling is a very subdued seaman compared to Commodore Hawser Trunnion in Smollett's second novel *Peregrine Pickle.* Trunnion—with his violently nautical language and kind heart underneath—is a stage sailor, an eccentric, a "humor" in the Jonsonian sense; he and his companions, Hatchway and Pipes (living together in a fortified house which Dickens remembered when he described Wemmick's "fortress" in *Great Expectations*), lie behind a host of later military and naval fictional characters from Uncle Toby in *Tristram Shandy* to Captain Cuttle in *Dombey and Son*—and beyond. Such characters are the products of a flamboyant imagination, which Smollett certainly possessed, and in spite of being two-dimensional, they can operate with great moral force in the novel in which they play their part. I say *moral* force, because Trunnion, with his combination of good heart and picturesque violence of nautical language, can speak out on the side of the good in critical situations in a way that clears the moral atmosphere and lays bare the moral pattern which sustains the work as a whole. And in *Peregrine Pickle* we need every possible device to suggest a pattern, for the shape of the novel continually gets lost in its doggedly episodic progression. The novel lacks the brutal vigor and the sense of earthy reality we find in so much of *Roderick Random,* and its succession of practical jokes, tricks, acts of vengeance, beatings up, absurd physical accidents, and farcical situations sometimes seems to be the product of a desperately searching inventiveness. Smollett took a peculiar pleasure in accidents involving gross physical discomfort. A good example of this is in Chapter 42, where Peregrine is in Paris. He has fallen in with a couple of eccentric Englishmen, a stupid and ignorant painter named Pallet and a self-important young doctor who always swears that the ancients did everything better than the moderns. To demonstrate this, the doctor arranges a dinner in the manner of the ancient Romans, to which are invited not only Peregrine and Pallet but also (at Peregrine's malicious suggestion) "a French marquis, an Italian count, and a German baron, whom [Peregrine] knew to be egregious coxcombs, and therefore most likely to enhance the joy of the entertainment." Here is part of Smollett's account of the dinner:

> The Frenchman, having swallowed the first spoonful, made a full pause, his throat swelled as if an egg had stuck in his gullet, his eyes rolled, and his mouth underwent a series of involuntary

contractions and dilations. Pallet, who looked steadfastly at this connoisseur, with a view of consulting his taste, before he would himself venture on the soup, began to be disturbed at these emotions, and observed, with some concern, that the poor gentleman seemed to be going into a fit; when Peregrine assured him, that these were symptoms of ecstacy, and, for further confirmation, asked the marquis how he found the soup. It was with infinite difficulty that his complaisance could so far master his disgust, as to enable him to answer, "Altogether excellent, upon my honour!" and the painter, being certified of his approbation, lifted the spoon to his mouth without scruple; but far from justifying the elogium of his taster, when this precious composition diffused itself upon his palate, he seemed to be deprived of all sense and motion, and sat like the leaden statue of some river god, with the liquor flowing out at both sides of his mouth.

The doctor, alarmed at this indecent phenomenon, earnestly inquired into the cause of it; and when Pallet recovered his recollection, and swore that he would rather swallow porridge made of burning brimstone than such an infernal mess as that which he had tasted, the physician, in his own vindication, assured the company, that, except the usual ingredients, he had mixed nothing in the soup but some sal ammoniac, instead of the ancient nitrum, which could not now be procured; and appealed to the marquis, whether such a succedaneum was not an improvement on the whole. The unfortunate petit maitre, driven to the extremity of his condescension, acknowledged it to be a masterly refinement; and feeling himself obliged, in point of honour, to evince his sentiments by his practice, forced a few more mouthfuls of this disagreeable potion down his throat, till his stomach was so much offended, that he was compelled to start up of a sudden; and, in the hurry of his elevation, overturned his plate into the bosom of the baron. The emergency of his occasions would not permit him to stay and make apologies for his abrupt behaviour; so that he flew into another apartment, where Pickle found him puking, and crossing himself with great devotion; . . . when our hero returned to the dining-room, the German got up, and was under the hands of his own lacquey, who wiped the grease from a rich embroidered waistcoat, while he, almost frantic with his misfortune, stamped upon the ground, and in High Dutch cursed the unlucky banquet, and the impertinent entertainer, who all this time, with great deliberation, consoled him for the disaster, by assuring him, that the damage might be repaired with some oil of turpentine and a hot iron. Peregrine, who could scarce refrain from laughing in his face, appeased his indignation, by telling him how much the whole company, and especially the marquis, was mortified at the accident; and the unhappy salacabia being removed, the places were filled with two pyes, one of dormice, liquored with syrup of white poppies, which the doctor had substituted in the room of roasted poppy-seed, formerly eaten with honey, as a dessert; and the other composed of an hock of pork baked in honey.

And so the party proceeds, until the final course is brought in. The doctor describes it to his guests:

"That which smokes in the middle," said he, "is a sow's stomach, filled with a composition of minced pork, hog's brains, eggs, pepper, cloves, garlic, aniseed, rue, ginger, oil, wine, and pickle. On the right-hand side are the teats and belly of a sow, just farrowed, fried with sweet wine, oil, flour, lovage, and pepper. On the left is a fricassee of snails, fed, or rather purged, with milk. At that end next Mr. Pallet are fritters of pompions, lovage, origanum, and oil; and here are a couple of pullets, roasted and stuffed in the manner of Appicius."

The painter, who by wry faces testified his abhorrence of the sow's stomach, which he compared to a bagpipe, and the snails which had undergone purgation, no sooner heard him mention the roasted pullets, than he eagerly solicited the wing of the fowl; upon which the doctor desired he would take the trouble of cutting them up, and accordingly sent them round, while Mr Pallet tucked the table-cloth under his chin, and brandished his knife and fork with singular address; but scarce were they set down before him, when the tears ran down his cheeks, and he called aloud, in a manifest disorder,—"Zounds! this is the essence of a whole bed of garlic!" That he might not, however, disappoint or disgrace the entertainer, he opened his instruments to one of the birds; and, when he opened up the cavity, was assaulted by such an irruption of intolerable smells, that, without staying to disengage himself from the cloth, he sprung away, with an exclamation of "Lord Jesus!" and involved the whole table in havoc, ruin, and confusion.

Before Pickle could accomplish his escape, he was sauced with a syrup of the dormice pye, which went to pieces in the general wreck; and as for the Italian count, he was overwhelmed by the sow's stomach, which, bursting in the fall, discharged its contents upon his leg and thigh, and scalded him so miserably, that he shrieked with anguish, and grinned with a most ghastly and horrible aspect.

There are no moral implications in an incident of this kind. It is knockabout farce, presented as pure entertainment. There is more of it in *Peregrine Pickle* than in any other of Smollett's novels, and the reader has to have a very strong appetite for this sort of thing not to get occasionally wearied. Some accidents and misadventures, on the other hand, do have moral implications, such as the farcical coincidences which prevent Peregrine from carrying out his seduction of the lady he met in the diligence on the way to Ghent or some of the troubles he meets with in Paris as a result of his quarrelsomeness, arrogance, and lust. For Peregrine is a much more dubious character than Roderick Random, and for large parts of the novel carries with him much less of the reader's sympathy. He even attempts to drug and so seduce the beautiful and virtuous Emilia, who of course in the end forgives him and whom he marries in the happy ending. True, he is persecuted (for reasons never convincingly explained) by his mother, and by his weak-minded father who is subservient to his mother, but on the other hand he is loved and protected by Trunnion, and he goes abroad, not as a desperate fortune hunter, but well provided with money and servants, in order to learn more of the world. For all his faults, he has at bottom a generous heart and a capacity for shedding tears of sensibility. His relations with his sister, the only member of his immediate family who will have anything to do with him, are tender and loving; when they met after a long absence she "shed a flood of tears in his bosom" and he reciprocated: "he embraced her with all the piety of fraternal tenderness, wept over her in his turn, assured her that this was one of the happiest moments of his life, and kindly thanked her for having resisted the example and disobeyed the injunctions of his mother's unnatural aversion." Then there is his tender reconciliation with Mr. Gauntlet, Emilia's brother, after learning his history:

> Peregrine's generous heart was wrung with anguish, when he understood that this young gentleman, who was the only son of a distinguished officer, had carried arms for the space of five years, without being able to obtain a subaltern's commission, though he had always behaved with remarkable regularity of spirit, and acquired the friendship and esteem of all the officers under whom he had served.
> He would at that time, with the utmost pleasure, have shared his finances with him.

—but he wants to find indirect ways of doing this, since he doesn't want to wound Gauntlet's sensitivities. All in all, Smollett allows Peregrine's "pride and vanity" (which he describes as "the ruling foibles of our adventurer") to take him as far as possible on the road to unscrupulous behavior without allowing him to lose his potential capacity for sensibility. Such a capacity does not, of course, in any way inhabit his relish for mischief. Time and again we are told how Peregrine promises himself "store of entertainment" by stage-managing embarrassments or fights or ludicrous situations for other people, such as the occasions when he contrives to get the doctor and the painter to fight a duel (in a scene reminiscent of the way Sir Toby provokes Sir Andrew Aguecheek into challenging the disguised Viola in *Twelfth Night*) or his device for making Pallet believe that the rabbit he was eating was really a cat. This last, incidentally, is an incident deriving from *Gil Blas,* which Smollett himself had translated (or the translation of which he had supervised) and which clearly had a strong influence on all his work—to an even greater degree than Cervantes, Defoe, and Swift, from whom he also learned.

As always in Smollett there are autobiographical elements, and private grudges are ventilated in the presentation of some of the characters. There are also interesting traces of humane political sympathies in his account of the Jacobite exiles of Boulogne making their daily pilgrimage to the shore to look across the Channel towards their native land to which they could not return. We are reminded that, though (in the words of an early biographer) Smollett "had been bred a Whig," the Battle of Culloden and its aftermath had provoked him to write "The Tears of Scotland," a poem of patriotic indignation.

> Mourn, hapless Caledonia, mourn
> Thy banish'd peace, thy laurels torn!
> Thy sons, for valour long renown'd,
> Lie slaughter'd on their native ground!
> Thy hospitable roofs no more
> Invite the stranger to the door;
> In smoky ruins sunk they lie,
> The monuments of cruelty.

After the death of his protector, Commodore Trunnion, Peregrine is his own master, and he embarks on a series of misadventures, humiliations, and disgraces during which he seems to be more the object of the author's satire than a hero. But these do not last long. After his encounter with the "Lady of Quality," whose excessively long reminiscences divide the novel roughly into two and whose style of sentimental elegance in narrating her misfortunes reminds us of the very similar style in which John Cleland clothed his bawdy *Memoirs of a Woman of Pleasure* (otherwise known as *Fanny Hill*), he sets up with his misanthropic friend Cadwallader Crabtree as a fake fortune-teller, before proceeding to a variety of other adventures which eventually land him in the Fleet. Once again the prison gives Smollett an opportunity to present not only inset moral stories told by some of the inhabitants (again, stylized to a degree, as all such inset moral stories are in Smollett) but also morally significant situations and incidents, such as the determination of the faithful Hatchway and Pipes to share his fate—something that Dickens remembered when he made Sam Weller insist on sharing prison life with Mr. Pickwick. The death of his unkind father, intestate, restores him to fortune and happiness. Peregrine "found himself delivered from confinement and disgrace, without being obliged to any person upon earth for his deliverance;

he had it now in his power to retort the contempt of the world in a manner suited to his most sanguine wish; he was reconciled to his friend, and enabled to gratify his love, even upon his own terms; and saw himself in possession of a fortune more ample than his first inheritance, with a stock of experience that would steer him clear of all those quicksands among which he had been formerly wrecked."
A *Bildungsroman* indeed!

Peregrine's fortune is now £80,000, £10,000 more than the £70,000 to be left to Ernest Pontifex by his Aunt Alethea in Samuel Butler's *The Way of All Flesh*, which enables Ernest to revenge himself upon his parents. Ernest's laughing reply to his detested father when his father asks him why the money was not handed over to himself or to his brother John savors of the same kind of vengeful use of final prosperity of which I earlier noted a trace in *Peregrine Pickle*. Only Butler's revenge is more savage:

Theobald flushed scarlet. "But why," he said, and these were the first words that actually crossed his lips—"if the money was not his to keep, did [Mr. Overton, Alethea's trustee] not hand it over to my brother John and me?" . . .

"Because, my dear father," said Ernest still laughing, "my aunt left it to him in trust for me, not in trust either for you or for my Uncle John—and it has accumulated till it is now over £70,000. . . ."

It may seem a long way from Smollett to Butler, but we can go even further, to Butler's great admirer Bernard Shaw. For Chapter 87 of *Peregrine Pickle* contains a story which was almost certainly the inspiration of Shaw's *Pygmalion*. Peregrine finds on the road an attractive, but ragged, filthy, and ill-spoken, beggar girl, and he is seized with the whim to turn her into a presentable lady by improving her speech, manners, and clothes. He has her sent to his home, where the first thing that she has to undergo is an unaccustomed bath and a thorough scrubbing. Peregrine had

observed, that the conversation of those who are dignified with the appellation of polite company, is neither more edifying nor entertaining than that which is met among the lower classes of mankind; and that the only essential difference, in point of demeanour, is the form of an education, which the meanest capacity can acquire without much study or application. Possessed of this notion, he determined to take the young mendicant under his own tutorage and instruction. In consequence of which, he hoped he should, in a few weeks, be able to produce her in company, as an accomplished young lady of uncommon wit and an excellent understanding.

He succeeds brilliantly, though he has difficulty in overcoming the lady's "inveterate habit of swearing." The time comes when she could be safely presented to the beau monde, and this is duly done. All seems to be going well until

one evening, being at cards with a certain lady whom she detected in the very act of unfair conveyance, she taxed her roundly with the fraud, and brought upon herself such a torrent of sarcastic reproof as overbore all her maxims of caution, and burst open the floodgates of her own natural repartee, twanged off with the appellation of b--- and w---, which she repeated with great vehemence, in an attitude of manual defiance, to the terror of her antagonist and the astonishment of all present: nay, to such an unguarded pitch was she provoked that, starting up, she snapped her fingers in testimony of disdain, and, as she quitted the room, applied her hand to that part which was the last of her that disappeared, inviting the company to kiss it by one of its coarsest denominations.

For a novelist as little read as Smollett, his influence has proved surprisingly pervasive.

The Adventures of Ferdinand Count Fathom, Smollett's third novel, is the only one of his novels which can be classed as picaresque in the sense in which Parker has defined that genre, for it has a true delinquent as hero. Indeed, Parker calls it "the last European novel of any consequence that is directly within the tradition started by *Guzmán de Alfarache*." Smollett was a little nervous of working within the rogue tradition, as his preface indicates:

Let me not, therefore, be condemned for having chosen my

principal character from the purlieus of treachery and fraud, when I declare my purpose is to set him up as a beacon for the benefit of the inexperienced and unwary, who, from the perusal of these memoirs, may learn to avoid the manifold snares with which they are continually surrounded in the paths of life; while those who hesitate on the brink of iniquity may be terrified from plunging into that irredeemable gulf, by surveying the deplorable fate of *Ferdinand Count Fathom.*

Smollett is not being hypocritical here, and we do not have here the problem we have in, say, Defoe's *Moll Flanders,* where obvious enjoyment in the presentation of a criminal life coexists with the professed aim of edification. Though *Ferdinand Count Fathom* sustains the reader's interest with the provocative liveliness of its main narrative, the instances of treachery, betrayal, double-crossing, and perfidy on the part of its hero really do arouse the reader's moral indignation, as they are intended to do. We do not need the interpolation of moral vignettes, in the standard Smollett manner, to establish the moral pattern, for nowhere are we tempted to admire Ferdinand or to have any feeling towards him other than one of moral detestation, even though his adventures are continually *interesting.* To sustain interest without sympathy is difficult in any kind of narrative, and Smollett's technical feat is considerable.

But Smollett did not trust his account of his villain's villainy to make its own moral point. "That the mind might not be fatigued, nor the imagination disgusted, by a succession of vicious objects," his preface continues, "I have endeavoured to refresh the attention with occasional incidents of a different nature; and raised up a virtuous character, in opposition to the adventurer, with a view to amuse the fancy, engage the affection, and form a striking contrast which might heighten the expression, and give a *relief* to the moral of the whole."

At one point, when Ferdinand has apparently driven to her death the beautiful and innocent fiancée of his friend and benefactor, after having maliciously estranged them from each other in the hope of seducing the girl himself, Smollett breaks out: "Perfidious wretch! thy crimes turn out so atrocious, that I half repent me of having undertaken to record thy memoirs." But he goes on to point out that "such monsters ought to be exhibited to public view, that mankind may be upon their guard against imposture; that the world may see how fraud is apt to overshoot itself; and that as virtue, though it may suffer for a while, will triumph in the end, so iniquity, though it may prosper for a season, will at last be overtaken by that punishment and disgrace which are its due." Smollett's answer to the old question, "Why do the wicked prosper?" is that in the long run they don't; sooner or later, and quite often sooner, they overreach themselves and are destroyed or forced to repentance. You will see why earlier I called Smollett an optimist.

Ferdinand, like all Smollett's villains, is villainous by nature; we are not given any psychological explanation of his evil disposition—unless his mother's having been a *femme de guerre* with various European armies and having had the habit after a battle of murdering wounded soldiers for their possessions can be considered as providing a hereditary reason for his delinquency. But he early acquires a generous patron and is given an excellent start in life. He is a brilliant actor and a consummate hypocrite, dissimulation and deceit being at the center of his villainy. He even lacks physical courage, but what Smollett calls his "sagacity and presence of mind" manage to supply the place of it. Throughout the whole of his life as a villain he is playing a part, in order to obtain money or position or to seduce a girl or sometimes simply to amuse himself. If in Dickens hypocrisy is so central a clue to moral evil, here again we can see the influence of Smollett.

In displaying the virtuosity of Ferdinand's hypocritical role-taking, Smollett is able to attack a host of contemporary follies and villainies, for generally it is the folly or villainy (or both) of society that makes it possible for the hypocrite to prosper. Ferdinand's career as a medical practitioner enabled his creator, who had studied medicine at Glasgow and had himself practiced as a doctor, to give his views on the abuses of medical practice. Anyone interested in the social role of the doctor in the eighteenth century, and in the difference in function and social prestige between the apothecary, the surgeon, and the physician, will find much illumination in this novel. I have myself found the novel richer in social details than any other of Smollett's. For instance, I had occasion not long ago to inquire into the degree to which the habit of whisky drinking (as distinct from gin drinking) had come into London from Scotland and Ireland by the third quarter of the eighteenth century, and sure enough we find that Ferdinand, in order to make people think that he was busy with his medical practice, would keep his carriage conspicuously waiting while he, supposedly attending patients, would in fact "glide into some obscure coffeehouse, and treat himself with a dram of usquebaugh."

Ferdinand's double-crossing of his friend and benefactor, Renaldo, a type of the virtuous man of feeling, and his driving of Renaldo's fiancée Monimia to apparent death, precipitates the climax of the plot. For, in a characteristic Smollett *anagnorisis,* Monimia turns out in the end, not only to be alive, but to be identical with Serafina, the daughter of the Spanish Don Diego whom Ferdinand had swindled out of all his money in Paris. Don Diego had fled from Spain in the belief that he had been responsible for the deaths of his wife and daughter (a belief now revealed to have been totally unfounded). His discovery that he was innocent of the deaths of these two women, together with the revelation that Monimia-Serafina was not dead after all, is what makes the happy ending possible. For Don Diego was not the virtual murderer he thought he was, and Ferdinand, evil though his behavior had been, was not after all responsible for the ruin and death of Monimia. Ferdinand's most ambitious and complicated plot not only failed, but hadn't really taken place: he *thought* he had committed this evil, but in fact he hadn't. This reminds us of Shakespeare's *Measure for Measure,* where forgiveness all round is possible because in the end it is revealed that nobody (except Lucio) was actually guilty of what they believed themselves to be guilty of: Angelo had not viciously trapped Isabella into yielding her body to him, for the girl he had spent the night with, unknown to him, was his own former fiancée and virtual wife. This device is taken to extraordinary lengths in *Ferdinand Count Fathom,* where in the end, the past is—one might say—*undone;* it is revealed *not to have occurred*—and this in spite of the vivid detail in which it was earlier described.

But, after all, this is only a device to enable Smollett to wind up the novel in the true spirit of moral edification and to provide a context in which Ferdinand's penitence, which comes about as a result of the final failure of all his schemes and his subsequent imprisonment and degradation, can be accepted. It also enables Smollett to shift the emphasis in the end to Renaldo and Serafina and to their triumphant union as an ideal, and an ideally happy, couple. The last section of the book is mostly taken up with the restored fortunes of this couple and of Don Diego. That their fortunes are restored is largely due to the good offices of a benevolent and sentimental Jewish moneylender (once again, Dickens remembered this, in the character of Riah in *Our Mutual Friend*). This Jewish man of feeling, who provides interest-free loans to enable gentlemen in distress to recover their fortunes and gives plain gifts on other occasions, is a new phenomenon in English fiction. At the various revelations of the identity of lost characters, there is, of course, weeping all round, and when Don Diego discovers his supposedly dead daughter Serafina, even Joshua, the Jew, bursts into tears of sensibility, Smollett's final seal of approval. ". . . as for Joshua, the drops of true benevolence flowed from his eyes, like the oil on Aaron's beard, while he skipped about the room in an awkward ecstacy, and in a voice resembling the hoarse notes of the long-eared tribe, cried,—'O father Abraham! such a moving scene hath not been acted since Joseph disclosed himself unto his brethren in Egypt!' "

In the end Ferdinand Count Fathom weeps too. Renaldo, to whom he has behaved with such baseness, forgives and helps him. The penitent Ferdinand seeks an interview with his benefactor, who has now married his Serafina and has entered into his inheritance to become Count Melvil:

Ovewhelmed as I am with Count Melvil's generosity, together with a consciousness of my own unworthiness, it ill becomes a wretch like me to importune him for further favour; yet I could not bear the thought of withdrawing (perhaps for ever) from the presence of my benefactor, without soliciting his permission to see his face in mercy, to acknowledge my atrocious crimes, to hear my pardon confirmed by his voice, and that of his accomplished countess, whom I dared not even at a distance behold; and to express my fervent wish for their prosperity.

Renaldo replies in words of encouragement and forgiveness, and extends his hand, which Ferdinand bathes in tears. Ferdinand, now married to a girl he had seduced quite early in his career of vice, retires with his wife to his retreat somewhere in the north of England, "which he found extremely well adapted to the circumstances of his mind and fortune," to lead "a sober and penitent life." Our last view of him, however, is not in this novel at all but in Smollett's last novel, *Humphry Clinker*. Matthew Bramble runs into Renaldo and Serafina in Yorkshire, when all three are on their way to Scotland, and by another of Smollett's characteristically manipulated coincidences, they find at the same time that a country apothecary named Grieve is really the reformed Ferdinand. Bramble is present at the recognition scene, which is precipitated by the discovery that Grieve's daughter is called Seraphina Melvilia after "the two noble persons abroad to whom he had been obliged for more than life." Bramble sums up the position in a letter to his friend Dr. Lewis:

Being a sincere convert to virtue, he [Ferdinand] had changed his name, that he might elude the enquiries of the count, whose generous allowance he determined to forego, that he might have no dependence but upon his own industry and moderation. He had accordingly settled in this village as a practitioner in surgery and physic, and for some years wrestled with all the miseries of indigence, which, however, he and his wife bore with exemplary resignation. At length, by dint of unwearied attention to the duties of his profession, which he exercised with equal humanity and success, he had acquired a tolerable share of business among farmers and common people, which enabled him to live in a decent manner.... In short, the adventurer Fathom was, under the name of Grieve, universally respected among the commonalty of this district, as a prodigy of learning and virtue.... I make no doubt that Grieve will be pressed to leave off business, and re-unite himself to the count's family; and as the countess seemed extremely fond of his daughter, she will, in all probability, insist upon Seraphina's accompanying her to Scotland.

So the wicked Ferdinand Count Fathom is finally absorbed into the moral pattern of Smollett's last novel, a novel where in the end everything—irascibility, petulance, eccentricity, pride, silliness, and even evil—softens into a moral landscape in which sensibility and rural content are the principal features. The Man of Feeling has triumphed over the satirist.

The irascibility and the satire remain, however, as an important part of Smollett's literary character. His *Travels in France and Italy* show him nosing his way through those countries with an extraordinary mixture of censoriousness and sheer curiosity. Sterne, whose *Sentimental Journey* appeared two years later, in 1768, contrasted his own ability to take pleasure in everything with the querulous attitude of Smollett: "The learned SMELFUNGUS travelled from Boulogne to Paris—from Paris to Rome—and so on—but he set out with the spleen and jaundice, and every object he pass'd by was discoloured or distorted—He wrote an account of them, but 'twas nothing but the account of his miserable feelings."

But an account of his feelings, whether miserable or not, was precisely what the Man of Feeling was expected to give, and, for all Sterne's antipathy, he and Smollett shared a belief in the primacy of feeling. Of course, feeling could be peevish and splenetic. Smollett's most sustained work of deliberate and even nasty offensiveness is his *Adventures of an Atom,* a hard-hitting (and wide-hitting) political satire attacking pretty well everything that had happened in English politics for several generations, in the thinly disguised form of an account of an early period of Japanese history; it is very much a work of personal feeling. Satire and sensibility, censoriousness and a capacity for deep yet easily released emotion, the man of wrath and the Man of Feeling, are closely allied (we can compare the modern hippy). Smollett's literary career shows this clearly. His work provides an important clue to the development of taste, ethical attitudes, and patterns of moral emotion in eighteenth-century England—and Scotland. It provided all kinds of suggestions and situations for later novelists, including Scott, Dickens, and Thackeray. And if his novels are not among the very greatest in our literature, they are, at their best, vivid, entertaining, provocative, and disturbing. A generation which is interested in the nature of violence and in the relation of violence to moral feeling might well find Smollett's novels, in one of their favorite words, extremely "relevant."

3 | SCOTT AND PUSHKIN

John Henry Raleigh

Before examining the influence of Scott's historical fictions on those of Pushkin, it is best to emphasize how ready Pushkin was to receive that influence and how concerned he and his age and generation were with history and historical questions. Pushkin's own evolution as a writer was from lyricist to historian, from Byronic poet to the historian of the Pugachev rebellion and the author of *The Captain's Daughter.*

By discussing these matters first, I am making in some sense an artificial separation, since the historiographical interests of Pushkin and his age were greatly stimulated by the enormous popularity and wide currency of Scott's novels in Russia at this time, Pushkin himself being one of the most enthusiastic admirers. But even if Scott had never existed, Pushkin's interests would inevitably have evolved in the way they did. Scott's example was important to him, but the "whatness," the subject matter of Pushkin's historical fictions, was given to him, one could say forced upon him, by that mighty and tumultuous Russian past that he thought about and studied with increasing obsessiveness as his life went on.[1] Where Scott was most important to him was in the "howness," embracing, on the one hand, specific

---

[1] Most of the historians and literary critics cited in the footnotes that follow have been extensively relied upon. But I wish to single out in particular Paul Avrich's excellent *Russian Rebels, 1600–1800*. This is the first large-scale study in English of the four Cossack-led rebellions in the south and east of Russia in the seventeenth and eighteenth centuries. Two of these rebellions, and their leaders, were of great

dramatic situations and characters borrowed from or suggested by Scott and, on the other hand and most important of all, Scott's demonstration of the form of the historical novel: what the basic elements were to be, what were to be the proper proportions of these elements, and how to orchestrate these proportions into an overall unity.

I.

Of all the cursed questions with which Russian intellectuals, the thinking aristocracy, grappled in the late eighteenth and early-nineteenth centuries, the most important was the question of history itself: What was the "true" past of Russia, or did it have one? What should be its relation to the West? Above all, what was to be its future? This interest in history accelerated and intensified during Pushkin's brief lifetime from 1799 to 1837 and permeated all media from history proper to poetry, fiction, opera, drama, and journalism. Such instances of a consuming interest in history could be cited for all the European countries at this time, but not with the particular intensity that they generated in Russia. Karamzin's conservative *History of the Russian State*, which dramatized the continuity of Russian history and celebrated the autocracy, became for some people virtually canonical and was instrumental in turning

---

importance to Pushkin the historian and the historical novelist, as I have tried to show in the text.

Not cited in the footnotes are other books consulted and found useful: Philip Longworth, *The Cossacks* (New York: Holt, Rinehart and Winston, 1969). Raymond T. McNally, *Chaadayev and His Friends* (Tallahassee, Fla.: Diplomatic Press, 1971); *The Major Works of Peter Chaadaev*, trans. Raymond T. McNally (Notre Dame and London: University of Notre Dame Press, 1969); David Magarshack, *Pushkin* New York: Grove, 1969); George Verdansky, *The Tsardom of Moscow, 1547–1682, Part 2* (New Haven: Yale University Press, 1969).

My colleague at the University of California, Simon Karlinsky, has read the original manuscript with a sharp and knowledgeable eye and has saved me from many egregious errors in matters concerning Russian literary culture. He is absolved of blame for those that remain. I am also indebted to my colleague in English, Ulrich Knoepflmacher.

Pushkin himself from his youthful radicalism to his mature conservatism. In his letters Pushkin speaks of Karamzin's *History* with constant enthusiasm, both for its historical and its literary excellences, and sometimes with a kind of ecumenical awe. In a letter of 1824 to his brother and sister, he states: "The Bible is for a Christian what a history is for a nation. Karamzin's *History* at first begins with this phrase, turned around. I was present when he changed it." Pogodin the historian, like Karamzin a friend of Pushkin, declared: "The historian represented the crowning achievement of a people, for through him the people came to an understanding of itself."[2]

On the other hand, there was the famous "Philosophical Letter" of Chaadaev, another close friend of the poet and himself a Catholic mystic, which was published in 1836 and which, said Herzen, was like "a pistol shot in the night." It said that Russia was a barbarian enclave, which, properly speaking, had no history at all: "We are not of the West or of the East, and we have the traditions of neither." For this the autocracy declared the author insane and had him placed under daily medical observation. Chaadaev later appeared to recant in *"L'apologie d'un fou,"* which in fact is either wholly or partially ironic, but his shot in the night was the opening salvo in the Slavophile-Westerner conflict. Although Pushkin did not live to see the full-scale elaboration of the conflict in the 1840s, he was, nevertheless, intensely involved in the very issues that animated it. In Russian literature Pushkin is like God on the day of the Creation: everything he does, or is involved with, is a "first." And like God too, he is somewhat inscrutable. He neither wholly agrees nor disagrees with the extreme positions of either Karamzin or Chaadaev. If he turned conservative, the rebel in him never really disappeared. If he was a Rus-

---

[2] *The Letters of Alexander Pushkin,* trans. with preface, introduction, and notes by J. Thomas Shaw (Bloomington, Ind.: Indiana University Press, 1963) I, 192–93 (Karamzin's *History* begins, "History in a certain sense is the holy book of nations . . ."). Pagodin quoted by Nicholas Riasanovsky in *Nicholas I and Official Nationality in Russia* (Berkeley and Los Angeles: University of California Press, 1969), p. 102.

sian patriot and a believer that Russia did indeed have a history—and a magnificent one, as he spelled out in a letter to Chaadaev in 1836—he never lost his sense of the powerful barbarian element in Russian civilization.

By 1830 Pushkin the poet had lost a good deal of his popularity; in addition, the radicals thought he had sold out. *Poltava,* 1828, had been a popular failure. Further, his own poetic impulse was slackening, while his interest in prose and history was on the increase. There was nothing unusual in this change of interest. The study of history in Russia and elsewhere was not yet professionalized, and there were no clear boundaries between literature, history, and journalism. Thus it was possible to move from one area to the other with relative ease. Pogodin composed imaginative works; Karamzin had first made his mark as a creative writer with *Poor Liza.* Pushkin's own age in life probably had something to do with the shift as well. Karamzin in his journal for 1803, about to embark on his historical researches, had written: "At a certain stage in our life, history occupies us more than do novels; the mature mind finds in truth a peculiar charm, which invention lacks."[3]

Pushkin's drama *Boris Gudonov* (for whose historical background he had drawn on Karamzin) and some of his verse had been historical in subject anyway. Furthermore, as a cosmopolitan Russian who looked to Europe, Pushkin shared in that general efflorescence of historical interests of the Europe of the late eighteenth and early nineteenth centuries, partly the legacy of the Enlightenment, partly the impulse arising from the nascent romantic and professional tradition that was coming into being in Germany and elsewhere, although Pushkin's heart was always with the Enlightenment historians. He had been acquainted with Voltaire from his earliest days, and to Peter Vyazemsky he wrote in 1824: "The French are not a whit below the English in the field of history. If primacy is anything, re-

---

[3] Quoted by Richard Pipes in *Karamzin's Memoir on Ancient and Modern Russia,* a translation and analysis (New York: Atheneum, 1966), p. 54.

member Voltaire was the first to take the new road—and to bring the lamp of philosophy into the dark archives of history. Robertson said that if Voltaire had taken the trouble to indicate the sources of what he said, then he, Robertson, would never have written his *History*" (*Letters*, I, 164).

By the evidence of his correspondence and the contents of his library, Pushkin appears to have known Thierry, Thiers, Mignet, Michelet, Guizot, and Barante; Hallam and Gibbon (both in French); Hume and Robertson (both in French); and Niebuhr, whom he disliked (German pedantry). He also appears in the 1830s to have become more and more interested in ancient history as well. From his early years he was familiar with Tacitus and refers to him, especially in reference to Tiberius, in his correspondence both early and late. In the 1830s he contemplated a Roman story and even began it: "Caesar was on a journey and with Titus Petronius I followed him at a distance."[4] There is also among his literary remains what was probably a projected play about medieval Germany connected with the invention of gunpowder.

But all this paled before the fascination of Russian history itself, which for him became a kind of supreme "fiction." There were things in it that no mere single human imagination could conjure up by its own efforts and powers. On the other hand, it was just waiting to be called up by the wand of the sorcerer-writer, to come into being shaped and formed and living before the eyes of the present. This was the one subject about which his enthusiasm never diminished, even in his dark later years. In 1831 he requested from the Tsar, who was his personal censor, permission to work in the St. Petersburg archives, the proposed subject to be a history of Russia from Peter the Great to Peter III; he worked there intermittently for the rest of his life.

The flavor of Pushkin's enthusiasm is best given in his

---

[4] Quoted in John Bayley, *Pushkin* (Cambridge, Mass.: Harvard University Press, 1971), p. 331.

own words in his correspondence. By 1833 he was convinced that he needed a professional associate and tried, unsuccessfully, to persuade Pogodin to leave Moscow and to join him in the archives. He wrote to the historian that he had cleared the matter with the Tsar and that Pogodin would have access to all the archives, "except the secret one": "How many different books can be compiled here! How many creative ideas can acquire their full development here! . . . you will produce such marvelous things that we and our posterity will pray God for you, as we do for Schlözer and for Lomonsov" (*Letters*, II, 566-67). In 1836, a few months before his death, he wrote to Modest Korf: "What a field modern Russian history is! And when you reflect that it is as yet completely untilled, and that except for us Russians nobody can undertake it! But history is long, life is short, and worst of all, human nature is lazy (Russian nature especially)" (*Letters*, III, 778-79).

His fullest statement on the subject was in a letter of October 19, 1836, his response to Chaadaev's "Letter." (There were eight of Chaadaev's letters in all, and Pushkin had read them in manuscript long before publication). Pushkin's letter was never sent for fear of the censor's reaction to his agreement with Chaadaev that the present state of Russia was dismal. As Pushkin said, there was no real public opinion; there was a general indifference toward duty, justice, and truth, and a cynical disdain for human thought and dignity. But he disagreed equally with Chaadaev's assertion that Russia had no history at all.

In the letter Pushkin marches through the whole span of Russian history: its beginnings, the invasion of the Tatars, the development of national power and unity, the two Ivans, Boris, and "The Time of Troubles": "—is all this not to be a history, but a pallid and half-forgotten dream?" Pushkin continues: "and Peter the Great, who in himself alone is a universal history! and Catherine II, who placed Russia on the threshold of Europe: and Alexander, who led us to Paris? And (cross your heart) do you find nothing impressive in the present-day situation of Russia which will strike the future historian? Do you believe he will place us outside Europe?" Not for anything, says Pushkin, would he change his fatherland, "nor . . . have any other history than that of our ancestors, such as God gave it to us" (*Letters,* III, 780).

When Pushkin himself looked back from his own perspective at Russian history, two figures in particular caught his creative eye: Peter the Great and Emalian Pugachev, the Cossack leader of a powerful rebellion during the reign of Catherine the Great—that is to say, the mightiest of the Tsars and the mightiest of the rebels against the Tsar. The contrast between the two was classical: the dread Westernizer and builder of the Stone City in the North; and the Cossack leader of the most extensive of the cyclones or whirlwinds that swirled up in the seventeenth and eighteenth centuries among the Cossacks, the peasantry, the Old Believers, the lower orders of the clergy, the urban poor, the factory workers, the wanderers, the deserted soldiers, the escaped convicts—the whole flotsam and jetsam of a frontier country of south and east Russia that, spreading north and west, actually threatened Moscow and the monarchy itself. The two figures, Peter and Pugachev, are tied together in that each was a manifestation of a central national question which Pushkin shared: Was Russia to be reformed from above or from below?

Peter the Great loomed as large in historic memory as he had in his own lifetime and in his person (he was almost seven feet tall)—and not only for Pushkin, but for most other writers as well. Nicholas I, like Catherine before him, was obsessed with Peter, who was the patron saint of Imperial Russia. So was Pogodin, who wrote about Peter both as an historian and as a creative writer (a five-act tragedy in verse), and so were other historians. Each time Pogodin contemplated lecturing or writing about this most potent of the Tsars, he quailed because he thought he could not do justice to this giant, both "the key and the lock" to Russian history, and he imagined that Peter himself was there observing him, oak cudgel in hand.[5] In June 1831, Pushkin

---

[5] Pogodin quoted in Riasanovsky, *Nicholas I,* pp. 105–10.

wrote to him: "Write Peter; don't be afraid of his oak cudgel" (*Letters,* II, 498). But Peter and his oak cudgel were equally intractable to Pushkin the historian and Pushkin the historical novelist—disregarding for the moment the poet of *The Bronze Horseman, Poltava,* and "The Feast of Peter the Great." Pushkin appears to have been assiduous in his historical researches, but his proposed history of Peter remained a collection of notes, and his historical novel, *The Negro of Peter the Great,* is only a fragment.

Significantly, *The History of the Pugachev Rebellion* (1834) and *The Captain's Daughter* (1836) did get written, and well written. The *History* is described by Prince Mirsky as a "masterpiece"; by Michael Karpovich as "the first Russian monograph in social history"; by Philip Longworth as still quite valuable, since it drew on archival material no longer available; and by Paul Avrich as "the starting point for all subsequent research."[6] The rebel in Pushkin never died, even if it went underground. If one contrasts the two best of his creative works where his two key historical figures appear, *The Bronze Horseman* (Peter) and *The Captain's Daughter* (Pugachev), there can be no doubt where his instinctive human sympathies lay: they were with the rebel, even if, in his famous phrase, Russian rebellions were "senseless and merciless."

Along with his lifelong interest in Peter and the reform from above, there was an equally consuming interest in its opposite, the rebellion from below. There had been four such major rebellions, each symbolized by and embodied in the name of a Cossack leader who announced himself either as the true Tsar or as the representative of the true Tsar: Bolotnikov, 1606–7; Razin, 1670–71; Bulavia, 1707–8; and Pugachev, 1773–74. Of the four leaders,

---

[6] Prince Mirsky, *Pushkin* (New York: Dutton, 1963), pp. 187–88; Michael Karpovich, "Pushkin as an Historian," *Centennial Essays for Pushkin,* ed. Samuel H. Cross and Ernest J. Simmons (Cambridge, Mass.: Harvard University Press, 1937), p. 197; Philip Longworth, "The Last Great Cossack-Peasant Rising," *Journal of European Studies* 3 (1973), p. 2, n. 2; Paul Avrich, *Russian Rebels, 1600–1800* (New York: Schocken, 1972), p. 303.

Razin was the most colorful and was to become the most legendary, while the outburst that went under the name of the *Pugachevshchina* was the most widespread and the most powerful—and the last—such revolt. In Pushkin's day, and for long after, the names Razin and Pugachev possessed potent symbolic powers.[7]

In Pushkin's Mikhailovsky period, 1824–26, he composed some folk poems—including *Songs About Stenka Razin*—with Razin as a legendary hero. In a letter to his brother of November, 1824, he requested, among other things, "the historical dry information about Stenka Razin, the only poetic figure in Russian history" (*Letters*, I, 189).[8]

---

[7] I stress the words "major rebellions" because restlessness among the lowly and a "pretender"-leader who capitalized upon that unrest were endemic in seventeenth- and eighteenth-century Russia. According to Philip Longworth, there were in the seventeenth century twenty-three pretenders; in the eighteenth, forty-four. Catherine II alone—triply vulnerable as a German, as a woman, and as a tsar who had achieved the accession by a coup—had twenty-six. "The Pretender Phenomenon in Eighteenth-Century Russia," *Past and Present*, No. 66 (February 1975), passim.

[8] What Pushkin meant by this is clear when Stenka (diminutive for Stephen) Razin's career is set forth. A cossack, he came from a respectable home-owning family. In his earlier years he had been entrusted with governmental and military missions, and he once led a detachment of Don Cossacks against the Tatars. It was thought at one time that he would become ataman of the Don Host. But instead he was to become first bandit and then revolutionary, one of the reasons being that a brother named Ivan—when fighting with the army in the Ukraine—suddenly, like a cossack, decided he would go home and was hanged as a deserter. Razin became associated with the pauper cossacks, the escaped serfs, and others who had fled to cossack territory, and first led them on a piracy raid in the Caspian sea.

At the time of his rebellion, he was about forty years old: strong and powerful in physique, adventurous, fearless, indomitable, and dynamic. He appears to have been sociable and accessible to his followers; he could be both magnanimous and very cruel; he loved drinking bouts and gaiety; above all he was a bold and resourceful leader with considerable strategic abilities. At the height of his powers and ambitions, he announced that he would bring the Cossack form of government to Moscow. For all these reasons he captured the folk imagination and became in collective memory the Russian Robin Hood.

But he was already on the trail of Pugachev as well, and in that same month he had asked his brother to send him *The Life of Emelka Pugachev,* which had been published in Moscow in 1809 (*Letters,* I, 187).

Some years later, as Pushkin worked in the archives, his interests appeared to shift from Peter to Pugachev. On February 9, 1833, he wrote to Alexander Chernyshev, the Minister of War, asking for certain military documents. Ostensibly he was doing research on Suvorov, the great eighteenth-century general who had finally run down Pugachev; in fact, Pushkin had evidently once seriously considered doing a history of this subject. Of the four requests made, three were for documents about Suvorov. But this may well have been a smoke screen, for the fourth request was for the official dossier about the investigation and interrogation of Pugachev (*Letters,* II, 565). Chernyshev sent him the Suvorovian items but informed him that the Pugachev material was in Moscow. Pushkin's researches in this area appeared to have made his censor, Tsar Nicholas, somewhat uneasy, and on one occasion he blocked Pushkin's access to relevant documents: "What does he want these papers for? They have been lying untouched in the archives since my grandmother ordered them placed there. Even I have not read them. Does he wish to obtain from them scandalous material paralleling the canto of *Don Juan* in which Byron dishonored the memory of my grandmother? No, indeed."[9]

In the fall of 1833 Pushkin requested and was granted permission to visit the Pugachev country. To his wife he wrote on September 2, 1833, "Here I've been spending my time with old men, contemporaries of my hero; I've gone over the environs of the city [Kazan], I've looked over the sites of the battles, . . . " (*Letters,* III, 608). In October in the village of Perdy he had the great good fortune to meet and, for a price, to talk with a seventy-five year old Cossack woman who had had sexual relations with Pugachev.

---

[9] Quoted in Ernest Simmons, *Pushkin* (Cambridge, Mass.: Harvard University Press, 1937), p. 351.

(When she was fourteen or fifteen Pugachev had seen her and ordered her taken to a bath for him). He discovered too how much alive was the memory of Pugachev in the Urals. When he asked an old man what he remembered of Pugachev, the old man angrily replied, "For you he is Pugachev, but for me he was the great sovereign, Peter Fyodorovich."[10] (Pugachev had proclaimed himself Peter III.) Some of the legends were touching and moving in their simplicity:

> Emelian, our own dear father,
> Wherefore have you forsaken us?
> Our resplendent sun has gone down.[11]

Razin legends were still alive as well. Near Sartov, one of the towns on the southern Volga that Razin had captured, is a cliff that bears Razin's name; it is "commemorated by one of the most beautiful of revolutionary songs. Legend says that he who mounts the cliff by night will learn Razin's secret. The secret was class war."[12]

An anecdote in Pushkin's *Table Talk* links together his three Russian heroes: Peter the Great, Razin, and Pugachev. Tradition had it that when Pugachev was a prisoner in Moscow, he told a tale of Peter, on a campaign in the south, ordering the funeral mound of Razin to be opened so he could gaze on the remains of the folk hero. As Pushkin says, Razin's remains were actually disposed of in Moscow—what was left had been thrown to the dogs—but this did nothing to dispel the myth that the grave of Stenka Razin was in his own country.[13]

Upon his return Pushkin finished his history, and on December 6, 1833, he wrote to Benkendorf, the chief of police and the intermediary between Pushkin and Nicholas, asking permission to send the *History* to His Highness for examination (*Letters,* III, 621). (In that same letter he sent forward his greatest narrative poem, *The Bronze Horse-*

---

[10] Avrich, *Russian Rebels*, p. 257.
[11] Ibid., p. 251.
[12] Bernard Pares, *A History of Russia*, (New York: Knopf, 1965), p. 161.
[13] Bayley, *Pushkin*, p. 111, n. 1.

man, which embodies his most powerful evocation of Peter as the Dread Tsar, both the builder of cities and the destroyer of individuals). When Nicholas I heard that Pushkin's history was to be called "The History of Pugachev," he objected on the grounds that a rebel had no history; thus it was called *The History of the Pugachev Rebellion* upon publication in 1834. In the background of all this was *The Captain's Daughter*, which Pushkin began in 1833 but did not finish until 1836. But even after the publication of the history, Pushkin's interest in Pugachev remained very much alive, and in January 1835, he wrote to Benkendorf to find if he could read the Pugachev dossier in the archives, not for purposes of publication but to "set my historian's conscience at rest" (*Letters*, III, 703). He was given eight binders but was still unable to find Pugachev's own deposition. He was still in pursuit of it in 1836, the last year of his life, although whether he ever found it is unclear.

The personal depositions of these rebel leaders were of great importance, because they were all Pretenders and were (especially in the case of Pugachev) skillful and assiduous propagandists, assuring the masses that the long-awaited "true Tsar" had arrived to grant them their freedom, thus helping to keep ever fresh that seemingly indestructible peasant belief in a kind of secular Second Coming.

Some of the rebels for their part tried to hold out against making any kind of "confession." Razin, with incredible fortitude under hideous tortures, refused to make any admissions. One contemporary account of his execution has it that on the execution block in Red Square, with his hands and feet already cut off, he roared at his brother who had been brought to witness the execution, "Hold your tongue, you dog."[14] Pushkin in his *History* had published a probably apocryphal but revelatory anecdote of Pugachev's original interrogation by General Panin, who first examined him:

Panin: "Exactly who are you?"

[14] S. Konovalvo, "Razin's Execution: Two Contemporary Accounts," *Oxford Slavonic Papers*, 12 (1965), 94–98.

Pugachev: "Emelian Ivanovich Pugachev."
Panin: "Then how dare you, a brigand [*vor*] call yourself the sovereign?"
Pugachev: "I am not the raven [*voron*] but his offspring. The raven himself is still flying."[15]

Herzen picked up the metaphor of the raven still flying, and there are no doubt those in the Soviet Union today who believe or would like to believe, that the raven himself is still flying. Against the wishes of her advisers, Catherine had forbidden that Pugachev be tortured. But at the execution block he earned himself an easier death by replying that he was a Cossack, when he was commanded to tell who he was.

Thus the major creative effort of Pushkin's last years went into two versions of an historical event that was still politically explosive. Nobody in Pushkin's day knew that Pugachev's rebellion was to be the last such uprising; what they did know was that it had been the biggest. One authority has estimated that at its height the rebellion affected an area of some 400,000 square miles and 4,500,000 people, or one-fifth of the population of Russia.[16] It was, in fact, the greatest mass upheaval in Europe between the Puritan and the French Revolutions. Foreign observers took a great interest in it, and Pugachev, who appears to have been an excellent military commander, was often compared to Cromwell. For Russia it was the largest outbreak prior to the revolutions of 1905 and 1917.

Further, it had all happened relatively recently. When Karamzin was eight or nine years old, his father barely escaped capture, and thus certain death, when Pugachev's legions were operating in the Simbrisk region in 1774–75. In 1834 Nicholas told Pushkin that the Pretender's "sister" had just died in prison. Actually it was Pugachev's last surviving daughter. Pugachev's two wives and three children had been put in jail for life; one of the children had managed to survive in the dungeons for sixty years.

[15] Quoted from Avrich, *Russian Rebels,* p. 260.
[16] Longworth, "The Last Great Cossack-Peasant Rising," p. 24.

Most important, the memory of Razin and Pugachev never died, as the authorities were well aware. As late as the 1840s Nikolai Kastomarovo, a Russian historian, met an old peasant on the Volga who was convinced that Pugachev had been the "second coming of Razin after a hundred years." When Nicholas I died in 1855, rumors of a new *Pugachevshchina* swept the land, and a government spokesman declared: "We are not afraid of Mirabeau, but we are frightened by Emelka Pugachev. . . . No one will side with Mazzini, but Stenka Razin has only to say the word."[17] Gorki, who was born in 1868, records in *My Childhood* that his grandfather, in a discussion of Napoleon, in this context a man who wished to make all men equal, told him that Russia had had two "Bonapartes": Razin and Pugachev. On May 1, 1919, by the execution block in Red Square, Lenin evoked Stenka Razin as his forebear in the struggle against slavery. One further irony: Razin was first defeated at Simbrisk, which is now called Ulyanovsk and was the birthplace of Lenin.

It was by the agency of Pushkin that serious, empirical historical research was begun on Pugachev and his rebellion and that a composite Stenka Razin–Pugachev figure or character was immortalized in *The Captain's Daughter*.

II

The most potent outside force in the stimulation of Russian historical interests was Scott. Speaking of the multitude of Western literary influences on Russia at this time, James Billington says: "Perhaps the most important of all was Sir Walter Scott, whom Gogol called 'the Scottish sorcerer,' and whose works inspired the writing of history as well as historical novels."[18] In Pushkin's words in 1830: "The influence of W. Scott is felt in all branches of contem-

---

[17] Quoted from Avrich, *Russian Rebels*, pp. 122, 261.

[18] James Billington, *The Icon and the Axe* (New York: Knopf, 1970), p. 353.

porary letters."[19] Gogol at one time had tried to turn himself into a Russian Scott. *Taras Bulba*—to the beginning of which Pushkin paid the compliment of saying it was worthy of Scott himself—was one result of this effort.[20] Karamzin was said to have remarked that if he ever had a home he would put in his garden a monument of gratitude to Sir Walter Scott for the pleasure he had had from reading his novels. Among literate people in the 1820s and 1830s, the Caucasus was often associated with the Scotch Highlands.[21] Evidently most of Scott's novels got to Russia, usually in French translations at first; only his biography of Napoleon was banned.

Pushkin appears to have read Scott's poetry and novels first in French translations and later in English. Pushkin was introduced to the study of English in 1820; by 1828 he appeared able to read it, although not readily, and in his library he had Scott in both French and English editions. The first mention of Scott in his letters occurred in 1824 in a letter from Odessa to his friend Bustuzhev whose "Castle Neuhausen" was written in imitation of Scott. Near the end of this letter, he said, "Farewell, my dear *Walter*" (*Letters*, I, 148). From Mikhailovskoe in 1824 in the same letter to his brother in which he had asked for information on Stenka Razin, he called out for "Some poems, poems, poems! *Conversations de Byron!* Walter Scott! That is food for the soul" (*Letters*, I, 188). He transferred his enthusiasm for Scott to two protagonists of poems, Eugene Onegin and the hero of "Count Nulin." Scott appeared to have been on everybody's mind, including the Tsar's or his ad-

---

[19] Quoted in Tatiana Wolff, *Pushkin on Literature* (London: Methuen, 1971), p. 242.

[20] Walter Schamschula in his *Der russische historische Roman von Klassizimus bis zur Romantik* (Frankfurt: Frankfurt University Publications, 1961) expresses skepticism about both Scott's influence on *Taras Bulba* and the artistic worth of Gogol's novel, sentimentally patriotic and thus lacking Gogol's real forte, irony. Schamschula also points out that Taras Bulba himself, an *übermensch*, was the opposite of the usual Scott hero, colorless and meditating.

[21] Militsa Greene, "Pushkin and Sir Walter Scott," *Forum for Modern Language Studies*, 1 (July 1965), 207–15.

visers'. When in 1826 he submitted *Boris Gudonov* (originally entitled "The Comedy of Tsar Boris") for the Tsar's censorship, Pushkin was told by the Tsar that his aim would be better fulfilled if, along with the necessary expurgation, he would change his drama into a historical tale or novel similar to those of Sir Walter Scott. (This suggestion, which Pushkin declined, appears to have come to the Tsar from one of Pushkin's literary rivals, Bulgarin.) Writing in 1831 from Moscow, where *Boris* was much criticized, to Pletnev in St. Petersburg where, so he had been told, it was a great success, Pushkin tried to figure out the reasons for the St. Petersburg acclaim—one of them being, perhaps, the popularity of Scott (*Letters*, II, 452).

In 1834 and 1835 Pushkin returned to reread Scott. Between September 13 and October 18 in 1834 he was at his father's estate in Baldino, where he wrote to his wife: "I'm reading Walter Scott and the Bible, and I keep on thinking of you (*Letters*, III, 696). In September 1835, he was at Mikhailovskoe and borrowed some Scott novels from neighbors to read. They were evidently in French, for he regretted that he had not brought the English with him (*Letters*, III, 724). On September 25, he wrote to his wife from Trigorskoe "I am behaving myself with modesty and decency. I go on jaunts on foot and horseback. I'm reading Walter Scott's novels, which I'm in rapture over (*Letters*, III, 725).

Literary influences are intricate affairs and are often overstated or oversimplified in the telling, and the most famous, and most often cited, incident in the Scott-Pushkin relationship has usually been both overstated and oversimplified. Jeanie Deans's pleading with Queen Caroline, successfully, for her sister's life in *The Heart of Midlothian* is supposed to have been a source for *The Captain's Daughter,* which has Maria pleading with Catherine the Great, successfully, for the life of her affianced, Peter Grinev. Scott's Jeanie Deans–Queen Caroline incident was based on the real story of Helen Walker, who had refused to save her own sister by perjuring herself and yet was able to effect a commutation of her sister's death sentence by making her way to London to the Duke of Argyle, who granted the pardon. As for the similar episode in *The Captain's Daughter,* Pushkin explicitly said that he got the idea, not from Scott, but, like Scott, from a real event, the story of an officer in Catherine's army who went over to the enemy during the Pugachev rebellion, was condemned as a traitor, but was pardoned by Catherine at the request of the officer's aged father, who threw himself at the empress's feet (*Letters,* III, 782). Further, there is little resemblance between the respective scenes in the two novels. Scott's treatment is lengthy and complex and involves four people in a very complicated, delicate, wavering situation that is touch-and-go for a variety of reasons through a lengthy dialogue, until finally it becomes certain that Caroline will grant the pardon, with the reader fully understanding why she finally does so. Pushkin's version is stark simplicity, as was his wont. Only two people, Catherine and Maria, are involved; Maria pleads briefly and gives Catherine a letter which explains the innocence of Grinev. Further, Maria herself is the daughter of the heroic Captain Mironov who had bravely defied Pugachev and was hanged by him. For these reasons, Catherine grants the pardon. Unlike Scott's novel, Pushkin's narrative contains two meetings between subject and sovereign. In short, the differences between the two versions far outweigh the resemblances.

However, the relationship between *The Heart of Midlothian* and Pushkin does not end here. Scott's story was based to some degree on Shakespeare's *Measure for Measure.* Once he got over his youthful admiration for Byron, Pushkin's favorite authors were Scott and Shakespeare: while composing *Boris* he was reading Shakespeare, with ever-increasing enthusiasm, and was trying himself to write a Shakespearean rather than a French tragedy: " . . . but what a man this Shakespeare is! I can't get over it. How paltry is Byron as a tragedian in comparison with him" (*Letters,* I, 237). Like Scott, Pushkin was especially fascinated by *Measure for Measure,* and he, like Scott, wrote his own version, *Angelo,* in 1833. *Angelo* was a Pushkinian reduction of Shakespeare's play into a short narrative poem, with the spotlight on Angelo, or Pushkin's version of Angelo. The poem follows the Pushkin dictum that there is no need to spell matters out. Since Pushkin was well acquainted with both Scott and Shakespeare, he would undoubtedly have seen the lineaments of *Measure for Measure* in *The Heart of Midlothian*, which in turn could well have inspired him to do his own version of the story in *Angelo*. Finally, to make the wheel come full circle, nothing rules out the possibility or even the probability that the Jeanie Deans–Queen Caroline episode—a young woman pleading for a life to a female sovereign—could well have encouraged Pushkin to do his own, quite different, version.

One more illustration will make much the same point. Belinsky thought that Savelich, Grinev's indefatigably faithful, humorous, lovable, serf-retainer-valet in *The Captain's Daughter*, was taken from Scott's Caleb in *The Bride of Lammermoor*, and the resemblances are manifest, up to and including their heroic efforts to obtain food for their respective masters. From his earliest years, however, Pushkin had himself had a serf-valet, Nikita Kozlov, who taught his young master to read and write Russian, was always at his side, and finally accompanied his coffin to his grave. Considering the stormy character of Pushkin's life—the constant traveling, sometimes in primitive regions; the gambling, drinking, dueling, and womanizing; the usually desperate financial straits; the mercurial temperament of the poet himself—it is clear that the author of *The Captain's Daughter* did not have to look far for a model of the faithful retainer, although in fact Savelich is a far more "sympathetic" character than Caleb, who is cantankerous and fanatical. At the same time, this resemblance does not rule out the supposition that Pushkin could have gotten the idea for portraying Kozlov in his own historical fiction from reading *The Bride of Lammermoor*. There is a further complication in that several Savelich-like characters appear in Russian eighteenth-century comedies.[22] In other words, in

[22] This fact was pointed out to me by Simon Karlinsky.

conceiving the character of Savelich, Pushkin was artistically overdetermined.

Such examples as the above could be multiplied; I offer only these two as examples of the complexity of the possible interrelationships between Scott and Pushkin. The many explicit parallels between the work of these two writers have been drawn frequently by Russian, German, English, and American scholars, and they will not be my primary concern here.[23] Instead I propose an examination of the Scott-Pushkin relationship by way of a literary variation of Aristotle's four causes, as presented in the *Metaphysics:* the material ("the bronze of a statue and the silver of a cup"); the formal ("the *form* or pattern; that is, the essential formula"); the efficient ("The source of the first beginning of a change or rest"); and the final ("The same as 'end' ").[24]

Scott did not operate on Pushkin as a cause in all four senses. The final cause of Pushkin's writing was nothing less than his whole aim as a human being, as a poet, a writer of prose, a historian and historical novelist, and a Russian patriot and secular prophet. The material cause of Pushkin's historical fictions, as well as much of his poetry, was Russian history itself, just as in Scott's case the material cause was, first, Scotch history and then English history and finally European history. For both of them—for Scott because his national patrimony and culture were disappearing before his eyes, and in fact had been eroding at least since the union of the English and Scotch crowns in 1707, or even before, and for Pushkin because his national

---

[23] Militsa Greene, "Pushkin and Sir Walter Scott," points out many parallels between *The Captain's Daughter* and not only *Waverley* but other Scott novels as well. The fullest list, to my knowledge, is given by Walter Schamschula in *Der russische historische Roman:* some seven exact resemblances and six other points of contact between *The Captain's Daughter* and Scott's work. Schamschula's most interesting point is that in an earlier version of *The Captain's Daughter* Pushkin conceived of his hero as Byronic, but in the final version turned him into a Scott hero, i.e., a rather nice young man who gets the happy ending he deserves. Pugachev remains the Byronic figure.

[24] Aristotle, *Metaphysics*, trans. Hugh Tredennick (London: Heinemann, 1933), pp. 211–12.

patrimony and culture were still being formed, for good or ill, in an extraordinarily dramatic manner before his eyes—history was a more pressing concern than it was for most of their European contemporaries. It is thus no accident that the seminal historical novelist was Scotch and that the greatest historical novelist, Tolstoy, and the author of one of the most brilliant of short historical fictions, Pushkin, were both Russian. It was from these ends of Europe—not from central Europe, which in Hegel produced the philosopher for the whole affair—that the most vital and reverberating conjunctions of history and fiction issued forth. (Manzoni in Italy was in a similar circumstance to Pushkin.) If one thinks Victor Hugo and the French historical poets, dramatists, and novelists should be brought in here, I can only quote Pushkin from a long and negative discussion of attempts by de Vigny and Hugo to "do" Cromwell and Milton: "After the preposterous fantasies of V. Hugo and Count de Vigny do you want to see a scene painted in a simple manner by another artist? Read in *Woodstock* the meeting of one of the characters with Milton in Cromwell's study. . . ."[25]

Where Scott enters in is in respect to the formal and efficient causes. As for the efficient cause, the example of Scott's novels acted as a catalyst on Pushkin and on other Russian novelists, both before and after him, and encouraged them to attempt for Russian history what Scott had done or was doing for Scotch, English, and European history. Most important, Scott enters in as a formal cause. It is customary to say that as writers Scott and Pushkin were at opposite ends of a scale that is labeled elaboration at one

---

[25] *The Critical Prose of Alexander Pushkin*, ed. and trans. Carl R. Proffer (Bloomington: Indiana University Press, 1969), p. 219. The quotation is from Pushkin's "On Milton and Chateaubriand's Translation of *Paradise Lost*," published in *The Contemporary* in 1837. The ellipsis at the end of the quotation is Pushkin's, who evidently intended to insert a quotation from *Woodstock*. He would have been hard put to find it, since Milton is not a character in *Woodstock*. Elsewhere in *The Critical Prose* Pushkin says, "They equate Count de Vigny's mediocre *Cinq Mars* with the great creations of Walter Scott" (p. 159).

end and concision at the other. And this is true. The soul of Pushkin's wit is his brevity. For Scott, on the other hand, no words were ever to be spared in explaining, illustrating, underlining, even padding, the human and historical events under the province of his pen. Further, the usual inference that is drawn is that the advantage here is mostly Pushkin's: the beauty of concision. But this assertion is true neither as a general principle or proposition nor as an indication of Pushkin's superiority over Scott as a writer. Concision and expansiveness alike have the virtues of their defects and the defects of their virtues. Indeed in that most often cited contrast, Jeanie Deans–Queen Caroline and Maria Morovna–Queen Catherine, the comparison, in respect to human complexity and sociological intricacy, is in Scott's favor.[26] What I mean then by "formal" in this context is Aristotle's sense of ratio. What Pushkin learned from Scott was a sense of *proportion* or formula or ratio in re-creating the past in fiction: how much real history in relation to how much imaginary history; how many real historical characters in relation to how many imaginary historical characters; the proportional ratio between horror and humor (always more of the latter) in the historical canvas; the proper proportions between numbers of the social "high" and the social "low," with the corresponding ratio between peasant vernacular speech and educated speech; the intricate balance to be maintained between the imaginary private love story (boy meets, loses, and gets girl) and the real and often sanguinary historical event, war or rebellion or climactic historical moment (historical loser—often admirable, even lovable—after putting the fear of God into the powers that be, loses, and history goes serenely marching on). For the end of all this is to be—the Scott formula—a wedding and an affirmation of human progress.

Two other proportional relationships were suggested by

---

[26] See my own rather lengthy and detailed analysis of the scene in the introduction to my edition of *The Heart of Mid-Lothian* (Boston: Houghton Mifflin, 1966), pp. xx–xxiii.

Scott. First, there were to be just the right shades and touches to make the fiction an evocation of the national soul or spirit or ethos, neither chauvinistically conceived and uncritically celebrated, on the one hand, nor abased and diminished, on the other; rather it is all to be humorous, shrewd, down-to-earth, showing forth a common residual humanity but with all the unique and distinctive features, warts and all, of the national character in its myriad manifestations. The national sense of humor is all-important; foreign foibles are laughable, but native ones are both laughable and lovable.

Second, it was all to be a fictional democracy: the peasant is equal in novelistic value, interest, and importance to the king; no one is "historic"—making solemn or grand speeches about how important is the historical occasion in which he or she is involved or how memorable these events will be to future generations.

Few other European novelists grasped the sense of proportions in Scott's work, and his special tone and ambience, as well as did Pushkin, as he himself seems to have been aware. In "Of Walter Scott's Novels" (1830), not published in his lifetime, Pushkin said: "The chief fascination of Walter Scott's novels lies in the fact that we grow acquainted with the past, not encumbered with the *enfleur* of French tragedies, or with the prudery of novels of sentiment, or the *dignité* of history, but in a contemporary, homely manner." Shakespeare, Goethe, and Scott, he continued, "have no slavish passion for kings and heroes. They don't (as French heroes do) resemble menials mimicking *la dignité et la noblesse, Ils sont familiers dans les circonstances ordinaires de la vie.*" And in a review in 1830 of Zagoskin's *Yury Miloslavsky, or the Russians in 1612* (1829) Pushkin said: "Today by a *novel* we understand a fictitious narrative describing a historical epoch. Walter Scott gave the lead to a whole host of imitators. But how far removed are they all from the Scotch wizard! Like Agrippa's pupil, having summoned up the demon of the past they could not control him and became the victims of their own audacity." Thus, these imitators of Scott burden the reader with a plethora of historical details, but the characters are only and merely your own friends and neighbors: "how many absurdities, unnecessary details, important omissions; how much refinement! And, above all, how little life!"[27]

One of the things that Pushkin prized in Scott was his earthiness. He regretted the prudery that had come into being in Russia, as in most of the European countries, in the nineteenth century, and he was even fearful that the Russian language itself, whose written form he had been influential in crystallizing, would be bowdlerized. To Vyazemsky he wrote in 1823: "... I should like for a certain biblical obscenity to remain in the Russian language. I hate to see in our primitive language traces of European affectation and French refinement. Rudeness and simplicity are more becoming to it" (*Letters*, I, 146). Speaking of the genteel literary language of his own day and the concern by some journalists and authors over what was fit for feminine eyes, Pushkin said: "But our ladies (God be their judge) don't listen to them and don't read them, but they do read that coarse W. Scott, who simply doesn't know how to replace simple colloquialism with simple-mindedness."[28]

In respect to language itself, both authors inherited a similar, although not strictly analogous, linguistic situation. Both were in a sense bilingual, with a native language that was earthy, racy, colloquial, of the folk folksy, the language of the heart, and a nonnative language that was formal, cerebral, refined, the language of the mind and of polite and civilized discourse. With Pushkin the case was much more clear-cut, since the alternatives were two distinct languages, French and Russian. Three-quarters of his letters are in Russian; one-quarter in French. He found it easier, for example, to converse with women in French, but his correspondence with his fiancée-wife reveals a significant evolution. To his fiancée most of his letters are in French—except for one in which he is scolding her, something, he

---

[27] Quoted in Wolff, *Pushkin on Literature*, pp. 275, 235–36.
[28] *The Critical Prose of Alexander Pushkin*, p. 112.

said, he could not do in French. For this it had to be Russian, and after their marriage he writes to her only in Russian. At the same time, French remained his language for the discussion of general affairs and, especially, abstract thought. In a letter in 1831 to Chaadaev, who had expressly asked Pushkin to write to him in Russian, he replied in French, "My friend, I shall speak to you in the language of Europe; I am more at home in it than ours" (*Letters*, II, 500). Pushkin's linguistic spectrum then ran from Russian peasant vernacular colloquialisms and proverbs, the language of folk and homeland, through the Russian prose which he, Karamzin, and others were developing and which itself was the narrative base for Pushkin's creative writing, to French, the language of Europe and high thought.

Scott's Scots was not distinct from English in the sense that Russian was distinct from French; in fact, in origin it was a branch of English that had become arrested. In his youth he had heard it spoken by older people in what must have been a more pristine form (sounding Frenchified, so he said, probably because of the historic relationship with France). During his own lifetime the original spoken vernacular was finally disappearing, and the Scots dialect of his novels was an attempt to preserve an historical record of it or, at the least, a kind of written notation that would suggest what it was like. In any event Scots was the language of home and heart, colloquial and racy. For example, in a Scott novel a Scot speaking in Scots can use the word "bitch," something that could not happen in a dialogue in English or in a formal prose discourse in English, the language of high seriousness and high thought—the French to the Russian of Scots.

Those linguistic distinctions were of prime importance to the historical novelist: English and Russian for the narrative frame; in dialogue the intermittent use of the vernacular, Russian or Scots, for the authentic flavor of the native soil. There thus develops a counterpoint in the dialogue—what a novel needs is a lot of "chatter," said Pushkin—between the great dynastic events and the high characters and the obscure life of the lowly, with the resultant reminder that basic history is the history of the folk, the anonymous, communal, unrecorded, uncelebrated, long-suffering, and enduring masses.

Finally, Scott had demonstrated what so far had been the most successful temporal ratios in the composition of historical fiction: how far back in time to go and how to underline or dramatize the contrast and / or conflict between the present and the past. In *Waverley* Scott had gone back in history some sixty years, "the period of our grandfathers," far enough back in time to be historical yet still preserved in living memory. (With *Ivanhoe* and other novels he was to venture into another realm, but that is another matter.) But into that past period he had introduced a scale-of-civilization contrast: advanced England versus troglodyte Scotland. Thus there were in *Waverley* two past-present contrasts, one between this present and that past, the other within that past itself. And thus there are in his novels two time-clocks: the one is temporal and measures and records the distances and differences between the present and the past; the other is spatial as much as temporal and arranges the nations or the cultures of Britain and Europe on the scale of civilization (literal historical date to the contrary notwithstanding). For mankind in its various manifestations was always to be shown in evolution or contrast, no matter how far back in time the historical picture.

III

As a historical novelist Pushkin is, compared to Scott, a brilliant might-have-been. Of his several efforts, only the incomplete *The Negro of Peter the Great* and *Dubrovsky* have any substantiality; and only *The Captain's Daughter* is complete, and it is brief. In both *The Negro* and *Dubrovsky* can be seen the Scott proportions and ratios; the past versus the present; in that past another past versus the present syndrome; in that past also the dialectic between the high and the low, and in the dialogue between peasant proverbs and normative speech in *Dubrovsky* the comedy of the national character in all its manifestations, high, middle, low. The scale of civilization also appears in *The Negro,* with a decadent France playing the England to the Scotland of a semibarbarous Russia. Above all, social satire rather than historic solemnity is the mode. There are specific similarities as well. To mention only one cluster in *Dubrovsky:* Dubrovsky himself is a Robin Hood figure, an archetype to which Scott had given wide European currency through *Ivanhoe;* Dubrovsky's chief opponent is an inept chief of police, a kind of Russian Sheriff of Nottingham; as in *Ivanhoe* the efficacy of disguise is one of the mainsprings of the plot.

Pushkin completed *The Captain's Daughter* in 1836, the year before his death. Although he was unable even to begin the writing of his history of Peter the Great and broke off his novel on Peter very early, he was able to finish both his history and his novel on Pugachev. Here the example of Scott, especially of *Waverley,* was all-important, practically archetypal. Even the real historical situations upon which each novel was based were analogous, despite the fundamental differences between George III's Britain in 1745 and Catherine the Great's Russia of the 1770s. As Billington says: "In their conservative longing for a more godly ruling line, they [the Cossacks and peasants of southeast Russia] resemble the Jacobites of late-seventeenth and eighteenth-century England. Just as the Jacobite myth lived on in agrarian Scotland and northern England long after it had failed as an insurrectionary force, so the myth of peasant rebellion lived on in the mentality of southern Russia long after the last great insurrection under Pugachev."[29] Both authors were taking as a subject a lost cause, one that in fact had already suffered its final defeat, although Pushkin still did not know this half a century later about his cause, which still lived on in myth and memory as the very stuff of the poetry of the past.

For the frame of his story Pushkin borrowed a classical

[29] Billington, *The Icon and the Axe,* p. 200.

European device for the historical novel: he was not an author but the editor of the family memoirs of the Grinev family, petty provincial nobility—principally those of the son, Peter Grinev, who, after serving in the campaign against Pugachev, had been unjustly accused of treachery and condemned, but was finally reprieved. As in Scott, each chapter has an epigraph, drawn either from an earlier Russian author or from folk material, proverb, or song.

The resemblances between *Waverley* and *The Captain's Daughter* are manifest, as has often been pointed out, despite the fact that the much larger *Waverley* has far more characters and a much more complicated and intricate plot. To summarize some of the chief similarities briefly: both protagonists are scrappily educated young men, romantic and literary in inclination, who join the army, are engaged in putting down a rebellion, fall in love, become involved with the rebel leader (who in both cases is a pretender), are accused of treason, and are finally exonerated. The rebellion is crushed; each protagonist has a final interchange with the condemned rebel leader (Waverley talks to MacIvor in his prison cell before his execution; Grinev witnesses Pugachev's execution, and the rebel chief recognizes him and nods to him just before being beheaded). Both heroes marry and live happily ever after on their respective estates.

The attitude of both writers is similar: antiromantic, unheroic, and progressivist as to their historical outlook. Although writing historical novels, they both insist that they will not intrude upon the province of history proper; their real interest is in the humans rather than the history.

Scott: "It is not our purpose to intrude upon the province of history" (Ch. 57).

Pushkin: "I will not describe the siege of Orenberg, which belongs to history and has no place in a family memoir" (Ch. 10). "I will not describe our campaign and the conclusion of the war" (Ch. 13).[30]

---

[30] *The Complete Prose Tales of Alexander Sergeyvitch Pushkin*, trans. Gillon R. Aitken (New York: Norton, 1966).

Although they both describe military actions, the ones described are minor. Major and decisive turning points—Culloden and the final defeat and capture of Pugachev—take place offstage. No romance is allowed to war by either author. What Pushkin does tell us of the siege of Orenberg was that from the inside it finally came to be, of all things, a bore: "The inhabitants grew accustomed to cannon-balls falling in their courtyards; even Pugachev's assaults no longer aroused any excitement. I was dying of boredom. Time wore on" (Ch. 10). Waverley had expected plumed troops but found instead night marches, vigils, and couches under wintry skies. Military command in both novels is shown to be, as in Tolstoy, a mishmash of compromises insensibly issuing from the multiple clash of the egocentric and egotistical desires and wills of the chief advisors of the nominal commanders.

Scott had announced at the beginning of *Waverley* that he was dealing, not with moonshine, but with reality, and one of the basic rhythms of his novel is the constant undercutting of the hero's, and the reader's, romantic expectations. To take just one instance: Waverley is taken to the cave of Donald Bean Lean, a Highland outlaw. He expects to meet someone out of a canvas by Salvator Rosa, stern, gigantic, ferocious. Instead he is introduced to a short, slim man with sandy-colored hair and small pale features. Similarly Grinev is sent, for his first post, to the "Belogorsky fortress" and expects to find menacing bastions, towers, and a rampart. What he finds is a little village surrounded by a wooden fence, with one dilapidated cannon.[31] However, both authors, and their protagonists, remark on the

---

[31] In his history Pushkin had described what these "forts" were like: ". . . nothing more than villages surrounded by a wattle and mud or wooden fence. In them several old soldiers and local Cossacks, under the protection of two or three cannon, were secure from the arrows and spears of the wild tribes that roamed about the steppes of Orenburg gubernia and near its borders." Quoted in John T. Alexander, *Autocratic Politics in a National Crisis: The Imperial Russian Government and Pugachev's Revolt*, (Bloomington: Indiana University Press, 1969), p. 57.

wonders of reality itself. Waverley is intermittently struck with a sense of bemusement at what he has gotten into: a rebellion, Highland chieftains, the Scottish Highlands, and so on. Similarly, in *The Captain's Daughter* Grinev muses: "I could not help but marvel at the strange chain of circumstances: a child's coat given to a tramp had saved me from the hangman's noose, and a drunkard roaming from inn to inn was besieging fortresses and shaking the government" (Ch. 8).

Since both authors were describing the last stands of barbarian enclaves, they each celebrate human progress, which comes about, so both tell us, not from violence and revolution, but from the progressive spread of order and enlightenment and the diffusion of humane principles. Since in Scotland and Russia the last barbarian outbreak had happened relatively recently, both Pushkin, writing in the 1830s about events of the 1770s, and Scott, writing in 1813–14 about events of 1745, remark on the speed with which civilization proper had overtaken their hitherto disorderly societies. Both celebrate also the general softening of manners and morals in modern times, and Pushkin rejoices in the abolition of judicial torture and mutilation in Russia.

As for the humor and the horror, Scott had set the proportions and Pushkin preserved them. In novels about battles, men will be killed and wounded: that is a given of the situation, and in both *Waverley* and *The Captain's Daughter* men die or are wounded in war. But then there is the whole further matter of the cruelty and savagery that usually accompany such affairs, especially civil convulsions. The atrocities committed after Culloden were considerable; the barbarities committed by both sides during and after the *Pugachevshchina* were unbelievable. Few of the victims on either side enjoyed the luxury of a quick and simple death, and those that were left alive were often left mutilated. The only real difference between the two sides was that the rebels' cruelty was spontaneous while that of the government was calculated.

But the Scott ratio held that these matters were to be

minimized and to be suggested rather than explicitly dramatized on any great scale. There is little of human cruelty portrayed in *Waverley* as a whole, although at the end much is made of the fact that MacIvor is to suffer the traitor's death to the full: hanging, drawing, and quartering. Waverley and MacIvor discuss this prospect in their last conversation in Fergus's cell. Fergus even estimates the time involved: that it will take the executioner a half hour to accomplish his bloody work—but it appears to have taken longer by Waverley's calculation (although he is not a witness to the actual execution).

The 1745 in Scotland was child's play, in this respect, in comparison with the Pugachev rebellion and its aftermath. Accordingly, Pushkin's novel shows more savagery and suffering than did Scott's, but not remotely on the scale of actual history. In other words, he kept the Scott ratio, although his brief pictures are such as to give any imaginative reader the general idea. Thus, at the fortress of Belogorsky, Grinev sees an old Bashkir who had been mutilated after an uprising in 1741: ears and nose cut off and tongue cut out: "Never will I forget that man" (Ch. 6). In turn, Captain Mironov, a perfectly good man, was about to torture, as a normal procedure, the old Bashkir to get information from him; only his missing tongue saved him. When the fortress is captured, Grinev sees Captain Mironov and other officers hanged and sees the Captain's wife, stripped of her clothing, summarily dispatched by a blow on the head. Later in the novel he sees another unforgettable man, one of Pugachev's generals, Khlopusha, the nickname of Afanasy Sokolov, an escaped convict with no nostrils and red scars on his forehead. Khlopusha was an actual historical person, a former metalworker turned to brigandage, who became Pugachev's chief lieutenant; he had been four times beaten with the knout and had twice escaped from Siberia, with slit nostrils and a branded forehead. One of the most gruesome sights, once more based on what had really happened, was removed, along with other less gruesome incidents, from the novel (in English translations, it is usually printed after the end of *The*

Captain's Daughter as the "unpublished addition to Chapter Thirteen"). Grinev is crossing the Volga at night and sees, lit by the moon, a floating gallows, a raft with three hanged men dangling from the crossbeam. Grinev boards the raft and sees that their faces had been mutilated before they were hanged. Such a sight would not have been uncommon on the Volga in those days.

Moreover, Pushkin appears actually to have bowdlerized or softened some of his source material. The Belogorsky episode in *The Captain's Daughter*—in which a brave Russian officer defends his little fort, hopelessly, against Pugachev, is captured and hanged, his wife killed, his daughter preserved—was probably based upon a real incident that Pushkin reported in his formal history of the rebellion. A certain Major Kharlov was in command of a small fortress near Orenberg that was attacked by Pugachev. Kharlov was apparently drunk when the fortress was under attack. The fort was taken and Kharlov, though severely wounded, was hanged in the sight of his young wife. Pugachev then raped the wife, who became his mistress until she was killed by his followers, who feared her influence over him.[32]

But of humor there must be plenty, not only of situation but of character as well. Most important of all: it is the humor of national types. Baron Bradwardine, David Gellatley, Duncan MacWheeble, among others, of *Waverley* are quintessential eccentrics (Scott, not Dickens, invented the breed) and uniquely Scotch. In *The Captain's Daughter,* there are the brave, simple, henpecked Captain Mironov; his indefatigable wife; and, above all, Grinev's serf-valet, the immortal Savelich. If Pushkin's own Nikita Kozlov, who appears to have been in reality a much more sophisticated man than the simple Savelich, was anything like this in his devotion, Pushkin need not have wondered, as he probably did in his last sad years, if anybody loved him. Of such characters Gogol said that they were the first real Russians to be portrayed in fiction. Savelich himself is one of the

[32] Bayley, *Pushkin*, pp. 352–53.

first serfs to be presented in the foreground and as a complete human being in Russian fiction. For what gives the classical historical novel its élan is not its historical solemnity or grandeur or even its depth in time but its comedy of the national character.

Finally, at the center, along with the hero, is the rebel-king. In *Waverley* Bonnie Prince Charlie is portrayed, although briefly and from a distance. Thus Waverley's personal feelings are displaced to his lieutenant, MacIvor, and to MacIvor's sister, Flora. The mixture of emotions of Waverley for MacIvor is complex: admiration for one side of his character (his great abilities), distaste for the other (his personal ambition), disapproval of what he is trying to do (the rebellion), but, to the end, a lingering affection and admiration for him and a genuine regret for his grisly end. Pushkin puts Grinev into an analogous, although not completely parallel, relationship to Pugachev.

Pugachev is introduced to the novel and to Grinev by a device out of *Rob Roy*. At the beginning of *Rob Roy*, when Osbaldistone is on his way to the North, he dines at an inn; partaking of the meal is a real, an authentic, Scotsman, the first Osbaldistone has ever seen, who goes by the name of Campbell. A lean, vigorous, athletic man, with decided opinions, speaking a strong Scots, he turns out to be, naturally, Rob Roy himself. Similarly, at the beginning of *The Captain's Daughter*, when Savelich and Grinev are stranded in their sledge in a snowstorm, a figure appears out of nowhere and guides them safely to a nearby inn. Here they see their guide, who is about forty, of medium height, lean, broad-shouldered, with large, lively eyes, and a face with an agreeable but roguish expression, speaking Russian thieves' slang and proverbs and drinking spirits (this appears to be an accurate picture of the real Pugachev). It is Grinev's giving his hareskin coat to this stranger that leads later to Pugachev's saving his life, and that more than once. This action then is the mainspring of the plot.

The basis for this idea, a rebel leader taking under his personal protection an officer of the enemy, comes, I believe, not from the life of Pugachev, but from that of Stenka

Razin, the only poetic figure in Russian history. In August 1669 Razin and his forces went by boat down the Volga to Astrakan, on the Caspian sea. Prince Lvov, one of the commanders of the city, made an offer of peace which was accepted, and the Cossacks entered the city peacefully. Prince Lvov entertained Razin as his houseguest and some kind of bond was created between the two men. In June 1670 Lvov, with some 2600 soldiers, was sent to intercept Razin, who was once more on his way down the Volga. When the two armies met, Lvov's men refused to fight and went over to the enemy. All the officers of Lvov's group were killed except two, one being Lvov himself, who was spared, against the wishes of most of the rebel host, by Razin—who, except when drunk, appeared to have been less bloodthirsty than many of his followers. Later in 1670 Razin assaulted and captured Astrakan; an orgy of looting, torturing, and killing followed, but, once more, Lvov was spared. Unlike *The Captain's Daughter,* however, this story did not have a happy ending. In July 1671, the Cossacks who were occupying Astrakan in Razin's absence went on a rampage, killing all gentry and officials. Lvov himself was beheaded, and the house where he had entertained Razin was given over to plunder.

There appears to have been one other characteristic of Razin that Pushkin incorporated into his picture of Pugachev. All the rebel leaders had announced themselves as the enemies of the rich and the protectors of the poor, but Razin in particular had come to be a kind of Robin Hood in the popular imagination. And Pushkin, with a characteristically brief touch, adds a Robin Hood dimension to his picture of Pugachev. When Grinev is captured by Pugachev's men the second time and is taken to the leader, he had been on his way to try to rescue his beloved, Maria Mironov, now an orphan and the captive and recipient of the unwelcome attentions of Shvabrin, the villain of the piece. When Pugachev asks him what he is up to, Grinev replies:

"I was going to the Belogorsky fortress to rescue an orphan who is being persecuted there."

Pugachev's eyes glittered.
"Which of my people dares to persecute an orphan?" he cried. "Be he as wise as Solomon, he will not escape my judgment." (Ch. 11).

Scott's heart was always, and for good historical reasons, on the side of the losers and the underdogs; in *Ivanhoe*, for example, his real affections go out to Rebecca, a Jewess, to Robin Hood, an outlaw, and to Gurth and Wamba, two Anglo-Saxon slaves, and not to the mighty above them. Such instances could be multiplied in all his novels. This same instinctive inclination is similarly evident in Pushkin, and in *The Captain's Daughter* he finally makes the rebel leader actually likable in the eyes of Grinev and thus in the eyes of the reader. The whole matter is prefigured in the dream that Grinev has near the opening of the book. When Pugachev, then unknown, is guiding the sledge through the snowstorm, Grinev falls asleep and has a dream in which he is back home; his mother tells him his father is dying and wishes to bid him goodbye. But instead of his father, he finds in the bed a black-bearded peasant looking at him "gaily" or "merrily," (depending on the translation). His mother tells him that the peasant is his father by proxy and that he should kiss his hand, which Grinev refuses to do.

Then the peasant leaped out of bed, seized an axe from behind his back and began to swing it about in every direction. I wanted to run . . . but I could not. The room was full of dead bodies; I kept stumbling against them and slipping in the pools of blood. . . . The terrible peasant called to me gently and said:
"Don't be frightened. Come and receive my blessing." (Ch. 2)

"The peasant with the axe" was the most potent symbol in Russian history, the emblem of the ultimate revolt and the nightmare for centuries of the aristocracy and the autocracy. In *The Captain's Daughter* it is a reminder that Pugachev—despite the fact that we are to come to like him—and his followers were bloodthirsty fellows, as indeed they were. The dream prefigures other aspects of the novel as well. Later on, Pugachev is to demand that Grinev kiss his hand to acknowledge him as "the true Tsar," which Grinev refuses to do (and gets away with it). And while Pugachev is that "terrible peasant" to everybody else of Grinev's class and station, he is not to the hero. He becomes instead a proxy father, his savior and protector; Grinev in turn becomes his proxy father's confidante, the one person to whom the "true Tsar" can speak the truth. After he saves Grinev's life a second time, Pugachev says, "you see, I'm not as bloodthirsty as your brethren say I am" (Ch. 11). Shortly after this he confides to Grinev that he is not his own master, that his followers have their own ideas, and that they will finally betray him (all this is historically accurate). Grinev urges him to cut loose from them and to throw himself upon the mercy of the empress. But it is too late for that, and Pugachev replies—by way of a folk parable about a raven who feeds on carrion and an eagle who feeds on live blood—that it is better to be an eagle for a day than a crow for centuries. When he takes his last leave of Pugachev, Grinev thinks: "At that moment, I felt strongly drawn to him. I fervently wished to take him away from the environment of the criminals he commanded, and to save his head while there was still time" (Ch. 12).

The most significant revelation of the hero's true feelings about the Pretender occurs when he hears of Pugachev's capture.

> But in the meantime a strange feeling poisoned my joy: the thought of the villain, smeared with the blood of so many innocent victims, and of the execution awaiting him involuntarily troubled me.
> "Emelya, Emelya," I thought with vexation, "why didn't you throw yourself on a bayonet, or get hit by grapeshot? It would have been the best thing you could have done." (Ch. 13)

Thus Pugachev is a "villain," and yet. . . . The full force of this passage is lost in most translations into English by the leaving out, in order not to confuse the reader, of the phrase, "Emelya, Emelya" (an affectionate diminutive)—the one time that Grinev refers to Pugachev by his given name. But it is a deft Pushkinian sign pointing to where the heart's affections really lie.

Pushkin, then, blended Stenka Razin and Pugachev for what was to be his final portrait of a Russian leader. If he tried to make Peter the Great homely and familiar in *The Negro of Peter the Great,* and failed, he nonetheless succeeded in making Pugachev agreeable, merry, and likable. His characterization probably does not give us the full truth about the real Pugachev, but it does tell us a lot about Pushkin: that—during his last years and as a historical novelist, especially in *Dubrovsky* and *The Captain's Daughter*—he was what George Sand said Scott was: the poet of the peasant, soldier, outlaw, and artisan.

4 | THE REGENCY NOVEL OF FASHION

Francis Russell Hart

The social and historical consciousness of the later eighteenth century evolved in significant measure through a growing concern with that feature of social change called "fashion." The idea, of course, was already ancient; so, too, was its equivocal place in moral and social criticism. René König traces a radical ambivalence toward fashion from the fulminations of Isaiah to the ironic worldliness of Mandeville's *Fable of the Bees* (1714). But a late-enlightenment society that came to adulate Brummell came, also, to use the word *fashion*—and its cognates *ton, exclusive, the world*—in a sense and with an intensity that were significantly new.[1] Its "fashionable" novelists, writing normally in the voices of traditional moralism, nonetheless led the way toward a new social consciousness.

The concept of fashion as formulated by modern social theorists is, of course, not to be confused with the problem of fashion as explored by novelists of almost two centuries ago. For the theorist, fashion is a code of social styles and behaviors, characterized by rapid change, associated with historic periods when new social alternatives are numerous and available and when traditional modes

---

[1] René König, *A La Mode*, trans. F. Bradley (New York: Seabury, 1973); Ellen Moers, *The Dandy* (New York: Viking, 1960), pp. 25–26; Ingrid Brenninkmeyer, *The Sociology of Fashion* (Winterthur, Del.: Keller, 1962), pp. 6–7, 13.

of social control—custom, name, title, even wealth—have lost their credibility. Its spectacular character requires public visibility on a large scale. Its ephemerality makes for hectic instability. Its availability encourages a democratic competitiveness, which in turn generates a reactionary mystique of exclusiveness. Its coerciveness provokes a sense of insecurity, distress, even shame, among those who struggle vainly to emulate the shifting nuances of its styles. Such, in summary, is the concept. Aided by the perspectives it provides, we can discover the complexity and urgency of the problem explored by the novelists.

For them, fashion as a theme is a socializing of numerous interrelated themes—political, moral, even religious. The "fashionable" life is social life as spectacle, masque; it is dominated by an almost fanatical commitment to appearance, a slavish concern for reputation. It is lived in places merely spectacular or temporary: the townhouse, the opera, ballroom, club, or pleasure garden, the resort or retreat. In such places, life is specious ceremony, demanding at once an extravagant show of wealth and a "liberal" unconcern for wealth (as opposed to mercenary vulgarity). Fashion is antihistorical. It lives from moment to moment, keeps up with "the times," substitutes "establishment" for estate, status for name, credit for inheritance. Thus it fosters a false independence, a neglect of hereditary obligations, a worship of novelty and instability. Fashion adulates "personality," yet is antipersonal. For it encourages the false liberality that is libertinism, an emotional gambling that squanders personal integrity, a commitment to social role that atrophies the true nature. Most important, fashion worships "society," yet is antisocial. It is obsessed with etiquette, and an obsessive etiquette supplants true manners, a purely "public" life merely masks as society. The social dialectic of fashion generates its own antitheses: sentimental imprudence, cynicism, antisocial withdrawal. The social danger of these is the chief concern of many of the novels. For these are the mere negations of fashion. Its true contraries are the real social virtues whose specters it worships.

The affirmation of those real virtues in a time of social confusion and transformation, the search for new stabilities in a period of revolutionary change, the striving to articulate a proper balance of personal autonomy and responsible worldliness: these become the objectives of the novelists of fashion. The elements and objectives emerge gradually, to be sure. We can trace their emergence if we begin with Fanny Burney, glance next at her successors Maria Edgeworth and Susan Ferrier, turn then to Hook, Ward, and Lister, and end with early Bulwer and Disraeli. The lineage has been discussed before. But the complexity of its attention to the problem of fashion, and the significance of the social mythology it helped create, deserves fuller recognition. First, however, we need to understand the social instability of the period and to elaborate the concept of fashion provided by recent theorists.

I

Few epochs in British social history are more sharply definable or more often defined than the half-century from the 1780s to the 1830s. The 1780s are generally seen as the takeoff point in socioeconomic tempo. By the 1780s, observes Plumb, "the settled world, the world of Walpole and the Pelhams, had ended," and "the traditional structure of local society was crumbling under the weight of administrative problems of national complexity." By the 1830s, summarizes Morazé, "The social hierarchy was no longer a stable reality fixed by an immutable decree of providence. It was a turmoil of ambitions, failures and successes, which were undermining the old *elites* in order to make way for the new ones. The rapidity of change was such a new phenomenon that thinkers and artists became fascinated by the strange problem of progress."[2] It is not

[2] J. H. Plumb, *England in the Eighteenth Century* (Harmondsworth, Middlesex: Penguin, 1950), p. 140; Charles Morazé, *The Triumph of the Middle Classes* (Garden City, N.Y.: Doubleday Anchor, 1968), p. 192. George Rudé, *Europe in the Eighteenth Century: Aristocracy and the Bourgeois Challenge* (New York: Praeger, 1972), p. 49.

surprising that to mid-Victorians the Regency period should have seemed the end of the past.

It is convenient but simplistic to identify this half-century with "the dual revolution," political on the Continent, economic in Britain. Growth in population and trade, and revolution in agriculture, were advanced. Industrialization was not; and while its tempo picked up dramatically from the 1780s, industrial revolution did not become a social reality for the arts until the 1830s. As Morazé put it, "there was no such thing as an industrial revolution in 1780; it had not yet evolved from the revolution in social customs."[3] For images and expressions of this prior social revolution, we turn to the novelists of fashion.

Recent historians have seen the process in terms of a bourgeois "challenge" or "triumph," but the concept is complicated by evidence of a dissolution and multiplication of bourgeoisies. The bourgeoisie was losing the unity of legal status; traditional privileges were compromised by internal division. Bourgeois of trade and commerce merged with the new wealth and power of banking and credit. Political and professional bourgeois resisted merger with the new manufacturer, while "the industrial entrepreneur broke free from the social limitations that capitalists before him had imposed upon themselves."[4] Conflicts of social style accompanied the growth of power and wealth.

The picture of confusion in fashion suggests something other than self-confidence. When Watt's London mill was ready in 1786, Watt found pointless the proposal to celebrate the opening with a high society masked ball. Yet he

---

[3] Morazé, p. 8; cf. E. J. Hobsbawm, *The Age of Revolution, 1789–1848* (New York: N.A.L. Mentor, 1964) pp. 44–45.
[4] J.-F. Bergier, "The Industrial Bourgeoisie and the Rise of the Working Class, 1700–1914," trans. R. Greaves, in *The Fontana Economic History of Europe*, ed. C. M. Cipolla (London: Collins, 1973), p. 407. Rudé stresses the "challenge," while Morazé stresses the "triumph." Bergier (pp. 401–17) traces the dissolution of bourgeois unity; Hobsbawm (pp. 41, 153, 221) describes conflict between old and new bourgeois. R. J. White, *Life in Regency England* (London: Batsford, 1963), argues that sharp class divisions were largely mythic (pp. 49–50).

built himself a fine country house and laid out a park, following a fashion he "affected to despise." Boulton of Birmingham with similar inconsistency delighted in the visits of "the Great" to the "Toyshop of Europe."[5] And these men were still shut off from social power, and divided from the bankers and merchants who identified with Tory society, from whom they bought marriages, land, parliamentary seats, and military commissions. Meanwhile, a new class of fundholders, unconnected with either, had grown tremendously. The "bourgeois triumphant" is no simple, stable image.

Nor is the "aristocracy conquered." The "end of aristocratic society" need not mean the end of aristocratic principle or influence, and society remained aristocratic. "It was not only the direct impact of titled land-owning classes that made it so," writes Rudé, "but its ability during the great part of the [eighteenth] century to absorb and impose its image on other up-and-coming groups."[6] The old aristocracy was identified with the land. But the concept of land was rapidly changing from hereditary property to productive commodity. Landowners were caught up in agricultural improvement and experiment, while their continuing power in Parliament allowed for the passage of enclosure bills in ever-more-rapid succession. The growth and prosperity of large tenant farms gave birth to the new class consciousness of gentlemen farmers and (angrily caricatured by Cobbett) their idle "ladies." The farmhouse's elegance could not tolerate the dirty feet and uncouth manners of workers. Nearby, amassing wealth, the rural industrialists looked on with mixed feelings at the gentry and acquired their own social ideal: "a new feudalism," Plumb calls it, "whose centre was the mill or mine instead of the castle."[7] And all groups turned increasingly for ex-

[5] André Parreaux, *Daily Life in England in the Reign of George III*, trans. C. Congreve (London: George Allen and Unwin, 1969), pp. 63–64.

[6] Rudé, p. 77. Hobsbawm, pp. 33, 218; Morazé, p. 144; Parreaux, pp. 38–40.

[7] Plumb, pp. 145–46. G. M. Trevelyan, *English Social History* (London: Longmans Green, 1942), p. 472; E. W. Bovill, *English Country Life, 1780–1830* (London: Oxford, 1962), p. 31.

pertise to the technological elites of the late Enlightenment, who in turn were caught up in the patronage of a changing aristocracy. Here, then, is a composite of class consciousness, emulation, competition, and animosity.

The picture of shifting aristocracy is further complicated by evidence of aristocratic resurgence and defensive exclusiveness. The 1719 Peerage Bill had failed, but peerages were mostly limited to large landowners until Pitt's minor "revolution" in the 1780s. Seats in Parliament remained quite exclusive. Increasingly, justices of the peace were country gentlemen, socially acceptable parsons, or even aristocrats. The military ranks were growing increasingly exclusive. Aristocratic values were rationalized and reinforced as "the animating spirit or incentive throughout all walks of life" at the very period when aristocrats became more entrenched and rigid. Yet aristocracy had been corrupted by two developments: "its association with money and wealth, and its use by governments as an instrument of rule."[8]

For an increasingly unstable, segmented, yet interconnected social world, wealth was becoming the only common denominator. "The fundamental fact about Britain in the first two generations of the Industrial Revolution," writes Hobsbawm, "was that the comfortable and rich classes accumulated income so fast and in such vast quantities as to exceed all available possibilities of spending and investment."[9] The social historian is struck not just by this huge accumulation but by the instability of wealth and the expression of that instability in the cult of fasion. The growth of wealth in the late century can be seen in the rapid increase of banking, the spread of banks to rural districts, and the growth of banking credit. The entrepreneur became a crucial figure; the war made business a gamble and the merchant a profiteer. Frantic risk-taking was becoming a way of life, status of name and land was giving

---

[8] R. R. Palmer, *The Age of the Democratic Revolution: The Challenge* (Princeton: Princeton University Press, 1969), pp. 68, 71–79; Rudé, pp. 177–78, 215; Hobsbawm, pp. 32–33.
[9] Hobsbawm, p. 65. Rudé, pp. 69–70.

way to credit, and it is not surprising that gambling became a universal mania.[10] The mania would play a symbolic role in the mythology of fashion. For financial credit was the key to social credibility, and social credibility in a disoriented society became fixed to the fantastic currency of fashion. A self-conscious and unstable aristocracy spent that currency with an ostentation and a mystique that asserted its unique social credibility and simultaneously expressed its contempt for the wealth that made fashion available to all buyers. The effect is genuinely fantastic, and Plumb sounds this keynote in his vignette of aristocratic intoxication. "About their lives there is a touch almost of fantasy."[11] It was a world in which social spectacle tried to ritualize an elusive and bewildering social reality, and fashion tried to stabilize a chaos of styles.

"Fashion," wrote Edward Sapir, "is emphatically a historical concept." Under culture's surface are "powerfully psychological drifts of which fashion is quick to catch the direction." Custom-bound societies are characterized by slow changes of style; "it is not until modern Europe is reached that the familiar merry-go-round of fashion with its rapid alternations of season occurs."[12] Modern sociologists of fashion naturally avoid the urgent moralism of Regency essayists and analyze fashion as an authentic mode of social control and change, but they do recognize its problematic aspects. Sapir, for instance, notes that fashion differs from taste by dint of an inherent "measure of compulsion." König adopts the Steinmetz definition: "a periodic change of style of a more or less compulsory character" (a compulsion to change; a compulsion to adapt to the change). "In fashion, abrupt change and an equally abrupt tendency to stabilize, both demanding adaptation, constitute a paradoxical situation." Fashion may be "socially legitimized caprice" or a "new and unintelligible form of

---

[10] Plumb, pp. 147–49; Morazé, pp. 137, 147; Trevelyan, pp. 464, 467; Parreaux, p. 178; Bovill, p. 124.
[11] Plumb, pp. 84–85.
[12] Sapir, "Fashion," in *Encyclopedia of the Social Sciences* (1931), VI, 139–41.

social tyranny."[13] For the novelists of fashion it is both. For the novelists it threatens the proper balancing of personal taste and integrity with a due respect for "the world."

Blumer's analysis of the social functions of fashion relates its importance to distinctively modern periods of social change. First, it "introduces controlling social forms into a moving area of divergent possibilities." Second, it "provides for an orderly march from the immediate past to the proximate future" by detaching social forms from the "grip of the past" and offering means of adjusting them to changed circumstances. Third, it "nurtures and shapes a common sensitivity and taste"; it is "democratic," Brenninkmeyer argues; it "desires appropriate interpretation regardless of rank, birth or heredity,"[14] and is thus a means of broad socialization in a time of shifting social norms and boundaries. Such orderliness could hardly be apparent to a custom-oriented society for whom fashion seemed a tyranny of spasmodic rapidity and chaotic instability. Yet we can see in the novelists how the articulating of this sense of bewilderment could yield new patterns and norms and a new social consciousness.

König introduces an additional historical dimension. He stresses the public scenic aspect of fashion, its definitive need to see and be seen. He traces the loci of public display through Western history from agora to court to baroque theater, and notes that with the coming of the nineteenth century, cities became centers of "intense and sustained social activity," and hence of fashion. But König's most valuable perspective on the fashion problem is both psychological and aesthetic. He evokes the tragicomic insecurity and suffering of the fashionable *nouveau*, for whom any social disapproval is intolerable and whose restless urge towards conformity in change risks the loss of personality itself. "These are the hysterics of fashion, the true fashion snob." The snob "radiates a distinctly unhappy conscious-

---

[13] Sapir, p. 140; König, pp. 44–45, 54–55.
[14] H. G. Blumer, "Fashion," in *International Encyclopedia of the Social Sciences* (1968), V, 343–44; Brenninkmeyer, p. 61.

ness"; although he makes fashion his religion, he must fail; yet in failing, "he has the peculiar urge to seek contact with the very people who reject him. His insecurity leaves him no other way out than to exaggerate." Thus, while fashion may arise from a primordial impulse to levity, the "reputation of levity that fashion has acquired . . . is not quite correct. For this apparent levity hides a restless, consuming death-wish, which is realized at the precise moment when a fashion has reached its climax and basks in the eager acceptance of the great public. Hence the veil of melancholy that surrounds every fashion."[15] In a culture that relished graveyard poetry and Gothic melodrama and was to idolize Byron, the melancholy is inescapable, and we should expect to find it even in the fiction of social manners. But the pervasive note of hectic tragicomedy is a Burneyan invention, further sophisticated by Edgeworth and Ferrier, and turned to religious solemnity by Ward, to Byronic fantasy by Disraeli, and to Gothic mystery by Bulwer.

One more Burneyan invention finds a gloss in König: the central consciousness of social distress, shame and bewilderment, over the shifting nuances of etiquette. The disintegration of aristocratic power left a "strangely unreal and occasionally truly ghostlike afterlife, which we call 'prestige.' "[16] Such prestige mingled strangely with the new bourgeois ideals of distinction and gentility, especially since the bourgeois became a slavish imitator of aristocratic exclusiveness. Yet the imitation, mixed with contempt, was perforce specious; the basis for exclusiveness was eroded. The expression of such confusion and paradox in the novels is an ordeal of subtly distinct and easily confused social values. This is the ordeal that gives form to the novel of fashion. Indeed, the very adaptation of the novel to such themes is part of the process. For the novel, by tradition a middle-class genre, was being adapted to aristocratic fantasies and models for a wide new public. The novel was becoming fashionable. And when, at the end of our half

[15] König, p. 124; also, pp. 57, 62, 125.
[16] König, pp. 146–47.

century, we reach the first fashionable onslaughts of Disraeli and Bulwer, we will find novelist and protagonist alike striving to translate a phantom of prestige into new forms of social and political power.

"The fashionable novel tells us, in effect," writes one critic, "that the world is a place of make-believe and sham."[17] Perhaps; and yet the make-believe happens in palpably contemporary settings—such is one important Burneyan invention. The most distinctive new scene was urban. London, soon to be the spectacular place of Nash, Holland, and the Regency, remained small in area, and fashionable London was smaller still. Brummell apologized for "being found as far 'east' as Charing Cross" and joked about post-horses when invited to Bloomsbury.[18] Degrees of fashion were sharply demarcated in topography. "No capital in Europe, perhaps," writes Parreaux, "could incorporate such a complex and subtle hierarchy of class structure based on so many varying elements: occupation, district, street, type of house—whether it was owned or merely rented, and which part lived in." The narrator of Lister's *Herbert Lacy* (1828) anticipated him: "I cannot find that in any other city, ancient or modern, this 'pride of place' has acquired such strength as in London. . . . Many and nice are the gradations of square-hood: numerous are its steps of precedence."[19]

This was the great age of elegant interiors, yet foreigners noted the outward shabbiness of fashionable London homes. Two explanations are obvious: much of fashionable life was lived in public, and the exhausting season of fashionable residence was short. Families connected with Parliament might arrive in February; most fashionables came in April. The exodus to fashionable resorts might start after the "birthday" in June, but July closed the Season, and fashionable houses had their shades drawn in

---

[17] M. W. Rosa, *The Silver-Fork School* (New York: Columbia University Press, 1936), p. 15.
[18] Moers, p. 66.
[19] Parreaux, pp. 99–100; T. H. Lister, *Herbert Lacy*, 2 vols. in 1 (Philadelphia: Carey, Lea and Carey, 1828), II, 136.

August. But fashion was reaching into the countryside, and communications between city and country became a network of fashion. Styles of equipage multiplied and became fashionable indicators. New middle-class tastes for the villa filtered into aristocratic minds, and the fashionable country house must emulate the villa's convenient and compact elegance. The spread of elegance via an itinerant aristocracy to new farmhouses roused Cobbett's ire, but others saw positive values: the socializing of the aristocracy; the spread of knowledge and elegance to the countryside; the sharing of refinement among classes.

Evident here is a central stylistic paradox of social change in the period. Fashion was undermining an aristocracy of name and rank with a new elitism of taste. The shift was as evident in dress as in domestic architecture and carriages. The extravagance of male costume up to the 1780s gave way to casual dress, then to republican simplicity, and finally to the fastidious, simple elegance of Brummell's "style suitable for any man, king or commoner, who aspired after the distinction of gentleman."[20] Women's fashions followed a similar trend, becoming progressively more youthful and simple. Fashion was democratizing aristocratic tastes, and aristocratic emulation became more accessible. Perhaps as a reaction, the new social mode of fashionable aristocracy was an intricate and obsessive exclusivism. Widely adaptable styles of elegance were being established, yet exclusivism dictated a hectic changeableness. Regency style produced the middle-class universal of elegant gentility; Regency fashion dictated an "otiose and extravagant pastiche."[21] It is a genuine crisis of style, and it dramatically reflects the bewildering instability of social change and the bewilderment felt by those compelled to enter such a social world. The ordeals and temptations

---

[20] Moers, pp. 35–36. Parreaux, pp. 25–36.
[21] White, p. 65: "part Classic, part Gothic, with an admixture of Egyptian and Oriental, liberally tarted up with the picturesque: a composite which is the negation of a style. And there is indeed something monstrous about the works of the Regency."

THE REGENCY NOVEL OF FASHION | 95

of social bewilderment are the central motifs of Burney's novels.

II

"It is time," writes Lady Howard to Mr. Villars at Berry Hill, seven miles from the nearest town, that his seventeen-year-old ward "should see something of the world." Indeed, "she seems born for an ornament to the world. . . . I cannot but think, that it was never designed for one who seems meant to grace the world, to have her life devoted to retirement." After two visits to London, Evelina has had enough: "I desire not to see any more of the world! the few months I have already passed in it, have sufficed to give me a disgust even to its name." "What a world is this we live in! how corrupt! how degenerate!"[22] This is the dangerously antisocial impact of fashion.

Entering "the world" is learning what it is to be in society. What makes Burney's *Evelina* (1778) the first predominantly *social* novel in English is its obsessive preoccupation with being in society. The epistolary mode underlines the paradoxical quality of the obsession: Evelina is constantly in company, yet terrifyingly alone; she is solitary, far away from the authority and friendship of true guidance, yet always exposed. Society is nightmare. Her persistent response is mental pain, bewilderment, shame: "unused to the situations in which I find myself, and embarrassed by the slightest difficulties, I seldom, till too late, discover how I ought to act." She is "perpetually involved in some distress or dilemma." Her home, heart, pious nature are fixed in the total retreat of Villars; "the world" is terrifyingly public, an unstable, intricately codified sphere of scenes, ceremonies, specious "manners." Villars wants her

---

[22] Fanny Burney, *Evelina* (New York: Norton, 1965), pp. 7, 112, 246, 259.

not to enter it, yet she must; she must, says one critic, "come to terms with a society she has first seen through."[23]

"Seen through" is the key. Society is a world of appearances; appearances turn cruelly against her; she will never again "trust to appearances." Yet she must learn that in society the apparent is part of the real, and that the real test of prudence is the management of appearances. Distress arises from misapprehension and mystery; mystery pervades the book, surrounding name, status, inheritance. Evelina is as much of a mystery to the world as it is to her. Her name is not her own; her own is denied her. A changeling has replaced her, and there is a surreal quality about her sensations when she hears that her father's only daughter has appeared, hears her own praises sung, yet sees a double bearing her status. False appearances are so common as to seem diabolical; confusions of attachment and motive are rife, and true communication seems under a spell. Yet Evelina's appearance ultimately declares her true identity to her father and her "name" is restored.

Name means two things to Evelina. It means legitimacy and reputation, both matters of the utmost "delicacy." And "delicacy" makes difficult their vigorous and direct pursuit. Villars, however remote, is at the center of this dilemma: he would recover Evelina's name, yet his delicacy has led him to prefer a fiction of security, to keep Evelina from "the world" in the security of an adoptive name and inheritance. The actual pursuit must be left in grosser hands. Mrs. Mirvan would be more delicate, but the indelicate and aggressive Mrs. Selwyn is more available and effective. Villars can only rest in the paradoxical hope that while Evelina must change in "situation," she may remain unchanged in "disposition," the pious, domestic, and principled innocent of his nurture. Such a vision of social transformation suggests myths of social import.

The threat to name is the malicious misrepresentation

---

[23] *Evelina,* pp. 283, 229; Ronald Paulson, *Satire and the Novel in Eighteenth-Century England* (New Haven: Yale University Press, 1967), p. 287.

of appearances called slander. In the novel of fashion, where name and appearance are fragile idols, slander has a peculiar force; the delicacy of reputation makes slander uniquely evil. Sir John Belmont has originated the slander by denying his wife and destroying the marriage certificate. Evelina's unprincipled suitor Sir Clement Willoughby is most evil when he forges a letter from Orville, a slander that imposes a false style and hence a false name of indelicacy. In his manipulation of reputation, Willoughby anticipates the intellectual dandies of later novels. Evelina must "see through" the specious appearances of the social world, but Willoughby does so already. Seemingly a creature of society, he is ruthlessly antisocial; he tolerates the worst forms of social error—"the haughtiness of Mrs. Beaumont, the brutality of Captain Mirvan, the self-conceit of Mrs. Selwyn, the affectation of Lady Louisa, and the vulgarity of Madame Duval"[24]—in his reckless passion. His "duplicity of character" is one way of living in such a world, by compromising his own superiority of taste and intelligence.

The efficacy of slander is linked to the evils of secrecy. Where public approbation is necessary and honor is inseparable from appearance, secrecy is the hallmark of a dangerously antisocial motive. In this regard Evelina's plight is peculiarly difficult. She has "an aversion the most sincere to all mysteries, all private actions"; "concealment" for her is "the foe of tranquility." But delicacy and prudence dictate great care of exposure, and withdrawal from the world is a form of antisocial secrecy. Madame Duval makes everything public—self-publication is her extreme of vulgarity. Villars stands at the opposite extreme; he has kept Evelina's name and history secret, and "the name by which I was known, the secrecy observed in regard to my family, and the retirement in which I lived, all conspired"[25] to further the scheme whereby another could usurp Evelina's name and inheritance. It seems proper that Evelina should keep

---

[24] *Evelina*, p. 325.
[25] *Evelina*, pp. 245, 253, 355.

secret the confidences of Macartney, yet doing so dangerously misleads Orville; it is improper that she should conceal from Villars the forged letter, but to communicate a forgery is equally dangerous.

The dilemma is similar to Evelina's other dilemma of submission and self-direction. She is painfully anxious to conform to each new social usage, yet the result of her submission is an intense shame. Villars has admonished her to obey those in authority over her, and has made her dependent on dangerous guides; then, himself helpless, he urges her "not only to *judge* but to *act*" for herself. It is his most honest and paradoxical moment, for he confesses that "we are the slaves of custom, the dupes of prejudice, and dare not stem the torrent of an opposing world, even though our judgments condemn our compliance."[26] "Custom" is not yet "fashion," but the dominant dilemma of the novel of fashion is here.

Here, too, is its chief ethical problem. If the social world is such a place, must one enter it? Having entered it, can one ever recover the tranquillity and stability of withdrawal? How much withdrawal, or distance, is proper? Is Evelina made to "grace the world" or to be true to herself? The answers come through Lord Orville and lead to Evelina's aristocratic destiny. Orville is the key to the novel's social mode and to its imperatives of social discrimination. Walter Allen finds in Burney "the entry of the modern notion of class"; her fiction "is full of people who, absurd as it may seem to her, do not know their place." Montague and Martz agree that a social order "stands or falls by its ability to express and maintain a code of manners," and that Evelina is correct in "being anxious to measure up to the manners of the class to which she rightly belongs."[27] In fact, only Orville "measures up"; Orville is a man "almost as romantic as if he had been born and bred at Berry Hill,"

---

[26] *Evelina*, p. 149.
[27] Walter Allen, *The English Novel* (London: Phoenix, 1954), p. 90; Edwine Montague and Louis Martz, "Fanny Burney's *Evelina*," in *The Age of Johnson*, ed. F. W. Hilles (New Haven: Yale University Press, 1964), p. 180.

a man who is "really polite." And Evelina "saw that the rank of Lord Orville was his least recommendation, his understanding and his manners being far more distinguished." His "politeness . . . knows no intermission, and makes no distinction." He is distinguished by grace and elegance grounded in compassion and tact. His gentility is at once aristocratic and classless; and in Evelina, for all her "heedless indiscretion," he comes to see the same thing: "she has been extremely well educated, and accustomed to good company; she has a natural love of virtue, and a mind that might adorn *any* station, however exalted."[28] It is in *this* sense that she is made to be an "ornament" to "the world." Orville and Evelina confess their love before she achieves name and inheritance; his faith in her must be tested and proved without them, and only then is he worthy to supplant Villars—the aristocrat emulates the country parson— as Evelina's social model.

The snobbery of class belongs instead to those who falsely admire fashion, those for whom name and rank usurp the true distinction of social reputation, those who live in society merely to gratify their own vanity or malice. Nor are these of a single "class." It is easy to ridicule Madame Duval, the Frenchified barmaid, and her Cockney cousins the Branghtons with their pseudofashionable boarder Mr. Smith. But the most persistent social humor in *Evelina* is in the combats of Madame Duval and Captain Mirvan, and they are equally boorish and not socially discriminated. Indeed, such social mixtures as the Mirvans, boorish husband and fashionable wife, would quickly seem out of date to the Regency. Fashion is not yet a dominant social mode in *Evelina*. Mrs. Mirvan's "high life" season is not described. Mrs. Selwyn, the indelicate lady of ruthless wit, is a "mere country gentlewoman," and the haughty Mrs. Beaumont is obsessed with name and rank, but not fashion. Men of mere fashion such as Lovel and Merton are still conventional fops. Yet the types and dilemmas of

---

[28] *Evelina*, pp. 351, 265, 21, 102, 328.

fashion are latent, and *Evelina* clearly prepared the way for the novel of fashion without itself being one.

The significance of fashion as a condition of entering the social world becomes explicit in *Cecilia* (1782),[29] and with it the tragicomic instability of such a world. Once more the principled but naive heroine comes out of rural shelter into the bewildering city; but Cecilia's nurture is not the classless piety of a Villars. Her ancestors were well-to-do farmers; in her father "a spirit of elegance had supplanted the rapacity of wealth," and he had chosen to live as a private country gentleman. Cecilia is virtually an orphan, and the romance structure is organized around the social options offered by her three rival guardians. None represents a satisfactory style. Harrell lives in and for the world of fashion, a career of feverish, false gaiety based on debt and gaming and ending in desperation and suicide. Briggs epitomizes a mercenary vulgarity; a miser, he enters society occasionally in the style of Captain Mirvan and mocks fashion by masking as a monkey or savage. Delvile, the last hope, is regressive and inelegant; a pompous, cold worshipper of hereditary name, he despises the mixed world of fashion and money represented by the other two. Cecilia's problem is how to know the world, and how to be known right herself, in a network of false social alternatives. Her plight is worsened by the fact that her rural "protector," Monckton, acting *in loco parentis* and playing the *role* of a Villars, is secretly determined to win her inheritance for himself. The worst villainy in the book is Monckton's secret blasting of her reputation. Her situation becomes desperate because her lover, Delvile's son, is a prisoner of his father's obsession with "name." Cecilia's inheritance is hers only if her husband adopts her name; and young Delvile, volatile and imprudent, seeks to evade the problem by a secret marriage.

The structure of *Cecilia* is a large-scale anticipation of Austen's *Northanger Abbey:* the world of painful public frivolity is succeeded by a narrower world of rigid vanity; the

[29] Fanny Burney, *Cecilia*, 2. vols. (London: George Bell, 1904).

discomforts of both are aggravated by vulgarity—bourgeois avarice and pretension. The place of Macartney in *Evelina* is taken here by young Belfield, who is driven to affect a style of life more genteel than his shopkeeping kin. He and his family are just a few among the great abundance of minor characters. Burke, a keen admirer of the novel, found its only flaw in the number of characters; but they are necessary to Burney's aim. Her dramaturgical comic sense centers on the mixing and clashing in public life of various social styles, and it supports the claim of *Cecilia* to be the first novel of large-scale social discrimination. Burney's courtesy-book intentions are also evident:[30] she means to offer and test models of gentility that are independent of title, name, and fashion, to seek a true gentility and elegance fixed in landed wealth—the vision of the new bourgeois aristocrat.

This, like other meaningful patterns, is of course beyond Cecilia's comprehension. Bewildered and harrassed like Evelina, tricked by her attachment to the Harrells into growing debt, she is constantly misrepresented and constantly bewildered as to how to prevent it. Her inevitable independence grows painfully in the isolation of learning that all of her counselors are either illiberal or disingenuous. But her isolation is never a solitude, and she never seeks one. She flees from distress to active charity; she longs only for true society, idolizes reputation, abhors secrecy. Virtually the second half of this huge book is a Richardsonian ordeal wherein the heroine is driven by circumstance and Delvile to secret marriage. Only when his dying mother relents and his father proves unworthy of respect does she consent, and then unhappily. But with Delvile away, the word of her marriage gets out, she is deprived of her estate, and at the surreal climax, her very name a secret, she is homeless and desperate, almost a martyr to the regeneration of name and reputation.

Contemporary readers were disturbed by the depend-

---

[30] Joyce Hemlow, *The History of Fanny Burney* (Oxford: Clarendon, 1958), pp. 21–23. On the reception of *Cecilia*, see pp. 150–63.

ence of plot on the idolatry of name. And it is, of course, difficult to accept reputation as a solemn imperative when, throughout the book's first half, reputation has been treated as the empty compulsion of *ton* and credit. But this is the distinctive problem of the novel of fashion: how to preserve true reputation in a social world where reputation is corrupt and ridiculous; how to redeem from the suicidal tyranny of fashion the ideals of true elegance and courtesy. Elegance emerges as an ideal at once aesthetic, ethical, and economic. Elegance is liberality of mind and taste, comfort and stability. Elegance is closely tied to that central moral virtue of prudence, for both are directed to the most careful preservation of social and economic resources, as opposed to and threatened by waste at one extreme (Harrell the gamester and spendthrift) and miserliness at the other (Briggs and old Delvile the exclusive). But prudence without liberality is prudence without discriminating charity; without both, prudence is criminal, as in the slanderous Monckton. The true ethical expression of elegance is courtesy. Courtesy supplants name and title, and is the true social mode of which "fashion" is the antisocial specter. There is no Orville in Cecilia to teach or embody such an ideal; the heroine, in her anguish and bewilderment, must discover it for herself.

The heroine of *Camilla* (1796), subject to the same social agonies and bewilderments as Evelina and Cecilia, subjected to the same frightening and fugitive isolation, is less able to learn on her own. She is a "sweet, generous, inconsiderate girl, whose feelings are all virtues, but whose impulses have no restraints"; the "reigning and radical defect of her character" is "an imagination that submitted to no control." The evolving problem of fashion now focuses on the social dangers of unprincipled imagination. Camilla is peculiarly susceptible to the *momentary* impulses of fashion, and its worldly counsel can lead her

> into the semblance of a character, which, without thinking of, she was acting. Born simple and ingenuous, and bred to hold in horror every species of art, all idea of coquetry was foreign to

her meaning, though an untoward contrariety of circumstances, playing upon feelings too potent for deliberations, had deluded her into a conduct as mischievous in its effects and as wide from artlessness in its appearance, as if she had been brought up and nourished in fashionable egotism.[31]

The familiar Johnsonian theme, the precariousness of sentimental virtue without principled prudence, is adapted to a fiction of social discrimination. In Camilla, sentimentality causes reckless shame and blinds social judgment. She loves Edgar Mandelbert but supposes the feeling unreturned, and cannot follow her father's counsel of constraint and discretion. The sense that she is disobeying her father and will not be pardoned leads to a foolish concealment, the opposite of her natural openness, and brings her to desperate and homeless isolation. False shame has driven her to seek refuge, and the refuges offered have been invitations to the world of fashion, leading to further indiscretions and a crescendo of shame. Only a principled integrity can enter safely into the hectic social world that is "fashion."

The problem of fashion has now assumed a central position. Fashion no longer appears in its conventional comic guise as foppery; rather, it is a force of restless worldliness that corrupts true social impulses. In the bitter snobbery of Miss Margland the governess it is a rigid adherence to public etiquette accompanied by bad manners. Fashionable people are anxiously imitative, yet they act with reckless social indifference. The extravagant epicure Clermont Lynmere is highly fashionable yet antisocial, as, in their different ways, are Mrs. Arlbery and Mrs. Berlinton, two of Camilla's social guides. Both appear antifashionable, yet both are unprincipled in their contempt for a world that they exploit and upon which they are selfishly dependent. Camilla is deceived by Mrs. Arlbery's satiric animation and Mrs. Berlinton's sentiment; both seem careless of the obsession with reputation that marks fashion, yet both are

[31] Fanny Burney, *Camilla*, ed. E. A. and L. D. Bloom (London: Oxford, 1972), pp. 120, 84, 679.

slaves of that false ideal: " 'We are terribly in the back ground, General!' cried Mrs. Arlbery, in a low voice. 'What must be done to save our reputations?' " The friendship of Mrs. Berlinton makes Camilla fashionable, for "no contagion spreads with greater certainty nor greater speed than that of fashion; slander itself is not more sure of promulgation."[32] Yet Mrs. Berlinton's own extravagant carelessness leads to a sentimental liaison with Camilla's brother-in-law and to his accidental suicide.

Camilla's brother Lionel is a victim of fashion, for he is not "guided by his own natural judgment" but thinks only of carrying the "newest flourish of the *bon ton*" back to Oxford. The author's "strictures upon the Ton" are perhaps the earliest sociological analysis of the mystique of fashion in English fiction:

> Ton, in the scale of connoisseurs in the *certain circles,* is as much above fashion, as fashion is above fortune: for though the latter is an ingredient that all alike covet to possess, it is courted without being respected, and desired without beng honoured, except only by those who, from earliest life, have been taught to earn it as a business. *Ton,* meanwhile, is as attainable without birth as without understanding, though in all the *certain circles* it takes place of either. To define what it is, would be as difficult to the most renowned of its votaries, as to an utter stranger to its attributes. That those who call themselves of the *ton* either lead, or hold cheap all others, is obtrusively evident: but how and by what art they attain such pre-eminence, they would be perplexed to explain. That some whim has happily called forth imitators; that some strange phrase has been adopted; that something odd in dress has become popular; that some beauty, or deformity, no matter which, has found annotators; may commonly be traced as the origin of their first public notice.[33]

Ton and "fashion" are purely capricious and momentary forms of social leadership; they supplant birth and understanding, and hence they undermine true aristocracy and may be mistaken for new bourgeois ideals of elegance,

---

[32] *Camilla,* pp. 412, 443.
[33] *Camilla,* pp. 463–64.

taste, and good manners. They are covertly linked to "fortune," which they affect to despise.

In *Camilla*, the covert relation of fashion and money is central. Camilla's growing entrapment in the fashionable world and her growing alienation in secrecy, shame, and artifice from her natural and familial self result from her inability to avoid debts. Lionel is the primary cause. Led to help him and keep his debts secret, she is trapped into borrowing from her wooer, the dissipated Sir Sedley, which in turn leads to greater misunderstandings with her solemn lover Edgar. Lionel is an extreme form of Camilla. She is unreflective; he is averse to reflection, anxious to be fashionable, drawn to young men who gamble. The scale of social judgment has direct monetary equivalence; the test of judgment is economy. Camilla's father speaks for a true economy that reflects social judgment and integrity of feeling: "open oeconomy, springing from discretion, is always respected. It is false shame alone that begets ridicule."[34] False shame, an undisciplined social consciousness, leads Camilla to the brink of financial disaster, until she lies penniless, desperate, and ill at an inn nine miles from home. Instability of temperament, manifest in unprincipled virtue, leads to gambling, that sure sign of social excess and moral disaster in Burney—as in the careless Lionel, the desperate Bellamy, and even the sentimental libertine Mrs. Berlinton, whose desperate passion leads her to set up a Faro table in her fashionable home. Hereafter the novel of fashion will find in gambling a characteristic of the idolatry of fashion, a dangerous drug for the emotional and social recklessness that fashion generates, and a sign of the tragic hypocrisy of the fashionable world, which hides in contempt its obsession with money and risk.

A stable economy is reflected in a proper degree of worldliness. The plot of *Camilla* is managed so as to compare degrees of worldliness. Those who affect to despise "the world"—Mrs. Arlebery and Mrs. Berlinton—are as much enslaved by it as those who, like the brainlessly vain

[34] *Camilla,* p. 792.

cousin Indiana, live only in the world's image. The dangerous and absurd extremes of unworldliness are sentimentality and pedantry. The selfish pedant Dr. Orkborne is retained to transform Camilla's young sister Eugenia into a classical scholar. But Eugenia, crippled from childhood, must learn not to withdraw from the world. It is she who serves as touchstone in a society of marital gaming, where appearance alone matters. To her alone can Camilla, despondently alone as her social brilliance increases, turn for counsel.

III

For literary historians it is debatable whether Burney's followers from Edgeworth to the early "Silver Fork" novelists constitute a single generic development. For contemporaries it was less doubtful. A *New Monthly* reviewer saw *Tremaine* (1825) as in "the movement inaugurated by Maria Edgeworth"; *Vivian Grey* was a deliberate successor to *Tremaine*, and *Pelham* took both for antecedents.[35] In what follows I will suggest that the lineage is—as an evolution in social mythology—clear and meaningful.

Maria Edgeworth is remembered chiefly as a fine comic regionalist whose father's intrusive didacticism spoiled her novels of society. W. L. Renwick offers a fairer estimate: "Miss Burney invented the social novel; Miss Edgeworth made it."[36] *Belinda* (1801) he sees as her finest social novel. *Belinda* differs from a Burney novel by including few scenic representations of the fashionable world. It centers with psychological fullness and complexity on the heroine's

---

[35] Marilyn Butler, *Maria Edgeworth* (Oxford: Clarendon, 1972), pp. 348–49. Cf. Robert Blake, *Disraeli* (London: Eyre and Spottiswoode, 1966), pp. 34–35; and Michael Sadleir, *Bulwer: A Panorama* (London: Constable, 1931), pp. 117–18.

[36] W. L. Renwick, *English Literature, 1789–1815* (Oxford: Clarendon, 1963), p. 75. Maria Edgeworth, *Belinda*, Vols XI–XII of Tales and Novels of Maria Edgeworth (London: Baldwin and Cradock, 1833); *Patronage*, Vols. XIV–XVI of Tales and Novels (London: Baldwin and Cradock, 1833).

tragicomic relationship with a lady of fashion and the reckless desperation of her life. "Fashion," as in later Burney, is a socializing of the idea of "Fortune," and Lady Delacour is its slave. It is the specious extreme of worldliness, the capricious power of brief notoriety in public life, and it falsifies true social virtues and traps its slaves into roles that atrophy their true natures. Its contrary is not unworldly withdrawal, but domesticity; Lady Delacour's opposite is Lady Anne Percival, the unaffected but elegant and refined center of a happy family society.

Notably, however, while drawn to the Percivals, Belinda is pledged in compassion and trust to Lady Delacour, whose dreadful secret, a supposed cancer of the breast, she must keep even at the risk of her own reputation and happiness. Her problem is not to discover the hollowness of fashionable life; she knows it from the beginning, for Lady Delacour tells her. Her problem is to work within such a fallen world, to keep faith with its victims, yet to realize her own integrity as she heals them—not of their sins, but of their cynicism and despair. Her secular ministry is akin to that of the "sister" of *The Prelude* and Fanny Price in *Mansfield Park*.

The problem of appearances, no less central than in Burney, turns on such distinctions as false and true prudence, false shame and true delicacy, slander and candor, false and true independence, true wit and its specious versions, audacity and buffoonery. In the social world of *Belinda* such confusions are common, for social life is spectacle or masque. Masques abound from the beginning; masquerades are self-consciously theatrical. At their first appearance together, Belinda and Lady Delacour exchange roles as Tragedy and Comedy, which seems fitting, for Lady Delacour is trying to persuade Belinda that the world is a grotesque tragicomedy where high spirits hide pain and melancholy. Confusions of masque are sexual as well. The capricious false friend suitably named Mrs. Freke dresses and acts as a man, while on one occasion the hero Clarence Hervey—young man of fashion with a hidden sentimental life—masques as a woman. In a social world of confusing masques and distorted roles, Belinda and Hervey must learn and prove each other's true natures.

A further test comes with the entrance of two "romantic" alternatives. It is revealed that Hervey keeps a mysterious "mistress," "Virginia" to his "St. Pierre," in a cottage near Windsor. And Belinda acquires an attractive new suitor, Vincent, an unfashionable but aristocratic Creole. The tests are fitting, for Hervey, the "chameleon," must prove his integrity, and Belinda, the individualist, must prove herself free of romantic delusion. One must not be a slave to "the world," but one must not have contempt for the world either; in Edgeworth these are parts of the same romantic fatalism (and here is the germ of Ward's *Tremaine* and Bulwer's anti-Byronism). The test for Belinda is complicated when the Percivals, independent of fashion and "the world," press the suit of Vincent, while Lady Delacour urges her to secure Hervey. It is indicative of the novel's complexity that Lady Delacour's preference is correct, the virtuous, domestic Percivals are deluded, and the fashionable lady saves the day. The Percivals are fooled by the sentimental aristocrat from the West Indies. Vincent is caught gambling; Hervey saves him his fortune but Belinda knows she must reject him. He is not evil; he is a man of feeling, a chivalric sentimentalist whose morality is of impulse, and as with Burney's Mrs. Berlinton, this leads to emotional and financial recklessness. Belinda clings to her first love and is proven right.

But not until Hervey is freed of his romantic heresy. Ostensibly a man of fashion, he has fallen under the influence of Rousseau and St. Pierre and, while mixing in "the world," he educates himself a wife in total seclusion. Their history subtly counterpoints the illusory romance of Belinda and Vincent, confirms the admonition against sentimental unworldliness, helps elaborate the image of a society trapped in illusions, and elucidates the meaning of fashion in such a society. The illusion of fashion is merely a hectic and cynical negation of the romanticisms of Vincent and "Virginia." Fashionable people are deluded fatalists who act out of contempt for the world even as they slavishly fear and obey it. Vincent, in rejecting the fashionable world, is losing touch with reality and becoming prisoner of his own feelings. Hervey, in his chameleonic way, tries to sustain the role of man of fashion while pursuing in private a Rousseauistic illusion. Belinda is his escape, for only Belinda keeps faith with the social world and yet maintains her own rational integrity. The problem of fashion has become the problem of proper independence and true sociability.

The same complex of issues informs Edgeworth's most ambitious novel, *Patronage* (1814). "The patronage of fashion" has become a political force of social advancement. If we seek only a simple didacticism, the book appears to promote the independence of "private life" as opposed to the patronized life of unprincipled dependency. Mr. Percy and his virtuous family adhere initially to a code of withdrawn independence, while their cousins and antagonists the Falconers aspire to social and political power through patronage, and rise dishonestly only to fall abjectly. But the meaning is no such simple lesson of unworldliness. Percy has three able sons in the three professions (military, medical, and legal) who succeed admirably in their public roles and are patronized for their intrinsic merits. The chief patron Lord Oldborough, minister to the king, turns out to be a good patron and, however ambitious and ruthless with his enemies, a man and minister of integrity. Slander, as before, is a major evil, and it is closely linked with forgery, which almost brings the downfall of Oldborough and almost robs the Percies of their inheritance. It is fitting, moreover, in a novel of social appearances that legal insignia such as seals and documentary "wafers" should play an important role. Thus, the simple normative contrasts of dependent and independent, public and private, give way to more complex implications. And fashion is not treated with horrified rejection.

Many facets of the fashionable world are interrelated through a large assemblage of characters. Some who live by fashion are whimsical and good-natured about it. Lady Frances Arlington is a playful prankster, and Lady Jane

Granville, preacher of patronage and manager of marriages, is affectionate, whimsical about her tyrannies, and willing to admit her errors. But Edgeworth's tragicomic theme is here too. People caught in the public world of social and political fashion are often people of genuine natures who have been sophisticated into their roles and suffer accordingly. Poor Buckhurst Falconer, forced into the church and then into a miserable marriage, is almost a tragic figure, whose goodness never quite deserts him. His father is seen eventually as pathetic and weak rather than malicious, and the ambition of his fashionable mother is self-destructive. Even Lord Oldborough, noble stoic that he is, confesses his role has stifled his natural affections.

Finally, fashion provides a complex historical perspective on the subject of marriage. Edgeworth endorses class intermarriage as a social openness that is natural and good, an agency of assimilation and regeneration. But she is concerned with the *pace* of such change. She values the liberalizing process of cultivation and refinement. The refined merchant is ready for social leadership; his progeny is not. Fashion is a problem because it prescribes a rapid, arbitrary, and superficial refinement and generates in response an unnatural exclusiveness. People who become slaves of fashion are cut off from natural historical process. Currency of appearance and manner usurps the place and the goals of true liberality, elegance, and refinement. Fashion tends to corrupt the union in history of the practical work ethic of the bourgeois to the principled noblesse of the aristocrat. Edgeworth is a liberal patriarchalist, concerned for the regeneration of aristocracy, a process fashion seeks to pervert or forestall.

With this in mind, we recognize the link between Edgeworth's "tales of fashionable life" and her Irish novels. In *The Absentee* (1812), a "tale of fashionable life," fashion is identified with aristocratic absenteeism, an aristocracy's abdication of hereditary role and continuity. Lord and Lady Clonbrony should be home on their Irish estate, not aping the *ton* in London, "the nonsense of high life." We are shown in detail Lady Clonbrony's extravagant gala, but also the frantic intrigues by which she secures invitations: "Wheel within wheel in the fine world, as well as in the political world."[37] Surrendering their patriarchal humanity, the Clonbronys suffer from futile extravagance, social anxiety, and the derision of mimicry. At home in Ireland the poor still love them for what they were, charitable monitors of local life. In their absence, the poor sink into despair, dissipation, and exploitation. The point is clear: without the other, each class loses its true nature. Fashion is the tempter that causes such loss; fashion is a world where true social natures are corrupted.

But not irreversibly. Lady Clonbrony's "natural warm manner" breaks through her false refinement. The Clonbronys' son, Lord Colambre, and their supposed niece, Grace Nugent, are refined. Grace has an "air of fashion," an "elegant and dignified simplicity." Colambre has been at Cambridge, where "his ambition for intellectual superiority was raised, his views were enlarged, his tastes and his manners formed."[38] His liberality of ideas is the central point of view in the novel; his is an enlightened curiosity about the world. Initially his problem is that of the Burney heroine: public embarrassment at the folly and vulgarity of his kin. But it turns to a more positive uneasiness of cultural piety as he discovers the true Ireland.

To do so, he must contend with the novel's real representative of false fashion—not Lady Clonbrony, its foolish slave, but Lady Dashfort, its unprincipled and antisocial leader. Lady Dashfort is a destructive mimic, and Colambre must learn to see the truth beyond her cynical mimicries. Like Mrs. Freke of *Belinda* she thinks herself above the world and acts with libertine recklessness. She seeks to conquer Colambre imaginatively by convincing him that his country is what it appears to be—dirty, dissolute, backward. Her motive is to capture him for her daughter, a pseudoinnocent. The battle for Colambre's imagination centers

---

[37] Maria Edgeworth, *The Absentee*, Vols. IX–X of Tales and Novels (London: Baldwin and Cradock, 1832–33), IX, 80.
[38] *The Absentee*, IX, 8, 22, 39.

logically on slander. Lady Dashfort spreads the rumor that Grace's family, the women of the St. Omars, are uniformly unchaste, and while Colambre can see the truth about Ireland, he cannot so easily overcome his horror at the hint of unchastity and illegitimacy in his beloved Grace. Legitimacy is a positive counterforce to fashion; reputation is an essential aristocratic value, and his reluctance is fitting. It is also fitting that the true aristocrat, Count O'Halloran, should unearth the lost papers that refute the slander.

Fashion is social leadership, and it can be used for good or ill. Sir James Brooke recalls for Colambre the falsely fashionable state of Dublin society just after the Union: commerce and wealth pushed into the vacuum of rank and birth; the old hereditary leaders complained "that the decorum, elegance, polish, and charm of society was gone," and in disgust and despair fled to the country. But he perceives the long-term benefit of the influx of new ideas and the return of the old gentry,

"So that now," concluded Sir James, "you find a society in Dublin composed of the most agreeable and salutary mixture of birth and education, gentility and knowledge, manner and matter; and you see pervading the whole new life and energy, new talent, new ambition, a desire and a determination to improve and be improved—a perception that higher distinction can now be obtained in almost all company, by genius and merit, than by airs and address."[39]

Thus, fashion can be a mere negation, a restless slavery, or it can be a regenerative liberality. And Larry the coachman closes the novel with a letter to his brother Pat in London. Come home, he says; for "it's growing the fashion not to be an Absentee."

The integration of the novel of fashion with the novel of regional manners is increasingly evident in Edgeworth's Scottish counterpart, Susan Ferrier. Indeed, in Ferrier's third and last novel, *Destiny* (1831), the fashion problem has given way entirely to the problem of cultural integrity

---

[39] *The Absentee*, IX, 120.

in a regional context. But in her first two novels, the problem of fashion is central.

Ferrier's *Marriage* (1818) recalls the schematic exposition of *Cecilia* and *Camilla*. The dual heroines are daughters of a selfish and idiotic fashionable heiress and a poor Highland officer. Mary is raised in Scotland by a refined but domestic, kindly aunt-in-law, Mrs. Douglas, under the nearby influence of narrow, dull aunts and the local bluestocking Lady MacLaughlan. Her sister Adelaide grows up in fashion near Bath with their mother and two cousins. The sudden grotesque death of her grandfather obsesses Mary, spoils her health, and she is sent south to her mother at Beech Park for a few months of "improvement." In a Scottish presbyterian context, entry into "fashionable life" may be a flight from grotesque old mortality.

Trained by Mrs. Douglas in religious principle and domestic simplicity, Mary never mistakes what she sees in "the heartless bustle of Beech Park." Mrs. Douglas had had her own fashionable London season and learned the follies of fashionable life. She had also acquired its elegance and refinement, and she confirms that a retired domesticity need not be unrefined. But like Evelina's Villars, Mrs. Douglas is far away, and Mary must undergo the dilemmas and distresses of a Burneyan social entrance of her own. Her difficulties are of three kinds. She must decide how to behave when she finds that her mother is heartless and unworthy of obedience. She must decide whether to give up her suitor, Lennox, when she overhears his pious, blind mother urging him to love dutifully. And she must resolve the Burneyan problem of moving in a refined and elegant world with narrow, vulgar connections. The third is most important, and its development carries the book's meaning as a novel of fashion.

Vulgarity is seen initially in the narrow, provincial aunts of Glenfern. They belong to "the little departments of life"; "their walk lay amongst tapes and pickles; their sphere extended from the garret to the pantry." When Mary sees her aunt Grizzly in Bath, remote from Highland locale and childhood association, she discovers "the slight sensation of shame as she contrasted her awkward manner and uncouth accent with the graceful refinement of those with whom she associated."[40] But exposure to women of fashion renews appreciation: "the result of Mary's comparison was, that her aunts' feelings, however troublesome, were better than no feelings at all. 'They are, to be sure, something like brambles,' thought she; 'they fasten upon one in every possible way, but still they are better than the faded exotics of fashionable life.' "[41] In fact, vulgarity is independent of class and location, and paradoxically it finds its most extreme form among the speciously fashionable. Lady Emily defines the vulgar as "generally under-bred, consequently vulgar. They pique themselves upon saying good things *coute qu'il coute*. There is, in short, something quite professional about them."[42] Lennox, a military man, is gentlemanly, not "professional," hence not vulgar; he is "liberal" of mind. The Duke of Altamont likes only great dull dinners, a kind of "tasteless grandeur," and so he is "vulgar-minded," for there are vulgar-minded dukes "as there are gifted ploughmen, or any other anomalies." Vulgarity is a narrowness and superficiality of mind that is satisfied with mere worldly goods; it is not social pretension as such but a "lowness" independent of class, and for the presbyterian satirist in Ferrier it is akin to idolatry.

True elegance alone is no antidote. The only truly elegant man of fashion in the book is Mary's cousin Lindore, and he is clearly a Regency ideal. He calls for simple dishes; he walks part way home; in all his movements are the ease and grace "which a perfect proportion alone can bestow." His dress and deportment are "plain, even to simplicity"; "he had too much taste to carry anything to extreme; and, in the midst of incense, and adulation, and imitation, he still retained that simple, unostentatious elegance, that marks the man of real fashion—the man who feels his own

[40] Susan Ferrier, *Marriage,* 2 vols., 3d ed. (Edinburgh: Blackwood, 1826), I, 304; II, 244.
[41] *Marriage,* II, 73.
[42] *Marriage,* II, 357.

consequence, independent of all extraneous modes, or fleeting fashions."[43] His is fashion independent of "fashions." But he is unprincipled; the clue is that he reads Rousseau and Goethe and exalts "criminal passion." Lindore and his sister Emily are reminiscent of Austen's Crawfords. But in a fashionable world they set the tone and then serve to illustrate that it is not enough. By contrast, false fashionableness is absurd. It is epitomized in Mary's stupid mother when she buys an odd vessel of green mottled china: " 'O delicious!' cried Lady Juliana, clasping her hands in ecstasy; 'I will give a party, for the sole purpose of drinking tea out of this machine, and I will have the whole room fitted up like an Indian temple. Oh, it will be so new!' "[44] In such an impulse is the utter corruption of social and sacred ceremony, "the sad fruits of a fashionable education."

Why, then, risk the exposure? The answer is Mrs. Douglas's. Not to be educated in "the world" is to remain either narrow or romantic in seclusion. Mary must "make the trial" because she has "already lived too long in these mountain solitudes," and "if it is dangerous to be too early initiated into the ways of the world, it is perhaps equally so to live too long secluded from it."[45] So her "beloved pupil" mixes in society, meets the pious but refined Lennox, and comes into her worldly status and inheritance.

Worldly inheritance is a more agonizing and suspect, but nonetheless necessary, process in Ferrier's second novel. The heiress of *The Inheritance* (1824), Gertrude, must actually "fall" into fashion and lose her name and identity. Like Burney's Camilla, she is ardent, imaginative, and prone to illusion. Her "virtue was impulse—her generosity profusion." She is subject to false shame and reckless extravagance; elegant, repelled by vulgarity, she suffers the distress and disorientation of the Burney heroine. She

---

[43] *Marriage*, II, 345–46.
[44] *Marriage*, I, 234.
[45] *Marriage*, I, 335.

must learn that without religious principle and cultural piety, elegance and refinement are worthless; she must discover the "simplicity of manner, which is the characteristic of a noble, ingenuous mind."[46]

The learning is made difficult by the desperate guidance of her supposed mother. Mrs. St. Clair, née Sarah Black, introduces a new economic urgency into the novel of fashion. Widowed and poor, she sees the only hope of security in making Gertrude heiress to her brother-in-law, Lord Rossville. Having known only poverty, exile, and friendlessness, she has secretly adopted her nurse's infant as her only hope of security. But when Gertrude becomes countess, the nurse's supposed widower reappears to blackmail her. Commanded by a "mother" with some terrible secret, harrassed by the blackmailer, constrained by the dull, pompous Lord Rossville, surrounded by her mother's vulgar relatives, and subject to her own ardent illusions, Gertrude understandably falls in love with the true man of fashion, Colonel Delmour.

Delmour is the Regency ideal, a livelier Lindore. He has a "graceful high-bred ease," a "high hereditary air of fashion and freedom which bore the impress of nobility and distinction." Charming, sportive, "his presence was like sunshine upon frost-work, and an air of ease and gaiety succeeded to the dulness and constraint which had hitherto prevailed." In London he is leader of the *ton,* and here he instructs Gertrude in the "arbitrary and capricious mechanism of the fashionable world."[47] The mode is clearly becoming more self-conscious, more purely style. Only the *je ne sais quoi* gives consequence in "this magic circle," and to accomplish the entry of the new countess, Delmour calls upon Lady Charles Austin, an authentic vision of the mystery. Lady Charles is pure style; she is thin, unbeautiful, middle-aged, striking but unsingular in dress, quiet in manner, "but perfectly elegant, and the *tout ensemble* con-

---

[46] Susan Ferrier, *The Inheritance,* 3 vols. (Edinburgh: Blackwood, 1824), II, 311; I, 284.
[47] *The Inheritance,* I, 66; III, 79.

THE REGENCY NOVEL OF FASHION | 117

veyed that impression of high birth and high breeding, which is something too subtle and refined to be described or analyzed; something of so delicate and impalpable a nature, that it might sometimes escape notice altogether, but for the effect it produces upon others."[48] Gertrude is "soon in the vortex of elegant dissipation," becomes "the idol of the day," and ignores her obligations at home. Her extravagance is wild, her transformation is superficial and convincing, her reign is brief. She returns to Rossville, to blackmail and melodrama, to the revelation that she is no Rossville but the descendant of a poor croft girl, and to Delmour's desertion. But the poor croft girl was Gertrude's great-uncle Adam's lost love, and from this now-wealthy but unworldly nabob she receives her true inheritance, the exemplar of an older and a newer cultural aristocracy, grounded in folk tradition and local piety "improved" by mercantile wealth into modern comfort and refinement.

As in *Marriage,* true vulgarity is mental—the "vulgar sordid cares" of poverty are not so bad as "a vulgar sordid spirit." But fashion is a false option, appealing, "free," refined, yet subtly trapped in its own slavery to the world. *The world* has various levels of meaning. The book is grounded in religious orthodoxy and folk piety, yet it prizes certain essential worldly discriminations, even while recognizing their nullity in otherworldly perspective. For the fashionable, *the world* means fashion; for the religious it means a sphere of idolatrous attachments. For Gertrude, it means an array of appearances, while for Adam, the misanthrope, it means the universal folly of human nature. But his is not the religious perspective, and he is properly faulted for attempting to "walk as if uncontrolled by the scan of that dread power, commonly called the eyes of the world."[49] On one growing painfully into a true and aristocratic inheritance, the world imposes difficult but real discriminations of refinement and piety.

[48] *The Inheritance,* III, 83.
[49] *The Inheritance,* I, 207.

In the same year as Ferrier's *Inheritance* there appeared the first series of Theodore Hook's tales of fashionable life, *Sayings and Doings*. It is both inevitable and superficial that Ferrier and Hook should be seen together as founders of the "fashionable novel."[50] Hook was not a serious novelist like Burney, Edgeworth, and Ferrier—or, for that matter, Ward, Lister, Disraeli, and Bulwer; perhaps this is part of the secret of his phenomenal success. He was the public entertainer of a coterie to which he belonged—in the role of public entertainer. While filled with the mimicry of fashionable gossip, his fabliaux are not more "realistic" than his real pranks and entertainments. They exploit, sometimes brilliantly, the artifices of pure farce, and thus their stated exemplary purposes and moral tags are as suspect as their topical realism. In fact, it was Hook's role to reflect contemporary fashion as comic illusion, histrionic artifice, witty improvisation. And such is Hook's agility and duplicity of tone that, like the Fool of courtly tradition, he can mimic, flatter, and condemn all in the same performance.

In the tales as in his social performances, Hook's was a triumph of style and voice. He could graphically catalog the surface faults and frissons of an imperfect etiquette with authoritative specificity, the consummate stage manager, and scene designer, whose charm is the mystique of connoisseurship. When new wealth aspires to fashionable dinners,

> for instance, the butlers stand looking at each other, in attitudes with dishes in their hands, and hesitating where to put them down; then there is always a dreadful uncertainty about the wine; Lunel is detected in a long-necked bottle up to his chin in an ice-pail, presuming to do duty for St. Peray, *absent without leave;* the Claret is frozen hard, the Hock left luke-warm, and common red port put down upon the table as if people were to drink it; the fish is generally doubtful; the *entrees* cold, and the *soufflets* flat and heavy.

When semifashion, as in the family of old-fashioned attorney Abberley, dines at home:

---

[50] See M. W. Rosa, *The Silver-Fork School,* p. 55.

To grace the board, there was, first, a tureen filled with stuff, made at a neighbourhood pastrycook's (sent home in a copper-pan, upon the head of a dirty boy in a linen jacket, with a paper of sweet cakes under his arm,) called mock-turtle,—a glue-like mixture, *illustrated* with dirt boluses, much in use amongst modern Goths; secondly, the head and shoulders of a cod-fish, as large as a porpoise; and a haunch of mutton, kept till half putrid, decorated with a paper ruffle, to look, and, if possible, smell like venison.[51]

His diction conflates elegant allusion with current cant or slang and traditional moral tags (the "prodigal" in "state and glory" headed for "ruin"). His rapid impressionistic panoramas of fashionable life alternate between a colorful surface verisimilitude and a generalized impression of anxious vacuity and melancholy compulsion. They are unencumbered with complex characters. In place of character there are really only four personifications of stereotypical response: the vulgar and showy futility of the *nouveau* pretender; the grotesque ennui of the exhausted insider; the naive bewilderment of the neophyte; and the exuberant manipulations of the onlooking showman. All four are modes of imitation or disguise in a world without reality. And the lesson is mixed. To the ambitious outsider: the style is too intricate and beautiful for you to imitate, and you will fail foolishly. To the insider: you who manage the perfect imitation will suffer even more, become jaded, homeless, grotesque in age. One thinks ahead to the Showman of *Vanity Fair,* who delights in the brilliant bagatelle while despising the whole thing. Perhaps some such adjustive mechanism is what Hook's fabliaux gave to win his readers' accolades.

Certainly he offered them no serious new aristocratic alternative to the model of fashion, for the ultimate retreat from fashion in Hook is bourgeois domesticity. Danvers and the "prodigal" George Arden of "The Man of Many

[51] Theodore Hook, "Danvers," in *Sayings and Doings,* 1st ser., 3 vols., 4th ed. (London: Colburn, 1824), I, 117–18; "The Man of Many Friends," in *Sayings and Doings,* 2d ser., 3 vols., new ed. (London: Colburn, 1825), I, 315.

Friends" are simple-hearted young men who are seduced into the traps of fashion, and almost as quickly maneuvered or forced out of them, to end in domestic retreats with wholesome, unfashionable wives, saved from "the destructive follies of wandering libertinism" to find "true happiness only to exist in the magic circle of Home."[52]

The hero of *Gilbert Gurney* (1836), Hook's autobiographical (and best) novel, is more essentially histrionic. He longs to be a popular stage farceur. He gives up the reading of law, refuses his brother's offer of a commercial career in Calcutta, and falls prey to "that disposition to treat high and serious subjects farcically, which is engendered and fostered in the society of those who . . . are habituated to judge of real events histrionically."[53] He falls into the company of Daly, an actor and passionate hoaxer (like Hook), and by way of Daly's madcap company he enters fashionable circles. The most convincing depiction of fashionable society is the description of Mrs. Fletcher Green at home, but even here the fabliau atmosphere prevails. The most sensational is the fete at Lady Wolverhampton's, where Daly sneaks physic into the macaroon cakes. The scene is "beautiful and gay . . . all exceedingly fascinating and intoxicating," but dominated by "the fiend of fun"; fashion has become boisterous merriment. The narrator still wears his clever "insider" mask, avowing the "habit of constant intercourse with the principal actors of the stage—not of the theatre—but of real life," and mocking those who derive their knowledge of high society "from the misinformed collectors of fashionable intelligence for the newspapers."[54] But something has changed; fashionable life is remembered in *Gilbert Gurney* as a kind of boisterous pastorale, and Gilbert identifies the change:

It sounds odd, and even absurd to say so, but true it is, that religion has become fashionable, and its cultivation and pursuits

[52] "The Man of Many Friends," II, 57–58.
[53] Theodore Hook, *Gilbert Gurney*, 3 vols. (London: Whittaker, 1836), I, 54.
[54] *Gilbert Gurney*, I, 323–24; II, 18–19.

have taken place of what in the days of our grandfathers were called spirit and humour, which, in plain English, meant profligacy and dissipation. . . . If these outward signs of change in manners are so evident, still more so are those by which society, of a more refined character, is distinguished. Piety, charity, sympathy, and benevolence are its attributes.[55]

It is fitting that after countless pranks and farcical near-disasters, Gilbert finds his society with nabobs at Chittagong Lodge, is saved by his wealthy brother's return, and marries the daughter of a country rector.

Such marriages are not new to the novel of fashion; the first hero of the "Silver-Fork" had done likewise. There is general agreement that Ward's *Tremaine* (1825) "launched Colburn on his career as a publisher of fashionable novels," and that Colburn, "whose sense of judgment in such matters was unerring, exploited it to a fashionable audience" and made it a best-seller. But is it, Rosa asks, "a fashionable novel?"[56] Is *Tremaine* a novel at all? Exclaims the narrator, "I did not know I was writing one." His hypothetical readers ask, "May we venture to inquire, then, what you *are* writing?" "As I hope for readers, I intended it as a treatise of moral philosophy."[57]

The "treatise" is set on a country estate in rural Yorkshire and in a villa near Orleans. It consists chiefly of philosophical dialogues with a learned country rector, interspersed with genre vignettes of the life and duties of the country squire and justice of the peace, and with brief, unsatisfactory visits to fashionable Bellenden House, where London beaux and marriage brokers ply their arts for a rustic season. Fashion is foolish, mean, and dull; it confirms the rector Dr. Evelyn's diagnosis of originality "rubbed down into general fineness by a general admixing with the world." The third volume consists almost entirely of religious instruction leading to Tremaine's conversion. How,

---

[55] *Gilbert Gurney*, III, 207–8.
[56] Moers, p. 54; Rosa, pp. 64–65.
[57] R. P. Ward, *Tremaine, or the Man of Refinement*, 3 vols. (Philadelphia: Littell, 1825), I, 158–59.

then, can "the heart of the novel" be "a recapitulation of a dandy's life in London at the height of the Regency"?[58] If this fastidious, enfeebled misanthrope was ever dandy, he is no longer, and his fashionable career is recalled only in brief retrospect: "How different from the Tremaine of his youth, or even of his later years, when the hero of high life, in the assemblies of London or Paris, the champion of party, or the fastidious criticizer, yet devoted admirer of the sex, he sparkled through a whole night, amidst a blaze of artificial elegance, which, however flattering to his senses, never, as we have seen, satisfied his heart!"[59] The reason for this dissatisfaction, declares the narrator, "was plain, namely, that God and nature were not there." The book recounts the difficult return of Tremaine to God and nature, and his painful indoctrination into the duties and active charities of the traditional Christian squire, consistent with true refinement.

The process is difficult and painful because his flight from "the world" is from an imperfect motive to a specious refuge. His fastidiousness has rejected "all that wealth, pomp, luxury, and taste, can effect," but he has fled in a selfish despair that is merely the negative side of fashion, and he is still a slave of its tyranny. His flight is in ignorance of "very dangerous mistakes about solitude"; he has, like the young Teufelsdröckh, reached only the negative pole of Byronism, which he fails to recognize as the heritage of that "Swiss mountebank Rousseau."[60] Byronism and Rousseauism are merely fashionable rejections that affirm the power they flee. The true alternative to fashion is not a specious and self-absorbed unworldliness, not the pathetic folly of a half-mad recluse, not the misanthropic retreat fed by sentimental eighteenth-century philosophers or the romance of easy retirement from a world "where all is vulgarity, envy, or ennui." It is the "proper blending of [life's] simplicities with its elegancies, the wholesome union of

[58] Moers, p. 54.
[59] *Tremaine*, II, 234.
[60] *Tremaine*, II, 234; I, iv, 176.

public and private duty, the golden moderation recommended by Horace."[61] But this is a goal not be realized short of conversion to a lively Christian faith, and conversion is the climactic stage in Tremaine's recovery. The proto-Victorian change in social refinement recalled by Gilbert Gurney is already prominent in *Tremaine*.

Thus, the problem of fashion for Ward is not so much in its disruption or falsification of social life as in its negative impact on the aristocrat of refinement, its tendency to foster, not vulgarity and social exclusivism, but cynical unworldliness and selfish despair. Tremaine does not return to the fashionable world from his Arcadian fantasies. He marries simple Georgy Evelyn and assumes his role in a simpler social world. Ward is thus akin ideologically to Bulwer, and in his emphasis on simpler, truer refinement and a useful aristocracy, he is in the direct line of Edgeworth and Ferrier.

His concern with degrees and kinds of withdrawal from "the world" is associated with a sphere evidently of more interest to him in his second (and much better) novel, *De Vere; or, The Man of Independence* (1827). After Edgeworth's *Patronage*, his *De Vere* may lay claim to being one of the earliest of authentic political novels in English; indeed, as Lister, Disraeli, and Bulwer confirm, this was to be the generic direction of the novel of fashion, and its Victorian heir was less Thackeray than Trollope.

The hero is not a Byronic solitary but a proud and quixotic young squire who is deluded into an indiscriminate suspicion of all public officials. His uncle, Lord Mowbray, and his Oxford friends engage in unprincipled maneuvers for ministerial place or influence. His older counselors carry on lengthy philosophical discussions of misanthropic withdrawal. His rival in love and power, the Earl of Cleveland, is introduced as the "monarch of fashion," with a fashionable carriage-and-four and a mansion on the "pure Grecian model," but his fashionable significance soon gives

---

[61] *Tremaine*, I, iv, 15.

way to his political position as "the Richelieu of England." Cleveland's ally Clayton, characterized as "the Parvenu," is the political opportunist rather than the social pretender. The long climax to the first volume is a country fete at Mowbray Castle, and to this spectacle come various fashionable types. But the scene shifts to London, and here "the world" waits, not for fashionable conquests and scandals, but for ministerial resignation and the ruthless struggles of political succession. De Vere is courted and pushed by rival factions and, maintaining his independence, is distrusted and rejected by all—all but the good statesman Wentworth. What brief allusions there are to fashionable life are sketchy and derisive; the real thrust is political, and the aim is to persuade De Vere that his condemnations are too sweeping, his evasion of power struggles unfair and romantic.

De Vere has long since questioned his fastidiousness and suspected that "ambition is not only so natural to man, but so properly pursued, *when properly regulated,* that he would be an ill teacher who should propose to eradicate it from his mind."[62] He has known the fear that "if he renounced the world, he might renounce his duty to society," and on his picturesque travels he has visited numerous exemplars of selfish retirement. But now, wealthy and influential, his rivals disgraced, his friend Wentworth forming the government, he declines all urgings to office and, married to his beloved Constance, follows the lead of Tremaine.

In Ward's *De Vere,* the problem of fashion has receded into relative insignificance. In the year between *Tremaine* and *De Vere,* Thomas Henry Lister's first (and best) novel *Granby* (1826) provided the most sophisticated rendition to date of fashion as a problematic force in political society. Some features of *Granby* are familiar. The hero is an unaffected outsider; the suspense is over the mystery of his substantial inheritance. The problem is the threat to and the testing of his love by all the bars, secrets, and slanders

---

[62] R. P. Ward, *De Vere; or, the Man of Independence,* 3 vols. (Philadelphia: Carey, Lea and Carey, 1827), II, 182–83.

of fashionable society. The villainous Tyrrel knows that, being illegitimate (a well-kept secret), he must lose his father's estate to Granby; the Jermyns, not knowing this, have their own secret: their daughter Caroline, being female, cannot inherit and must therefore have a rich husband—i.e., not Granby. Thus the love of Granby and Caroline is wrapped in legal mystery and threatened by poverty; when Granby unexpectedly inherits, Caroline cannot reopen communications for fear of appearing mercenary. The love has long been imperiled by social appearances, and these include extraordinary uncertainties of communication and correspondence—forged letters, forced letters, late letters—exploited and aggravated by slanderers. Granby must somehow preserve his honor in society against slander, and Caroline's love must be based on a faith that survives false appearances.

Associated with slander in a world of fragile social credibility, as before, is the narcotic of gambling. Tyrrel is an infatuated but cleverly dishonest gamester who tries in vain to ruin Granby. Repentant and suicidal, Tyrrel blames his infatuation on the knowledge that he is illegitimate. Gambling is a reckless narcotic for one who sees his social life to be a lie, a fever of insecurity and deceit as in Burney, a metaphor for the society of which it is a characteristic illness. In what is called "the defensive warfare of society," the ablest warriors are those who, through careful misrepresentation and consummate acting, are the most skillful gamblers. Possessed of such powers, Tyrrel is limited by a certain coarseness, a "certain obtuseness of mental vision," which blinds him to "the finer springs of action."[63] Not so his fellow slanderer, Trebeck.

Trebeck is one of the most sophisticated characterizations in Regency fiction, and his moral implications coordinate the problem of fashion with central moral anxieties of Romanticism. Mephistophelian in urbanity, a social ventriloquist, he is a study in inauthenticity. Brummell and his biographers recognized in him a biographical portrait of

[63] T. H. Lister, *Granby*, 2 vols. (New York: Harper, 1826), II, 30–31.

truth and subtlety, but his significance transcends topicality. Ellen Moers sees him as the embodiment of Lister's own hidden love of fashion, but this is to misrepresent his negative, feebly opportunistic role in the novel's resolution, and to fall into the trap of those for whom Henry Crawford is the true hero of *Mansfield Park*. Trebeck is the outsider who masters and uses the fashionable world while professing to hold it in contempt. Superficially derided for "fineness" by "underbred" people who secretly worship "fine people," he is a confidence man who demonstrates that refinement can be unprincipled and also that it is independent of wealth and rank. As Granby's friend puts it, "fashion is not so aristocratic as many imagine; it may be bought, like most other things." But Trebeck disregards rank and would never sacrifice taste to wealth. He is anything but the foppish dandy of vulgar repute. Outside of "society" he enjoys "normal" people. To the prudent Caroline he affects independence:

> Do not associate me with the silly, worldly characters around me. I laugh at them, while I laugh with them. They are mere steps in my ladder. I regard them as tools, and treat them accordingly. Do not think that I am really heartless. How can I show that I have a heart, while I live with people who have none? Our best and warmest feelings require reciprocity for their display. With the world at large, I see the tone which best suits it. To you I am addressing a different language. Towards you I have no disguise.[64]

But this of course is one more disguise. He is, in fact, slavishly tied to a narrow social vision. As Caroline recognizes, he is essentially antisocial: "a heartlessness was in his character, a spirit of gay misanthropy, a cynical, depreciating view of society, an absence of high-minded generous sentiment, a treacherous versatility, and deep powers of deceit." He is dangerous because he carries cynical opportunism to a point of social and aesthetic genius. The description of his female counterpart, Miss Darrell, provides a further gloss on his enigmatic artificiality: "She was

[64] *Granby,* I, 94–95.

all brilliancy and effect; but it were hard to say she studied it; so little did her spontaneous, airy graces convey the impression of premeditated practice. She was a sparkling tissue of little affectations, which, however, appeared so interwoven with herself, that their seeming artlessness disarmed one's censure."[65] The presence of such figures makes *Granby* uniquely interesting as an anatomy of the social politics of fashion. But to be fair to the novel and its popularity, we should note that its chief preference is clearly for an elegant retirement.

Considering the success of *Granby* and the alleged rage for "fashionable" fiction, it is puzzling that Lister (via Colburn) should reappear in 1828 with *Herbert Lacy*, a novel in which fashion plays no significant role. The plot motifs, to be sure, are familiar. The suffering lovers are long separated by slander and class barriers. Herbert has been "nursed in lofty aristocratic feelings," has "trodden . . . the levelling maze of fashionable society," has been "taught invariably to connect vulgarity with low extraction," and does not at first suspect his own "illiberality." Agnes must feel "the vulgarity of her relations" and "the ridicule that their awkwardness and pretension must excite." Both agree that "people are seldom ridiculous, unless when taken out of their proper station, or when their vanity makes them strive to appear what they are not."[66] Slanders fail, divisions are overcome, pride and prejudice are chastened. Ian Jack's likening of the book to Austen's novels suggests properly that for all its slight "fashionable" aura, it is a domestic love story complicated by caste attitudes.[67]

Lister turned next, however, to the fashionable three-decker in *Arlington* (1832), and essayed a remarkable amalgam of current fashions in fiction: a society love story, a male version of Ferrier's *Inheritance*, slightly gothicized in the mixed mode Bulwer had by now popularized, utilizing the motif of amateur theatricals in the vein of *Mansfield*

---

[65] *Granby*, I, 77, 166.
[66] Lister, *Herbert Lacy*, I, 30–31, 68–69, 79.
[67] Ian Jack, *English Literature 1815–1832* (Oxford: Clarendon, 1963), pp. 248–49.

Park, and climaxing in the philosophical character of Ward. After his father's mysterious murder, Lord Arlington is exposed to the despotic "democracy" of a public school, the indulgent "aristocracy" of a university, and then the marital conspiracies of fashionable London. He is neither pedantically refined nor affectedly fastidious; he is not that "mawkish being, a modern Sybarite—a man-milliner-like creature of chains and essences, professing a perfumer's judgment in scents, a cook's in sauces, authoritative in pronouncing on a vintage, having 'a voice potential' to decide on the build of a carriage or the fashion of a seal, an Aristarchus of cravats and rings."[68] He must enter "the labyrinth of society" without true guides, "that society, which is scarcely society but in name." And for all his liberality, and his undying love for Lady Alice (whose parents are contemptuous of all fashion), he has a foible of vanity and is almost trapped into a fashionable marriage.

The fashionable world of London is urbanely analyzed. By its excesses Arlington is not fooled. Rather, his problem and Alice's is the now-familiar dilemma of how to *appear* disinterestedly devoted to each other in a world of cynical manipulation and false friends. Arlington's "friends" are two men of fashion (ostensibly patterned on Brummell and D'Orsay),[69] one an intellectual dandy, the other a decadent libertine, both accomplished and clever, both secret worshippers of social success and "the world." Denbigh practices a studied contempt of "fashion" and seeks to gratify his love of power through spoiling the love of Arlington and Alice by slander. Beauchamp, "the glass of fashion" in appearance, an epicurean roué, tries to marry his "friend" Arlington to the dazzling coquette Lady Julia in order to veil his own affair behind fashionable marriage. The web of decadence they weave around the hero is genuinely frightening. Arlington is saved by the temporary loss of inheritance.

He withdraws in despair and disgust from "the world,"

[68] T. H. Lister, *Arlington*, 3 vols. (London: Colburn, 1832), I, 85.
[69] Rosa, p. 71.

and blames his troubles on "the deceiving and corrupting influence of society. Society became the abstract monster, which he now loaded with all his faults; and when he looked back at any error, he would say to himself, 'How could I have avoided it in such a world?' "[70] In a "deep hue of misanthropic melancholy" he spends six years as a recluse. His only true friend, Hargrave, finds him in the condition of Tremaine at the outset of Ward's novel, and begins his volume-long philosophical cure to bring the misanthrope to "a more just and favorable estimate of society." After what we have seen, Hargrave's optimism is less than convincing, but it works, Arlington is reunited with Alice, and he will now live not *for* but *in* society, practicing the liberal benevolence of the country gentleman. It is an interesting amalgam, with a resolution that has now become traditional, an ideal of aristocracy regenerate in the enlightened country gentleman. But such an ideal could not satisfy the more ambitious and devious social activism of Disraeli and Bulwer.

IV

The development we have traced confirms Amy Cruse's view of the novel of fashion as an exercise in the politicizing of society; it does not fully explain Ellen Moer's conception of the dandy as a social subversive, a cryptoradical, using the training of fashion as a step toward power and revolutionary change.[71] Such novel complexities entered the tradition with Disraeli and Bulwer, whose first novels of fashion belong controversially to the time of Ward and Lister. The chief interest of *Vivian Grey* (1826) and *Pelham* (1828) is not simply in the evolution of the dandy, but in the new perspective on the problem of fashion to which that evolution belongs. The new perspective is inseparable, moreover, from a new complexity of mode. In *Vivian Grey*

---

[70] *Arlington*, II, 316.
[71] Amy Cruse, *The Englishman and his Books in the Early XIXth Century* (New York: Crowell, n.d.), pp. 144–48; Moers, passim.

we begin with a roman à clef of contemporary social artifice, move through political catastrophe to European wanderings of fantastic and farcical picaresque, and end in a satiric fantasy out of Voltaire and Juanesque Byronism. In *Pelham* the portrayal of fashionable artifice interweaves with and climaxes in Godwinian Gothic melodrama of obsession, underworld pursuit, and criminal detection. Thus, the setting of fashion is mimetically broadened and modally romanticized, and the prophetic satire of *Sartor Resartus*'s fashion myth seems close at hand.

The mastery of fashion now appears as a power of social impersonation and improvisation that aims at political and social change. The equivocal skills of the villain are part of the opportunistic postures of the hero. Pelham, *posing* as a dandy, is a master of self-impersonation. Grey, "with just enough of dandyism to preserve him from committing gaucheries," is a genius of improvisation.[72] Both know that they live in a world where society has become masquerade, and where the way to power is through mastery of masque. Their authors, likewise, are clearly seeking power behind the popular masque of the novel of fashion.

Imitation is the supreme skill, and yet social imitation has become stultifying and disintegrative. The continuity of custom has been overthrown, the caprice and ephemerality of fashion have replaced it, and society seems (for Vivian) "instinct with a spirit peculiarly active" with "so many openings . . . daily offered to the adventurous and the bold."[73] Both have friends and allies less skillful, less agile, than they and survive them. Grey manipulates the embittered Cleveland (a version of Tremaine) into leading his Carabas cabal, and when the plan is betrayed, he kills his passionate friend in a duel. Pelham's political friend Vincent is as much a pretender as he, but inattentive to appearances; Glanville is a melancholy Byronic obsessive, his promising political career ruined by a compulsion to

---

[72] E. Bulwer Lytton, *Pelham*, ed. J. J. McGann (Lincoln: University of Nebraska Press, 1972); Benjamin Disraeli, *Vivian Grey*, 2 vols. (New York: Dunne, 1904), I, 27.
[73] *Vivian Grey*, I, 32.

revenge, his life virtually ended by slander. Pelham and Grey are both troubled by the implications of the disingenuousness society imposes. Pelham, possessed of a true nature—principled and affectionate beneath the coxcombry—recognizes the process whereby artifice grows into nature. Grey is awakened by catastrophe to what he has made himself: "Am I, then, an intellectual Don Juan, reckless of human minds, as he was of human bodies; a spiritual libertine?" Chastened by disaster and healed by European wanderings, he hopes that "soon, very soon, . . . he should hail his native cliffs, a reclaimed wanderer, with a matured mind and a contented spirit, his sorrows forgotten, his misanthropy laid aside."[74] His Byronic destiny deems otherwise, for, while he grows in caution and knows genuine love, there seems no purpose in remorse or regret, and he appears at last a desperate, homeless rebel.

Grey never seems to transcend his (and Disraeli's) Byronism. Pelham, on the other hand, discovers in Byronism a crippling addiction to passion that incapacitates us for "our real duties" and perfects his practical vision. It is not clear that Vivian ever heeds his wise, refined father's warning: "You are now, my dear son, a member of what is called the great world; society formed on anti-social principles. Apparently you have possessed yourself of the object of your wishes; but the scenes you live in are very moveable; the characters you associate with are all masked; and it will always be doubtful whether you can retain that long which has been obtained by some slippery artifice."[75] Pelham, on the other hand, retains a practical vision of the truth behind appearances. He is set apart, his passion disciplined by *ton*, his ambition by principle. Close attention to social detail trains him in skillful observation, and when at last he must play the amateur detective, he is the exemplary man of action, a Trebeck of activism and principle.

His secret is to master the world without living purely for the world, for to live so is his idea of vulgarity, and even

---

[74] *Vivian Grey*, I, 164; II, 38.
[75] *Vivian Grey*, I, 201–2.

his mother has not escaped: "she lived, moved, breathed only for the world . . . . the very desire of supremacy in *ton* gave (Heaven forgive my filial impiety!) a sort of demi-vulgarism to her ideas; for they who live only for the opinion of others always want that self-dignity which alone confers a high cast upon the sentiments; and the most really unexceptionable in mode are frequently the least genuinely patrician in mind."[76] To live purely for the opinion of others is to be purely imitative, and universal imitation is the curse of contemporary society. A wise old beau analyzes the historical process. The influx of common persons leads "certain sets" to recede into exclusiveness and coterie. Isolation generates peculiar coterie manners, which in turn are imitated by other social leaders, and then by "the lower grades," and "thus manners, unnatural to all, are transmitted second-hand, third-hand, fourth-hand, till they are ultimately filtered into something worse than no manners at all."[77] His mother, trapped as she is in the process, is aware of it, and she blames it in part on the fashionable novelists. In fact, *Pelham* is frequently derisive of novels of fashion, as is *Vivian Grey,* and with them the genre has entered a sophisticated, some might say decadent, phase of self-mockery and self-exploitation. As Vivian puts it, "There is nothing like a fall of stocks to affect what it is the fashion to style the Literature of the present day, a fungus production which has flourished from the artificial state of our society, the mere creature of our imaginary wealth. Everybody being very rich, has afforded to be very literary, books being considered a luxury almost as element and necessary as ottomans, bonbons, and pier-glasses."[78]

In 1833, looking back on "the three-years' run of the fashionable novels," Bulwer sees the fashionable novelists as having "exposed the falsehood, the arrogant and vulgar insolence of patrician life," and having engendered "a min-

---

[76] Bulwer Lytton, *Pelham,* pp. 374–75.
[77] *Pelham,* pp. 342–43.
[78] *Vivian Grey,* I, 214.

gled indignation and disgust at the parade of frivolity, the ridiculous disdain of truth, nature, and mankind, the self-consequence and absurdity, which, falsely or truly, these novels exhibited as a picture of aristocratic society."[79] And in his 1840 recantation of *Pelham* he did claim that the book had made unfashionable the Byronic pose and had substituted the more "manly," socially useful pose of the dandy. But clearly the novel of fashion had done more. Socially it had articulated the consciousness of a growing divisiveness of caste in English society and had envisioned new and socially responsible ideas of aristocracy. For romantic critics such as Hazlitt it had provoked a restatement of the true social value of literature, which is not to inculcate the mysteries of social division, but to expand human knowledge and sympathy. For more Coleridgean critics such as Lockhart, it had dramatized the limits of "realism," proving that mere observation, without the "high faculties of imagination," could not achieve an "artist-like unity of form and purpose."[80] The two kinds of concern, both focused on disintegrity as a failure of imagination, are related. Imaginative literature for the romantic theorist, as we know from Wordsworth, Shelley, DeQuincey, and others, is a "great social organ" that works by the cultivation of imaginative sympathy and creative sensibility to overcome division—of man and the world, man and society, class and class—to improve social life by unifying it. Its antagonists are those intellectual and social forces that foster and rationalize division. Thus, the tyranny of fashion takes its place with the other despotisms of romantic myth. And the more accomplished novelists of fashion, in interpreting and dramatizing that tyranny, are not far from the mainstream of their romantic half-century.

---

[79] Bulwer Lytton, *England and the English,* ed. S. Meacham (Chicago: University of Chicago Press, 1970), pp. 287–88.
[80] William Hazlitt, "The Dandy School" (November 1827 in *The Examiner*), *Collected Works,* ed. Waller and Glover (London: Dent, 1904), XI, 343–48; J. G. Lockhart, review of *De Vere,* in *Quarterly Review,* 36 (1827), 269.

5 | THACKERAY'S DRAMATIC MONOLOGUES

Lionel Stevenson

In surveys of English literature a familiar truism is to the effect that the Victorian poets made their most significant and original contribution to poetic methods by creating the dramatic monologue. Though always associated primarily with Browning, this particular technique was developed simultaneously and independently by Tennyson and was promptly adopted by virtually all the poets—Arnold and Clough, Rossetti and Morris, Meredith and Swinburne. Though they had little else in common, they all found the dramatic monologue to be a rewarding vehicle for some of their best work.

The vitality of the new genre was derived from its fitness for conveying several potent impulses of the era. One was the burgeoning interest in psychology, the desire to delve as deeply as possible into the infinite varieties of individual identity. The concept of the unconscious had not yet been fully defined, but the authors were intuitively aware that there were depths in personality which could be revealed only obliquely, because persons are usually unaware themselves of their true motives and impulses. Everyone clings to an inner conviction of the rightness of his own position and resists conformity to externally imposed criteria.

A second influence toward the emergence of the dramatic monologue was the increasing flexibility of moral standards—the realization that every human being is a complex mixture of virtue and vice, of wisdom and folly, and that the old absolutes of right and wrong no longer applied in a relativist ethics. Furthermore, the newly spawned visions of democracy insisted that everyone, no matter how obscure, had the right to form his own opinions and to receive a fair hearing for his grievances.

So far as poetry was concerned, there was another pressure that forced it into a search for fresh devices. Literature was moving inexorably toward a stronger concern with realism, and the traditional genres of epic, lyric, and reflective meditation were inadequate for reproducing the vastly complex interrelationships of the modern world. Even the poetic drama was too formal and implausible to be accepted as an imitation of real life. Influential critics were declaring ruthlessly that poetry was obsolescent, a primitive survival from a simpler epoch. In the nineteenth century the novelists were advancing rapidly in their techniques for displaying individual characteristics and the tangled relationship between every human being and his environment. If the poets were to survive, they urgently needed to discover some medium that could combine the essential virtues of poetry—condensation, intensity, imaginative vividness—with the inescapable demands of fidelity to experience.

By a process of trial and error, Browning and Tennyson fumbled their way into a poetic technique that fulfilled all these requirements. Emotional intensity was achieved through forcing the reader to participate in the feelings of the speaker. Condensation resulted from the compression of a whole story into a single climactic or revelatory moment. Imaginative vividness came from the specific details of the occasion. Through the compulsory merging of the reader's personality with the speaker's, the dramatic monologue produced a subversive sympathy with the attitudes of human beings who were apt to be alien to the moral and intellectual standards that the reader customarily took for granted. The widespread difficulties experienced by readers and critics in grasping the principles of the dramatic monologue, their inability to comprehend that the "I" was an objective identity and not the voice of the poet, reveal the novelty of the experiments. The waxing sophistication of the Victorian reading public can be gauged by their increasing acumen in interpreting the hints that enabled them to recognize the distinctive traits of each persona and to reconstruct the whole situation that is revealed in the flash of the dramatic instant.

For literal-minded readers, the principal difficulty inhered in the fact that the dramatic monologue is essentially ironic. Such persons, intelligent though they may be, find it hard, if not impossible, to achieve the duality of perception that irony demands. In a dramatic monologue, indeed, the complexity of response may be more than merely dual. In addition to the literal data (what the speaker tells about the situation and his interpretation of it), there is not only the author's implication of what actually happened and what the speaker reveals about himself, but also the reader's eventual judgment on both speaker and author alike. Each element in the tripartite relationship exerts a perpetual and mutual influence on the other two. The consequent permutations of irony are inexhaustible.

It was fitting that this most personalized of poetic devices should have originated with the most evasive of English poets. Browning's compulsive insistence on his right to immunity from intrusion impelled him to develop a medium in which the author's identity could be concealed as deeply as possible behind objective masks. Naturally, no creative artist can obscure his unique individuality, but Browning fragmented his into multiple disguises. After a perceptive reader has absorbed the whole range of the monologues, the outlines of the poet's opinions and sympathies and prejudices emerge out of the mob of apparently disparate individuals. Thus we arrive at the point where we are aware of reading two poems at the same time—the one that expresses Browning and the one that explores the psyche of the dramatic speaker. Neither poem can exist in isolation, and superimposed upon each other they produce a unique illusion of double vision.

Any vital new literary phenomenon is not a miraculous parthenogenesis, but is bound to possess antecedents and analogs. The direct ancestry of the dramatic monologue, as indicated by the epithet itself and emphasized by Browning's early years of theatrical ambition, has been assumed to be the drama. Certainly the revelation of individuality by means of a character's own words is automatically achieved through dramatic dialogue and even more distinctly by the soliloquy. Some of Browning's poems, if they are to be strictly classified, are soliloquies, and Shakespearean echoes are perceptible. In certain essential respects, however, the new genre cannot be adequately described as a condensed play. A dramatic monologue is more than a detachable episode somewhere near the crisis of an action. Rather, it is a retrospective and prospective refocusing that disintegrates normal time sequence and reveals the inmost reality in psychological rather than chronological significance. Furthermore, the limitation to a single speaker is basically different from the technique of a play, in which each character talks in his turn. Nor is the parallel with the soliloquy fully applicable. In the Shakespearean model, a basic assumption is that every soliloquy is a valid exposition of the character's true thoughts. The only element of irony in a soliloquy of Hamlet or Macbeth or Othello—or of Malvolio or Falstaff—is in the contrast between the speaker's ideas and the hard facts of the dramatic action in which he is involved. At some expense of verisimilitude, Iago is cynically candid about his own unmitigated evil. When Browning depicts a similar being, such as Guido Franceschini or the Duke of Ferrara, the reader's reaction is far less direct.

Virtually no attention has been paid to the possible affiliation of the dramatic monologue with another literary form which for more than a century had been experimenting intermittently with the first-personal point of view. It was Defoe who first discovered the intensification of vividness and emotional identification effected by reporting the events of a story through the senses and the mind of a participant. Since the emergence of the dramatic monologue in poetry, the sense of irony has become so strong that many recent critics have been tempted to read it backward into Defoe's practice. To the modern sensibility there is something comic in the vision of Robinson Crusoe, the practical seaman and trader, setting up his efficient establishment on a desert island, or of Moll Flanders, the meretricious thief and prostitute, being converted to proper morality after making a modest fortune at her trade. There is little probability, however, that Defoe had any perception of such ambiguities. To him, the first-personal point of view performed its full function when it enabled the reader to project himself intimately into the experience of the narrator. Crusoe the mariner or Flanders the whore or Singleton the pirate was simply a talking machine to transmit the action, and the voice of each of them was the voice of Daniel Defoe. Dimly aware of this inconsistency, he explained in his role of "editor" that he had improved upon Moll's grammar and cleaned up her vocabulary so that she would be acceptable to genteel readers. When one of Defoe's locutors has thus been regularized, in conformity with neoclassical principles of generalization, the author's attitude is antithetical to the particularity that is essential to the dramatic monologue.

A more subtle intelligence was required for recognizing the potential irony that lurked in Defoe's new technique of fictitious autobiography. Captain Lemuel Gulliver is ostensibly such another honest mariner as Crusoe; but the acute reader soon realizes that his blunt common sense and his English chauvinism are being betrayed by the author's mischievous obliquity. Reluctantly, the reader acquires a new set of values, and regards Gulliver's criteria with unwonted skepticism. Not only do we share his experiences and grow fond of his innocent candor, but we also cringe at his insensitivity and challenge his standards.

Thus it was in *Gulliver's Travels* that the strategy of double vision inserted itself into English fiction; but the other principal satiric device in the book—the allegorical fantasy—was so much more conspicuous that the full import of the first-personal technique was not appreciated as providing anything beyond an illusion of plausibility. It is true that an elementary version of double vision for satiric purpose was represented in the "alien visitor" books, such as *The Citizen of the World*. The reader was expected to recognize the absurdities of his own culture in the distorting mirror of the foreign observer's astonishment. Here again, however, the narrator is not individually characterized, but functions obviously as a projection of the author's disillusioned vision.

Hence, in the next generation after Defoe and Swift, the same contrast between "straight" first-personal reporting and ironic double vision repeated itself with little if any perceptible development. By perfecting the technique of the epistolary novel, Richardson demonstrated the power of the participant's point of view to enhance immediacy and sympathy; but he did not explore its possibilities for involuntary revelation of character. All his locutors, like Defoe's, write very much alike, and all of them are to be accepted as reliable reporters. Pamela chronicles what happens to her from day to day and utters her fears and hopes with scrupulous accuracy. In *Clarissa* there is a greater opportunity for irony, as Lovelace reveals his nefarious plans side by side with Clarissa's anxieties; but the irony is dramatic and not psychological. Pamela, the proletarian servant wench; Clarissa, the prosperous bourgeoise; Lovelace, the polished worldling; Grandison, the benign aristocrat—all express themselves alike in the sonorous periods of Samuel Richardson.

Here again, as in interpreting Defoe, present-day critics have indulged in hindsight. Pamela can be regarded as a scheming minx, Clarissa as a sex-starved neurotic, Grandison as a pompous hypocrite; but these cynical twentieth-century views formed no part of the original novels, whether in Richardson's mind or in the reactions of two centuries of readers. They knew that Pamela or Clarissa or Sir Charles was a good character because she or he told them so; they knew that Lovelace was a scoundrel through the same sort of evidence. As complexities and inconsistencies did not exist, there was no need of a technique for displaying them.

When Fielding set out to ridicule Richardson's solemn moralizing, he displayed the ambiguity of Pamela's motives through the letters of Shamela, a very different sort of girl; but when he proceeded to more extended burlesque in *Joseph Andrews,* he rejected the epistolary structure as too cumbersome. Then, for his political satire on the Whig government, he practiced a form of ironic double vision that did not entail the first-personal point of view. In *Jonathan Wild* the narrator praises the highwayman for such virtues as courage, cleverness, and integrity, while the reader soon sees through the adulation and penetrates to Wild's unmitigated villainy. As in the instance of *Gulliver's Travels,* there is a complicating factor of ideological satire: contemporaries were expected to respond to the multiple irony of recognizing the misdeeds of the nation's political leaders in the humiliating guise of a common criminal, and thus to despise them and to laugh at them simultaneously. It is the standard practice of the cartoonist, and Fielding handles it effectively; but it is not related to the technique of first-personal point of view.

A quarter century later Oliver Goldsmith, with his intuitive originality, came nearer to using the device of unconscious self-betrayal in a work of fiction that had no ulterior purpose; but we cannot be sure whether he was aware of it. In *The Vicar of Wakefield* Mr. Primrose is offered as a model of Christian virtues, but we find him comic as well as benevolent, when his patience and naiveté prove to be mingled with vanity and even selfishness.

In the use of the first person, as in every other respect, a unique production, foreshadowing later developments, was *Tristram Shandy.* The narrator's identity permeates the whole fabric of the novel and supplies inimitable double meanings to every page. This identity is so elusive, however, that it can scarcely be defined. Ostensibly it is the eponymous autobiographer, who talks about "my father," "my uncle"; yet he must be assembling his data from other sources, since he does not exist during much of the recorded action. We are driven back to the assumption that the principal narrator is Yorick and Yorick in his turn is indistinguishable from Laurence Sterne. Thus the book—and the flock of imitations that followed—must be regarded as deflecting the first-personal point of view in fiction rather than as contributing to it. Perhaps such volumes should be classified as a species of personal essay instead of as novels.

Among the hundreds of epistolary novels in the second half of the century, there was only one that notably profited by the opportunities for character revelation and ironic ambiguity offered by the personal letter. This was *The Expedition of Humphry Clinker,* in which Smollett employs the idiosyncracies of the respective letter writers to produce not only rich humor but also ironic juxtapositions, as the reader witnesses each scene from several points of view. There can be no uncertainty as to the identity of each correspondent: Matthew Bramble's grumbling, his sister's peevish fussing, Winifred Jenkins's illiterate outbursts, Julia's adolescent sentimentality—each carries the very tone of the locutor. We quickly perceive the benevolence underlying Matt's vile temper; but there is no great subtlety in the balancing of the antipodal traits.

Clearly the sporadic occurrences of something like ironic ambiguity in first-personal narration and of unintentional revelation of personality on the part of fictional characters were so few and diversified in purpose and effect that no generic tradition was established. Apart from the handful of exceptional specimens discussed above, until well into the nineteenth century the first-personal narrative remained a conventional type of fictitious autobiography, the memoirs of a central character who seldom takes on individual traits. He goes through the necessary motions for keeping the action in progress, but the other performers become more vivid than he can be. At the outset of the nineteenth century the ablest novelists preferred the elbowroom of the omniscient point of view. Even Scott's practiced hand falters a bit when he undertakes the first person in *Rob Roy;* Frank Osbaldiston is one of his least vital heroes, handicapped by the necessity of maintaining proper modesty while recording his accession to maturity. The most powerful pre-Victorian novel of self-betrayal was James Hogg's *Confessions of a Justified Sinner,* which provides a horrifying picture of Calvinist megalomania. With supreme self-esteem the locutor chronicles the corrosive hatred that impels him to murder. One element of the authentic dramatic monologue is thereby obviated: the picture is so repulsive that no reader can experience the subversive sympathy arising from identification with the locutor.

In the 1830s, then, the standard model of the novel used the impersonal point of view and conveyed its story with the aid of copious commentary and analysis supplied by the author. No inference or indirection was possible within this rigidly explicit structure. Though prose fiction was on the threshold of its most rapid and explosive development, no conscious spirit of experiment had invaded the minds of its writers. Then, at the same juncture when Browning was impelled by his inner reticence to formulate by laborious trial and error the techniques of the dramatic monologue in poetry, a similar psychological compulsion pushed another author through the same process in prose. It is my thesis that Thackeray played a role in developing the strategy of ambiguous self-revelation in prose fiction parallel to that which Browning played in verse. The first experiments of the two authors were almost simultaneous: Browning's earliest monologues appeared in the *Monthly Repository* in January 1836, Thackeray's Charles James Yellowplush made his debut in *Fraser's Magazine* in November 1837.

William Makepeace Thackeray in his youth showed no tendency toward creative ambition. Indolent by nature, and heir to a comfortable fortune, he anticipated a life of elegant self-indulgence, including a dilettante dabbling in art and letters. He was exceptionally self-conscious, painfully aware of his great height, his awkward gestures, his weak eyesight, and his grotesquely battered features. From childhood onward he had learned to protect his sensitivity and his hunger for appreciation under an affectation of worldly cynicism. When he took part in undergraduate journalism at Cambridge, he needed to establish an objective identity as remote as possible from his own. Not bothering to invent one for himself, he snatched the first that came to hand.

Theodore Hook, a popular novelist and scurrilous journalist, was printing in his weekly *John Bull* a series of broadly comic "Ramsbottom Letters," purportedly written by a London merchant's widow describing her travels on the Continent. Crudely modeled on Mrs. Malaprop, with an admixture of Winifred Jenkins, Dorothea Julia Ramsbottom, who regards her social and intellectual status with great complacency, mutilates almost every word of more than two syllables. When Thackeray and his friends started *The Snob* in 1829, Mrs. Ramsbottom was an obvious specimen of the middle-class vulgarity that they intended to ridicule from the altitude of their sophistication. Bringing her on a visit to Cambridge, Thackeray contributed three of her letters to the short-lived *Snob* and one to its successor, *The Gownsman*. Even within these narrow bounds, a sort of plot began to develop. Mrs. Ramsbottom campaigns for a local parliamentary candidate; another correspondent reports that she has been brutally assaulted and driven insane; Mrs. Ramsbottom angrily writes to refute the canard. There could not have been a more utter divergence between two personalities: Dorothea Ramsbottom is elderly, obtuse, and a woman; the author is young, cultivated, and a male. Yet she is something more than a butt of ridicule. Her vitality and common sense are agreeable enough. Thackeray was not merely laughing at her crassness but was also using her for making fun of Cambridge; she retains something of the old "alien visitor" function.

The good woman's malapropisms can be illustrated by any random sentence: "I think the Library of Trinity College is one of the most admiral objects here. I saw the busks of several gentlemen whose statures I had seen at

Room, and who all received there edification at that College. There was Aristocracy who wrote farces for the Olympic Theatre, and Democracy, who was a laughing philosopher" (XXVIII, 8–9).[1]

Not only was Thackeray saved the trouble of inventing his own comic figure, he also had a guaranteed source of fresh material from one number to the next. He merely had to set the loquacious Mrs. Ramsbottom to expounding her views on another current topic. The humor of a single device, however, soon grows tedious, and Thackeray aparently tired of his impersonation, for she vanished before *The Gownsman* ended its brief existence. Nevertheless, by sheer chance he was launched at the very outset on the technique that he was to retain and refine throughout his career.

During the next eight years he showed but few symptoms of literary ambition; but then the loss of his patrimony and the failure of his dream of being a painter forced him into authorship—not as a genteel amateur, nor yet as an eminent creative author, but in the humiliating role of a hack journalist, eagerly grasping any assignment that came his way. During the 1820s a new medium had emerged, in the form of the popular magazine—the *London, Blackwood's, Fraser's*, the *New Monthly*. Probably in imitation of "Mr. Spec" and "Isaac Bickerstaffe" a century earlier, they adopted an editorial policy of pseudonymity; regular contributors came to be recognized by their fictitious identities. Lamb was Elia, Wilson was Christopher North, de Quincey was the Opium Eater, Maginn was Ensign O'Doherty or Oliver Yorke. When young Dickens came along, he followed the vogue by calling himself Boz. These were not so much imaginary beings as whimsical self-caricatures, in which the authors changed only a few incidental features of their actual circumstances. With Boz, in fact, there was nothing whatever beyond the pen name.

[1] Quotations are taken from *The Complete Works of William Makepeace Thackeray* (New York: Harper, 1904), with introductions by W. P. Trent and J. B. Henneman. Page reference follows volume number.

Thackeray, starting his professional career in the Fraserian circle, inevitably adopted the current practice; but he changed it in important respects. His purpose was not, like that of his colleagues, to establish an easily recognizable identity resembling his own, but to shroud himself in total obscurity, so that the former associates of his life as a gentleman should not suspect him of having degenerated into a disreputable vocation. Obsessively conscious of a gentleman's prerogatives, acutely aware of the incipient breakdown in class distinctions, he shared the public conception of journalists as raffish vulgarians who were destroying the dignity of literature. Particularly he wished to conceal the range of work he was grinding out each month for a variety of journals. Hence he created, not one disguise, but several, and he went to great pains to provide each one with circumstantial details remote from his own identity. These protective coverings released his inventive faculty in directions that might not have been possible for him in either the omniscient or the direct personal mode.

The earliest and in some respects the best of his comic impersonations occurred to him almost accidentally. As his first assignment for *Fraser's*, he undertook to review *My Book: or, The Anatomy of Conduct*, by John Henry Skelton, a retired London draper who had succumbed to the delusion that he should be the arbiter of elegance in dress and behavior. His pomposity, vanity, and ignorance rendered him an egregious example of the vulgar social pretensions that Thackeray despised. As the best means of caricaturing these qualities, the reviewer assumed the identity of a footman in a fashionable household. Since the chief qualification of a footman was a handsome physique to display the gorgeous livery, and his duties were usually minimal, footmen were regarded as stupid, lazy, conceited, and addicted to gossip. The most conspicuous trait of Thackeray's Charles Yellowplush is the phonetic spelling which reproduces his richly Cockney accent. His ineffable self-satisfaction served adequately to mirror Skelton's, and his ludicruous episodes of upper-class table manners were irresistibly farcical elaborations of such Skeltonisms as "When the finger-glass is placed before you, you must not drink the contents, or even rinse your mouth and spit it back" (XVII, 144).

The few pages of "Fashnable Fax and Polite Annygoats" sufficed to convince the magazine editor that a major comic character had been created, and he commissioned Thackeray to provide *The Memoirs of Mr. C. J. Yellowplush*, which ran for eight months in 1838. The series made no pretense to uniformity or structure. It started with a short story about one of Yellowplush's early employers, followed it with another dealing with his service under an aristocratic gambler, reverted to literary criticism to ridicule Lady Charlotte Bury's *Diary Illustrative of the Time of George IV*, then resumed the adventure of the Hon. Algernon Percy Deuceace in a longer narrative running through four installments. "Mr. Yellowplush's Ajew" supposedly brought the series to a close with a savage caricature of Edward Bulwer Lytton; but a year and a half later Yellowplush was brought back for a further assault on the same victim.

The unity of the series depends wholly on the personality of the locutor. The footman traces his career from infancy and exhibits the range of his traits. Identifying himself with his employers, he regards himself as their social equal, while respecting them for their arrogance. Utterly unscrupulous, he admires the clever and heartless gambler Deuceace with amoral enthusiasm. Hence, the ambiguity of double vision comes through strongly. While Yellowplush callously records other people's miseries, the reader responds all the more warmly to the pathos of the situations. Besides, Yellowplush sometimes reveals an unexpected impulse of pity under his cynicism. His association with the aristocracy has rendered him candidly contemptuous of upper-class mores. Thackeray was exposing not only the crassness of vulgar social climbers but equally the worthlessness of the caste they were seeking to emulate; and Yellowplush comes out the better in the contrast. In short, Thackeray, like Browning, had created a literary method in which the invented speaker is more important than what he is talking about.

It is a clue to Thackeray's creative process that he often became too fond of a character to abandon it at the end of the book. When he resuscitated Yellowplush after sixteen months, the phonetic spelling was almost all that set his mark on the essay. In the preceding paper, Bulwer had been legitimately burlesqued through the censorious eyes of the footman, but the "Epistles to the Literati" is essentially a piece of professional criticism. Even more indiscreetly, Thackeray reverted to Yellowplush five years later, after he had joined the regular staff of *Punch*. To satirize the current railway mania, Thackeray defies all plausibility in showing Yellowplush as making a large fortune through speculation, becoming a parliamentary candidate and fiancé of an earl's daughter, and finally, after losing everything during a panic, going to debtors' prison, whence he is bailed out by a devoted maidservant, whom he marries. The exposure of universal greed and aristocratic hypocrisy is effective in an obvious way, but the former image of Yellowplush has been irreparably damaged by all the burlesque melodrama. The motive of topical satire disturbs the artistic balance between character revelation and subject matter which made the original Yellowplush series a minor masterpiece.

By this time, Thackeray had no reason whatsoever for needing to rely on an outworn disguise, for he had invented a whole gallery of other personae. While the original Yellowplush memoirs were still running in *Fraser's*, Thackeray started a quite different serial for the rival *New Monthly*, and it was imperative that he should assume a mask utterly unlike his existing one. Several months before, he had signed a short story in *Bentley's Miscellany* with the name "Goliah Gahagan," but this had been merely to conform with the vogue for pseudonyms, and no effort was made to provide the name with an identity. The richly Irish resonance, however, must have lingered in Thackeray's mind; for his new serial he invented a full-scale figure to embody it, Major Goliah O'Grady Gahagan, a veteran of the Honorable East India Company's service. The stereotype of the braggart soldier was at least as old as Plautus, but fresh embellishments were provided. As Thackeray believed that the Irish were incorrigible exaggerators, the major's nationality compounds the self-glorifying tendency of his vocation, while the other Irish trait of eloquence supplies his magniloquent style. An accomplished name-dropper, he claims intimacy with leading celebrities of his era, from royalty downward; and compliments from these distinguished persons (including both Napoleon and Wellington) are cited in support of the major's most outrageous boasts. An element of individuality is contributed by the Indian setting, which Thackeray knew intimately from family tradition and early childhood memories. Half a century before Kipling, India had not yet figured much in English literature; and in spite of Gahagan's fantastic fabrications, the reader captures an impression of the country.

Some Passages in the Life of Major Gahagan may seem at first sight to be a simple if not tedious, burlesque on military memoirs, Irish verbosity, and exotic travelogues, following the familiar Munchausen tradition of the "tall tale"; but it proves to have complexities arising from the employment of duple vision. Somehow the major's self-magnifying mendacity does not disqualify him as a gentleman, and he even emerges as a competent and loyal officer. He is frank and sensible about the occasions when it is good tactics to retreat, as in a crisis when after his retirement from India he is serving as a brevet general with the Carlists in Spain: "Were I to say that I stopped to fight seventy men, you would write me down a fool or a liar; no, sir, I did not fight, I ran away. . . . I was running, running as the brave stag before the hounds—running as I have done a great number of times before in my life, when there was no help for it but a race" (XV, 339). The most interesting feature of the major's recollections, however, for modern readers is the inadvertent glimpses of the imperialist mentality and the sadistic behavior of the dominant race. Whether his readers in 1838 were aware of it or not, Thackeray was insinuating that their representatives in the subcontinent were disgracefully autocratic and atrociously cruel.

Another of his extensive dramatic disguises, which came three years later, was less exaggerated and farcical than the two previous ones, and represented a person whose caste and environment were more like the author's own. George Savage FitzBoodle is the very archetype of the London man-about-town—a fat, lazy bachelor who spends all his time at clubs and ekes out his scanty income by his winnings as "the third best whist-player in Europe." He seldom reads a book, and he expresses a sovereign contempt for literary men. The younger son of a baronet of ancient lineage, he was rusticated from Christ Church (traditionally the least intellectual and most patrician Oxford college) for impudence to a tutor, and after three months as a subaltern was expelled from the army for an affront to a superior officer. Thereafter he drifted around Europe, indulging in several unfortunate love affairs that left him a tolerantly cynical misogynist, preferring his pipes and cigars to womankind.

This series marks a long stride in Thackeray's control of point of view. The two-dimensional flatness of Yellowplush and Gahagan gives way to FitzBoodle's roundness, the result of closer similarity to Thackeray's own views. With his other two locutors, Thackeray enabled his readers to observe contemporary society through the eyes of a rascally servant and an alien soldier of fortune; his third one represented the values of the English upper class, which Arnold later termed the "Barbarians." FitzBoodle displays all the caste marks. He is gullible and sentimental under his worldly pose. From his school days he retains a smattering of classical allusions, but his literary taste is banal. He assumes as axiomatic that the manners and opinions of the gentry are of primary importance, and yet he is shrewd enough to recognize that their privileges are being eroded and that before long many of them must face the degradation of working for a living. Confident that the English are the finest race in the world, he sneers at the folly and stupidity of all foreigners.

As these traits are certainly to be perceived in Thackeray's own personality, we must accept FitzBoodle as partially his spokesman, in the same way that we see much of Browning in Lippo Lippi or Rabbi Ben Ezra and yet must beware of a one-to-one equivalency. The outcome is a complex example of multiple vision. Many of FitzBoodle's strictures about foreigners are valid, and yet as he utters them he reveals his own defects. As a psychological and social kinsman of FitzBoodle, Thackeray is thereby ridiculing himself; and as an author catering to the current English public, he is also ridiculing accepted criteria of his readers.

He felt so comfortably at home with FitzBoodle that he retained him as the narrator in a group of short stories with the general title of *Men's Wives*. One of these, "The Ravenswing," was on the scale of a substantial novella. FitzBoodle figures as a minor participant in the action of the stories, and his attitude of mellow detachment is pervasive; but if he had not previously been established as a fully objectivized individual, we should probably accept his voice in the stories as Thackeray's own.

The tendency to merge the author's identity with that of a congenial locutor had already existed for six years in Thackeray's most persistent impersonation, Michael Angelo Titmarsh. When he first appeared in *Fraser's Magazine*, half a year after Yellowplush, Titmarsh was similarly invented to serve a single specific occasion. Having an assignment to review the Royal Academy exhibition, and intending to express some subversive judgments, Thackeray needed a disguise to protect him from accusations of being a jealous amateur. Accordingly, he created Titmarsh, fresh from the ateliers of the Latin Quarter and—in his own opinion—a gifted painter of large historical canvases. Thus, he could utter the devastating remarks that would have been inappropriate for the gentlemanly Thackeray. It was therefore particularly necessary that Titmarsh's identity be clearly differentiated. He has a wife who weighs nineteen stone and a little son named Sebastian Piombo Titmarsh. He frequents low taverns, in which he is prone to get drunk. When Thackeray drew his portrait for illustrations, he was depicted as a small, plump man, whereas Thackeray was notoriously tall.

Titmarsh was revived a year later to review the next Academy show, and continued for a couple of years to provide critiques of exhibitions in London and Paris. Thus, what might otherwise have lapsed into perfunctory comments on a long list of pictures was enriched with the humor of the critic's personality and was rendered palatable to the readers of a popular magazine. Soon, however, Titmarsh became someone much more substantial than merely a mask for the author's ventures as an art critic. When Thackeray brought out his first book, *The Paris Sketch Book,* in 1840, he attributed the authorship to "Mr. Titmarsh." Though Titmarsh appears identifiably in only two of the pieces, the attribution is not implausible, for Titmarsh's familiarity with Paris qualified him to write the miscellaneous, gossiping impressions of life in the French capital. Next year Thackeray's second book, *Comic Tales and Sketches,* could be described only as "edited and illustrated by Mr. Michael Angelo Titmarsh," since the greater part of it consisted of the Yellowplush and Gahagan papers, which had their own separate locutors. By a deft trick, Thackeray superimposed one of his masks upon two of the others.

A similar device was employed in the same year with the serial publication in *Fraser's* of a short novel, *The History of Samuel Titmarsh and the Great Hoggarty Diamond,* "edited and illustrated by Sam's Cousin, Michael Angelo." Written in the first person, it is an unwontedly sentimental narrative of a naive and weak-willed young man, a junior clerk in an insurance office. He reveals his character innocently enough, and at the same time he records much about the background of the Titmarsh family. In this way his cousin Michael, to whom he intrusts the manuscript for publication, acquires in the reader's mind a solid relationship with a lower-middle-class environment.

Titmarsh assumed clearer status as Thackeray's alter ego in the two travel books that followed, *The Irish Sketch Book* and *Notes of a Journey from Cornhill to Grand Cairo.* In both, the material came directly from Thackeray's immediate experiences, but—as in the original art criticism—the frankness of the commentary was facilitated by the disguise. The Irish book aroused fury in English and Irish alike by its evenhanded reporting of faults on both sides; the other book was branded as blasphemous by the pious and as insensitive by devotees of the picturesque. The pseudonym was wearing thin by this time, as Thackeray penetrated his own disguise by signing his name to the dedications of both books. Nonetheless, Titmarsh was perhaps all the more a psychological necessity to the author. With his cocksure impudence, his invincible empiricism, his overt self-indulgence, he served as the spearhead of an assault on hypocrisy, sentimentality, and cant, which Thackeray was still reluctant to conduct in his own person. It may be suggested that Titmarsh and FitzBoodle both come to life because they are projections of two major elements in Thackeray's personality. FitzBoodle is the cosmopolitan gentleman, the sybaritic dilettante, lapsing into authorship under economic pressure and regarding the vocation with amused contempt. Titmarsh is the bourgeois professional writer, familiar with poverty, eyeing rank and prestige with disillusioned skepticism. The disparity between these ill-mated twins eventuated in the tensions that endow Thackeray's best work with its unique quality.

Once Thackeray's literary eminence had been established with *Vanity Fair,* he was under no further compulsion to retain the persona of Titmarsh, but for a number of years he continued to employ it in a particular genre, his so-called "Christmas books." Several of these—*Mrs. Perkins's Ball,* "*Our Street,*" and *Doctor Birch and His Young Friends*—reinforce our impression of Titmarsh's philistine background; but the final one, *The Rose and the Ring,* coming as late as 1855, is a playful fantasy that lies far beyond Titmarsh's blunt, literal mind.

It is unnecessary to list the other disguises which Thackeray adopted and discarded during the decade of his apprenticeship. Some are farcical caricatures, like Miss Tickletoby, the muddleheaded schoolmistress; others are mere names, such as Lancelot Wagstaff and Timothy Titcomb. Whether fully realized or merely perfunctory, the motley crew equipped Thackeray with the mastery of multiple vision which reached its artistic fulfillment in 1844, when *The Luck of Barry Lyndon* was serialized in *Fraser's*. While it was clearly suggested by *Jonathan Wild*, it went far beyond its model. In place of Fielding's political satire and his rather monotonous sarcasm in fulsomely praising a scoundrel, Thackeray keeps his attention fixed on the psychology of Lyndon as revealed in his own self-exaltation. He is vastly more complex than Thackeray's previous braggart, Major Gahagan. The result is a strangely disturbing experience for the reader, who finds himself compelled to proceed through several stages. At first he assumes that Lyndon is a reliable reporter of his exploits as a soldier of fortune. Upon becoming suspicious, the reader must start over again and arrive at his own interpretation of the persons and events that are chronicled. Next, he begins to analyze Lyndon's motives and the forces that shaped his personality. Finally, the reader arrives at insight that neither accepts Lyndon's self-righteousness nor remains satisfied with the disgust that it first evoked. We still respect the characters whom Lyndon vilifies, we abominate his arrogance and cruelty, we are sardonically amused by his greed and cowardice; and yet we find that we have acquired a reluctant affection for him. We cannot help admiring his ingenuity and resilience; we appreciate the perverse but very human rationalizing by which he justifies even his most heinous actions. Other dimensions of the irony include the challenge to accepted concepts of military glory and romantic heroism, and the revelation of the sordidness underlying the glitter of the eighteenth century. Barry Lyndon is not the villain-hero of Elizabethan tragedy or the satanic superman of Byronism, and yet he is a sort of hero—very human and even a little pathetic. Thackeray had finally acquired the essential strategy of the dramatic monologue, in which the reader is made to counterbalance moral judgment against sympathetic identification with an alien personality. The reading public of 1844, however, was not prepared for such subtlety: the editor of the magazine received letters of outraged protest against what was regarded as condoning of vice, and the author felt obliged to insert footnotes decrying Lyndon's iniquity.

It may have been this encounter with public obtuseness that persuaded Thackeray to undertake a different strategy for his next impersonation. For a series of essays in *Punch*, intended to display the ubiquity of shoddy values and hypocritical meanness throughout the social fabric, he chose the title *The Snobs of England*, "by One of Them." With this disarming gesture, Thackeray softened the cutting edge of his satire, while at the same time he alerted his readers to the inherent irony: the self-elected scourge of public depravity was so familiar with his subject because he was himself infected with the same virus in more subtle forms. By the deprecating stance, however, he was obliquely suggesting a further innuendo. If even the author were not free of blame, how could the reader remain smugly immune? The necessary condition of multiple vision was established, so that the reader with new ambivalence reconsidered his environment, the author, and himself.

The foregoing survey of Thackeray's varied experiments with dramatic personae and multiple vision forms a necessary background for the study of his handling of point of view in the major novels, a topic that has attracted critical attention in recent years. In the course of them he employed three distinct varieties of the ironically involved narrator. In *Vanity Fair* the identity is inconspicuous but gradually develops as a composite of George FitzBoodle and the persona of *The Book of Snobs*—a disillusioned worldling, immersed in upper-class English society. He is an inveterate gossip, piecing his story together from club scandal and backstairs malice. Anything but omniscient, he overtly resorts to guesswork or proposes alternative possibilities. Scrupulously avoiding slander, he leaves several crucial situations politely ambiguous, while as a suave gentleman he assumes enough sophistication in his readers that they can draw their inferences from the evasive hints.

This narrator has been personally acquainted with the characters through incidental encounters, and his attitude toward each of them is a constantly shifting mixture of sympathy and antagonism, pity and contempt.

With *Henry Esmond* Thackeray reverted to the old formula of the fictitious autobiography and practiced it so adeptly that generations of readers and critics have accepted it at face value as a reliable record, in which an admirable hero achieves an ideal balance of truth and modesty. When viewed, however, in conjunction with Thackeray's previous work in the same mode, *Barry Lyndon*, uncomfortable doubts intrude. Is Esmond's humility a form of inverted egoism? Is he perhaps guilty of covert spite and vengefulness? Just as Lyndon finally emerged as something more complex than the archetypal villain, so Esmond begins to seem less like the archetypal hero.

The third use of a dramatic persona is the most ingenious. Among the major novels, *Pendennis* is the only one that consistently maintains the objective, omniscient point of view. The early surroundings and career of this hero are so close to those of Thackeray himself that Arthur Pendennis can be assumed to possess many traits of the author, and yet he is convincingly developed as a distinct individual. When in two later novels, *The Newcomes* and *The Adventures of Philip*, Pendennis figures both as narrator and as an active participant in the events, he provides a peculiar illusion of authenticity. Since we are already acquainted with his own life story and have learned to like and respect him—all the more because we are aware of his peccadilloes and weaknesses—we accept him as a reliable reporter. Besides, since he knows the protagonists so intimately and has witnessed some of the scenes, we have no reason to doubt his credibility. Yet here again the possibility of ironic distortion is not absent, and the reader will do well to bear in mind the narrator's involvement. Indeed, in a remarkable passage in *Philip*, Pendennis himself warns us to beware:

> People there are in our history who do not seem to me to have kindly hearts at all; and yet perhaps, if a biography could be

written from their point of view, some other novelist might show how Philip and *his* biographer were a pair of selfish worldlings unworthy of credit: how uncle and aunt Twysden were most exemplary people, and so forth. . . . I protest as I look back on the past portions of this history, I begin to have qualms, and ask myself whether the folks of whom we have been prattling have had justice done to them; whether Agnes Twysden is not a suffering martyr justly offended by Philip's turbulent behavior, and whether Philip deserves any particular attention or kindness at all. . . . Perhaps I do not understand the other characters round about him so well, and have overlooked a number of their merits, and caricatured and exaggerated their little defects. (X, 367–68)

Perhaps nowhere else has a practicing author so clearly formulated the basic principle of the technique that I have been denominating "the dramatic monologue." With due allowance for the difference between the condensation of poetry and the expansiveness of the novel, it can be claimed that Browning and Thackeray introduced a new method that rendered their two media responsive to the subtleties and ironies of experience, to the complexities of individual psychology, and to the recognition of the relativity of truth that were coming to dominate the modern mind.

6 | SPECIAL CORRESPONDENT TO POSTERITY / How Dickens's Contemporaries Saw His Fictional World

Philip Collins

"Mr. Dickens," wrote the *Daily News* leader on his death, "... was emphatically the novelist of the age. In his pictures of contemporary life posterity will read, more clearly than in any contemporary records, the character of our nineteenth-century life. They will see us as we are, in our strength and our weakness, with all our social sores, and all the healing influences exerted to cure them. But Mr. Dickens has not merely shown us to posterity, he has shown us to ourselves."[1] This was not merely the pious tribute of that newspaper to its illustrious founder-editor. Many obituary assessments took the occasion to reflect upon his importance, for his contemporaries and for later readers, as

[1] 10 June 1870, p. 5, reprinted in my *Dickens: the Critical Heritage* (London: Routledge and Kegan Paul, 1971), p. 504. Many of the quotations for this paper also appear in that source; for such quotations, references will be given in the text, with the title abbreviated *DCH*. The paper is based on a lecture given in a series, "Dickens in His Times," at the Victorian Studies Centre, University of Leicester.

a depicter of the age as well as its great entertainer, a voice of its conscience, and its leading man of letters over so long a period as a third of a century. Such assertions had indeed been made about him throughout his career. A conspicuous literary figure with his first novel, and one whose fictions so evidently purported "to show the very age and body of the time his form and pressure" (or, as he himself put it in *Bleak House,* "to receive the impress of the moving age"), he was reckoned by readers of even his earliest fiction as likely to prove—in Walter Bagehot's happy phrase, which provides my title—"a special correspondent for posterity." Thackeray's prognostication, back in 1840, is well-known: "I am sure that a man who, a hundred years hence, should sit down to write the history of our time, would do wrong to put that great contemporary history of *Pickwick* aside as a frivolous work. It contains true character under false names; and . . . gives us a better idea of the state and ways of the people than one could gather from any more pompous or authentic histories" (*DCH,* 38). Such views were not unchallenged: various critics maintained that this or that part of *Pickwick* derived, not from the state and ways of the people, but from literary stock, or the theater, or the exigencies of being frivolous. But at least it seemed likely that this young author would be read by future generations unless, as some thought, he was too much the reporter, too localized in time and place, to survive. His popularity, reported the *Spectator* in 1838, though "one of the literary wonders of the day," was adventitious and precarious. His topicalities resembled "the passing hits of a pantomime—side-splitting at first, decreasing in effect at each repetition, and vapid or unintelligible by the end of the season": and his characters, too, belonged so much to "a fortuitous and temporary species, the product of a peculiar and local state of society congregated in large towns," that the *Spectator* doubted whether, even now, his novels were "greatly relished or read" in districts "removed beyond town impulses" (*DCH,* 69–70). "Class characteristics and local peculiarities are of a very transient nature," pronounced the *Saturday Review* twenty years later. "Fifty years hence, most of his wit will be harder to understand than the allusions in the *Dunciad;* and our grandchildren will wonder what their ancestors could have meant by putting Mr. Dickens at the head of the novelists of his day"(*DCH*, 384–85). To quote just one other prophecy—and there were many—that Dickens's contemporaneity would tell against him and would eventually prove fatal, here is Justin McCarthy, writing in the *Westminster* in 1864: "We cannot think that he will live as an English classic. He deals too much in accidental manifestations and too little in universal principles. Before long his language will have passed away, and the manners he depicts will only be found in a Dictionary of Antiquities. And we do not at all anticipate that he will be rescued from oblivion either by his artistic powers or by his political sagacity" (*DCH*, 452). These final phrases are to be understood ironically, of course, as McCarthy's previous argument has made clear.

One other contemporary prophecy about posterity's reactions: Mowbray Morris, in an interesting retrospective assessment in 1882, tried to surmise which parts of Dickens would survive and to adumbrate an historical approach at a level beyond simply consulting a dictionary of antiquities. "It seems impossible to imagine a day when the world will refuse to laugh with Dickens," wrote Morris, but it would, he guessed, be only "the careless glance of curiosity, or the student's all-ranging eye," that would "turn a century hence upon the Little Nells and Pauls, the Joes and the Trotty Vecks," and other such exemplars of his pathos (*DCH*, 611). Certainly, he argued, that all-ranging student would need to see Dickens *in* his times, as a way to understanding why he had invested so much effort in this pathos, and why it had seemed so effective. Indeed, in a larger way, Morris commended to posterity an historical approach to Dickens. For readers in a different world, without the great magician alive in front of them,

> ... a clear knowledge of Dickens's life and character, of his age and his position with regard to his age, ... will go far to explain and to account for many things in his writings which may puzzle

posterity. . . . It will go far, for instance, to account for the extraordinary one-sidedness and the consequent ineffectiveness of so much of his satire, and especially of his satire on the governing classes and the upper classes of society generally. . . . "I believe," he said . . . , "that virtue dwells rather oftener in alleys and byways than she does in courts and palaces." A judicious use of the historical method will no doubt help to explain the grounds for this belief. (*DCH*, 601–2)

And so on. This is rather like eighteenth-century Shakespeare criticism: some knowledge of Shakespeare's age and audience was useful to explain his faults and lapses. Some other Victorians, however, tried to show also how Dickens's central characteristics, including his strengths, were related to certain qualities of his age.

A variant on these speculations about how and what posterity would learn from Dickens was to posit instead an innocent foreigner reading him. An international darling within a few years, Dickens obviously was one of the means whereby overseas readers formed their notions of England—as, indeed, being one of the very few truly popular classics in the century since his death, he has inevitably given all of us, whether or not we are all-ranging students, some of our sense of the middle third of the nineteenth century, so that *Dickensian* remains, available as few literary terms are, for universally recognizable reference ("CITY TYPISTS WORK IN DICKENSIAN CONDITIONS," to quote one recent headline), and it makes sense to talk of "the Age of Dickens." Victorian reviewers' reference to foreigners had, however, the advantage for us that Dickens's overseas readers (unlike his then-unborn ones) could, and sometimes did, visit the milieux he had described. Before *Pickwick* was published, *Sketches by Boz* had been commended in these terms in the *Metropolitan Magazine* (March 1836):

We strongly recommend this facetious work to the Americans. It will save them the trouble of reading some hundred dull-written tomes on England, as it is a perfect picture of the morals, manners, habits of a great portion of English society. It is hardly possible to conceive a more pleasantly reading book; delightful from the abundance of its sly humour, and instructive in every chapter. The succession of portraits does not reach higher than of the best of the middle classes, but descends with a startling fidelity to the lowest of the low. . . . Taken altogether, we have rarely met with a work that has pleased us more, and we know that our taste is always that of the public. (*DCH*, 30)

In that last sentence, the reviewer spoke truly indeed; to his earlier point, about *Sketches by Boz* as a guidebook for Americans, it might reasonably be objected that akin though it is to Dickens's fictional art, this collection is a special case—more avowedly reportage, less affected by the imaginative and suasory purposes of the novels proper. Certainly part of his appeal for American readers then was, as Forster remarked, that his critical presentation of English society—assumed to be just and accurate—happily confirmed American suspicions about the wicked old country: he "was almost universally regarded by them as a kind of embodied protest against what was believed to be worst in the institutions of England, depressing and overshadowing in a social sense, and adverse to purely intellectual influences."[2]

To return to what reviewers thought overseas readers would get from Dickens: many of them thought that—in Tony Weller's phrase about bachelors' views on marriage—they would "think in their innocence it was all wery capital." Harriet Martineau, for instance, in 1855: "It is a curious speculation what effect his universally read works will have on the foreign conception of English character. Washington Irving came here expecting to find the English life of Queen Anne's days, as his *Sketchbook* shows; and very unlike his preconception was the England he found. And thus it must be with Germans, Americans, and French who take Mr. Dickens's books to be pictures of our real life" (*DCH*, 236). Or take this, from Professor William Edmondstoune Aytoun's sarcastic "Advice to an Intending Serialist" in *Blackwood's Magazine*, 1846. (Dickens is not named, but is understood when Aytoun addresses the ignorant and pre-

---

[2] John Forster, *Life of Charles Dickens*, ed. J. W. T. Ley (London: Cecil Palmer, 1928), p. 209.

sumptuous "Mr. Smith" he is ironically cheering on.) The intelligent foreigner, reading his works in translation, will be shaken out of his mistaken notions about British society and the national character:

> Above all, he will learn from you the true tone which pervades society, and the altered style of conversation and morals which is universally current among us. In minor things, he will discover, what few authors have taken pains to show, the excessive fondness of our nation for a pure Saxon nomenclature. He will learn that such names as Seymour, and Howard, and Percy—nay, even our old familiars, Jones and Robinson—are altogether prescribed among us, and that a new race has sprung up in their stead, rejoicing in the euphonious appellations of Tox and Wox, Whibble, Toozle, Whopper, Sniggleshaw, Guzzlerit, Gingerthorpe, Mugswitch, Smungle, Yelkins, Fizgig, Parksnap, Grubsby, Shoutower, Hogswash and Quiltirogus. He will also learn that our magistrates, unlike the starched official dignitaries of France, are not ashamed to partake, in the public streets, of tripe with a common workman—and a hundred other little particulars, which throw a vast light into the chinks and crevices of our social system. (*DCH*, 210–11)

If one turns from these predictions and warnings to what foreigners actually thought about Dickens's reliability when they came and saw his England, one finds his reports more positively regarded. Without being so literal-minded as to expect the streets to be crowded with tripe-eating magistrates, or everyone to be named Toozle or Sniggleshaw or Mugswitch, they found England (or rather, London) very redolent of Dickens—found his novels very suggestive of the state of the nation. Doubtless they looked for, saw, and attended to what he had long made them familiar with: or perhaps, as G. H. Lewes argued in a passage I shall quote later, they were "conned" into mistaking the world around them for the vividly but madly imaginative (and imaginary) world of Dickens's novels. As one English country cousin put it, "I saw wealth, and beauty, and power, so closely connected with crime, suffering, and poverty, that I thought the enjoyment of the former must be marred by the presence of the latter. Perhaps I looked on everything with an intensity which might be attributed to my having seen it all in fancy's glass, by the aid of that masterly delineator, Charles Dickens." To cite some American visitors: "When I got to London," wrote Francis Parkman in 1843, "I thought I had been there before. There, in flesh and blood, was the whole host of characters that figure in *Pickwick*.... The hackney coachman and cabman, ... the walking advertisements ... and a hundred others seemed so many incarnations of Dickens's characters." In 1856, Nathaniel Hawthorne was walking in Upper Thames Street and recalling that the Clennams' house in *Little Dorritt* (then being serialized) stood thereabouts—"But many of Dickens's books have the odor and flavor of courts and localities that I stumble upon, about London." About this time, Henry Adams arrived in London for the first time. Aristocracy, he found, was *real* here: "So was the England of Dickens. Oliver Twist and Little Nell lurked in every churchyard shadow, not as shadow but alive." For Moncure Conway, visiting England in the 1860s, Dickens was "the chief marvel of his time.... The more I saw of London the more I loved and honoured the London Dante who had invested it with romance, and peopled its streets and alleys with spirits, so that the huge city could never more be seen without his types and shadows"—a tribute which, however inexactly, recognized better than the others quoted that Dickens offers an imaginative rendering of London rather than a guidebook account of it. A decade later, Henry James, lodging in Craven Street (which runs from the Strand down to the river—authentic Dickens country, indeed), felt that "the whole Dickens procession marched up and down, the whole Dickens world looked out of its queer, quite sinister windows—for it was the socially sinister Dickens ... who still at that moment was most apt to meet me with his reasons."[3]

[3] Joshua Priestley, ed., *True Womanhood: Eliza Hessel* (Leeds: privately printed, 1859), p. 32; Mason Wade, ed., *The Journals of Francis Parkman* (New York: Harper, 1947), I, 221; Randall Stewart, ed., *The English Notebooks of Nathaniel Hawthorne* (New York: Modern Language Association of America, 1941), p. 283; *The Education of Henry Adams: An*

Earlier in his autobiography, James had spoken for his age—and for America too, where he had spent the years he was there describing—in his testimony to Dickens's enormous popularity and imaginative potency:

> How tremendously it had been laid upon young persons of our generation to feel Dickens, down to the soles of our shoes, no more modern instance that I might try to muster would give, I think, the least measure of . . . There has been since his extinction no corresponding case—as to the relation between benefactor and beneficiary, or debtor and creditor; no other debt in our time has been piled so high, for those carrying it, as the long, the purely "Victorian" pressure of that obligation. (*DCH,* 615)

One recalls, however, Henry James's earlier animadversions on Dickens as "the greatest of *superficial* novelists." This occurs in his review of *Our Mutual Friend* (*Nation,* 21 December 1865), in which he exclaimed: "What a world were this world if the world of *Our Mutual Friend* were an honest reflection of it! But a community of eccentrics is impossible. . . . Accepting half of Mr. Dickens's persons as intentionally grotesque, where are those exemplars of sound humanity who should afford us the proper measure of their companions' variations?"—a reminder, this, that the question of Dickens's accuracy as a social reporter, or special correspondent to posterity, was critically related to larger questions about the nature of his art. Thus, to use the simple terms favored by his reviewers: Were his figures characters or caricatures? And was his selection from human experience drastically biased in favor of the odd, eccentric, and therefore unrepresentative? As a reviewer in 1866 put it, "His characters, in fact, are a bundle of deformities. And he appears, too, to value them because they are deformed, as some minds value a crooked sixpence more than a sound coin. . . . Everything with him is not

---

Autobiography (Boston: Houghton Mifflin, 1918), p. 72; *The Autobiography of Moncure D. Conway* (London: Cassell, 1904), II, 6–7; Frederick W. Dupee, ed., *Henry James: Autobiography* (London: W. H. Allen, 1956), p. 572. I have used some of the materials cited in this note in my essay "Dickens and London," in *The Victorian Age,* ed. H. J. Dyos and Michael Wolff (London: Routledge and Kegan Paul, 1973), II, 537–57.

supra naturam, but *extra naturam.* His whole art . . . is founded upon false principles" (*Westminster Review; DCH,* 474).

Many of these questions had arisen early in his career, though his later work made critics more aware of, and more liable to discuss, the imaginative or fantastic or stagey or irresponsibly untrue elements in his fiction (it was called all these things, and I shall not at this stage question such statements). Back in the 1830s, *Sketches* and *Pickwick* and *Oliver Twist* and *Nickleby* gave critics ample occasion for defining the range (social and geographical) of his observation, for discussing his accuracy and for seeing him as, in sundry ways, an emanation of the age. He was, wrote T. H. Lister in the *Edinburgh Review* (1838), "the truest and most spirited delineator of English life, amongst the middle and lower classes, since the days of Smollett and Fielding" (*DCH,* 72). *Sketches by Boz,* said the *Sun* newspaper, "evince great powers of observation, and fidelity, combined with a humour which, though pushed occasionally to the verge of caricature, is, on the whole, full of promise. But their principal merit is their matter-of-factness, and the strict, literal way in which they adhere to nature" (*DCH,* 28). Perhaps it was all rather superficial? A favorite analogy for critics was the view from a cab: "Reading Boz's Sketches [said the *Spectator*] is like rattling through the streets of London in a cab: the prominent features of the town strike upon the eye in rapid succession, new objects perpetually effacing the impression of the last; all is bustle and movement, till the jerk of the stoppage announces that the "fare" or the "sketch" is ended. . . . This is just as much as the readers for mere pastime and present excitement require."[4] The cab analogy was used, in another early review, to draw attention to one of Dickens's mannerisms, particularly conspicuous in his earlier stories—the high degree of specificality about metropolitan localities. Here it is put

---

[4] *Spectator,* 26 December 1836, p. 1234. Raymond Williams has recently argued that Dickens has "a way of seeing men and women that belongs to the street" (*The English Novel from Dickens to Lawrence* [London: Chatto and Windus, 1970], p. 32).

unfavorably, and with a reference too (as in Bagehot's phrase) to the journalistic affiliation of Dickens's art: "The very spirit of a penny-a-liner" committed to "filling a certain quantity of pages per month" breaks out in "the prolix descriptions of the various walks through the streets of London, every turn in which is enumerated with the accuracy of a cabman" (*Fraser's*, April 1840; *DCH*, 90).

Inevitably, reviewers of the early fiction recognized London as Dickens's special (maybe his only effective) scene. Indeed, to give the whole of Bagehot's phrase: "He describes London like a special correspondent for posterity" (*DCH*, 394). As Forster remarked in the *Life* (p. 123), "There seemed to be not much to add to our knowledge of London until his books came upon us, but each in this respect outstripped the others in its marvels. In *Nickleby* the old city reappears under every aspect." And this is how Forster had reviewed *Nickleby* in 1839:

> Whatever Mr. Dickens knows or feels . . . is always at his fingers' ends. There is no beating about the bush for it. It is not carefully deposited, ticketed, labelled, elaborately set apart, to be drawn forth only as formal necessity may suggest, from the various cells of his brain. It is present with him through every passage of his book. It animates old facts with a new life, it breathes into old thoughts a new emotion. Who that has read his description of the various localities of London, as set down in this story of *Nicholas Nickleby*, can ever expect to forget them more? A fresh glow of warmth and light plays over the cheerful and familiar places, a deeper mist of misery and blackness settles on the darker scenes. . . . At all times, and under every aspect, he gives us to feel and see the great city as it absolutely is. Its interior life is made as familiar to us as its exterior form. We come to know better the very places we have known best. (*DCH*, 49)

This introduces two points much discussed by Dickens's reviewers: Dickens the explorer, and Dickens vivifying the known and familiar. One of his peculiar merits, wrote G. H. Lewes in 1837 (he later took a different view), was his "bringing before us things which we have all noticed hundreds of times, yet which we never thought of committing to paper" (*DCH*, 67). Or, as the obituarist in *Fraser's* put it, here was

... a series of books readable beyond rivalry, describing his own time to itself in a new and striking style; heightening the familiar so as to give it an artistic impressiveness, enriching it with humour, softening it with sympathies, mingling shrewd sense with a fanciful picturesqueness so as to produce the most unexpected effects out of commonplace materials, and discovering many quaint and strange things lurking in the midst of everyday life. (*DCH*, 526)

"Heightening the familiar": this is akin to Wordsworth's aims in the *Lyrical Ballads,* as described by Coleridge ("to give a charm of novelty to things of every day"), and Wordsworth was one of the few poets with whom Dickens was compared; Crabbe, suitably, was another, and in fact he owed something indeed to both, besides being analogous to them in several aspects of their art. As for discovering the quaint and strange: what had been particularly impressive, especially in *Oliver Twist* among the early books, was Dickens's social exploration of areas little known to genteel readers—an exploration directed, however, less by picturesque curiosity or a relish for the quaint than by compassion and political indignation. Richard Ford's remark, in the *Quarterly* for June 1839, is often quoted and was typical: "Life in London, as revealed in the pages of Boz, opens a new world to thousands bred and born in the same city, whose palaces overshadow their cellars—for the one half of mankind lives without knowing how the other half dies: in fact, the regions about Saffron Hill are less known to our great world than the Oxford Tracts, the inhabitants are still less."[5] There were, of course, genteel readers, such

---

[5] *DCH*, 81. In *Oliver Twist*, Dickens was particularly explicit about being the novelist-as-explorer. Thus, the Jacob's Island episode (Ch. 50) is introduced by a lengthy description, which begins with a reminder that this is not a fictional locale but an actual place ("the filthiest, the strangest, the most extraordinary of the many localities that are hidden in London, wholly unknown, even by name, to the great mass of its inhabitants"). He continues: "To reach this place, the visitor has to"—and there follows one of his cabman's-accuracy itineraries, ending with "the stranger" confronted with Folly Ditch, where "his utmost astonishment will be excited by the scene before him." Transparently, the imagined visitor or stranger is the reader, with the novelist as his guide-commentator.

as Lady Carlisle, who already knew that "there are such unfortunate beings as pickpockets and streetwalkers. I am very sorry for it and very much shocked at their mode of life, but I own that I do not much wish to hear what they say to one another" (*DCH*, 29). Or Lord Melbourne, having a literary chat with his young monarch: she "defended *Oliver Twist* very much," having found it "excessively interesting" partly because of its description of "squalid vice"— but, as she confessed, in vain, for Melbourne insisted, Podsnap-like, "I don't *like* those things; I wish to avoid them; I don't like them in *reality*, and therefore I don't wish them represented" (*DCH*, 44). But most readers went the way of their queen: all the more because Boz had the happy knack of alluding to pitch without defiling their minds. Throughout his career reviewers were almost unanimous on the purity of his writings, on the judiciousness of his selection from whatever sordid realities he depicted. The *Court Magazine*, for instance, in the year of Victoria's accession:

> The *vraisemblable* is not "Boz's" line of art; the *vrai* is with him all in all. What he gives you is literally true, but like a consummate artist, he does not give it to you literally. . . . [And] he never descends into vulgarity. The ordinary conversations of the loose and ribald multitude are faithfully reported, but by an adroit process of moral alchemy, all their offensive coarseness is imperceptibly extracted. . . . This is a peculiarity in the writings of "Boz," that reflects unbounded credit upon his taste. The subjects are passed through the alembic of his mind, and come, if we may say so, purified before the public.[6]

[6] *DCH*, 34–35. The description of Jacob's Island (*Oliver Twist*, Ch. 50) again provides an excellent example of this verbal and notional alembic. The "offensive," "repulsive," "loathsome" (etc.) sights are decently unspecified; readers who knew, or could guess, the enormities could mentally supply them, while readers like young Queen Victoria could register some sense of social shock (as well as literary *frisson*), but without being repelled by an explicitness they could not stomach. Contrast Henry Mayhew's brilliant but terrible description of Jacob's Island in *Meliora; or Better Times to Come*, ed. Viscount Ingestre, 2d ed., rev. (London: John W. Parker, 1852), pp. 276–80.

Some other recurrent and related questions emerged in these early reviews: the justice of Dickens's presentation of contemporary institutions and of controversial issues (his strictures on the New Poor Law in *Oliver Twist* being an obvious example here), the justice too of his portraits (or caricatures) of recognizable living individuals. How close, for instance, were Serjeant Buzfuz and Mr. Justice Stareleigh to the legal gentlemen whose names they echoed and whose natures they purported to represent? This debate continued, so far as the law of libel permitted, in many discussions (published or otherwise) of Fang, Squeers, Pecksniff, Skimpole, Boythorn, and other characters who clearly bore some relationship to identifiable and generally well-known public figures. The personal biases and convictions of the commentators colored these remarks, of course, and this, inevitably, was always the case with Dickens's presentation of controversial issues or of particular sections of society. Predictably, feminists such as J. S. Mill and enthusiasts for African missions such as Lord Denman, did not regard Mrs. Jellyby as a lifelike, or a representative, figure (*DCH*, 272, 297–98). Similarly, Mr. Chadband not only gave much offense to the godly (though, as Dickens-recitalists' programs show, he was much relished by popular audiences), but he also struck reviewers in the religious press, or those of religious disposition, as calumnious and wholly unreal: "Let any man search the dismal outskirts of Christianity for the foundation of this personage, and where will he find it?"[7] Few reviewers paused to enquire what kind of mimetic verisimilitude was appropriate in a novel which, while proclaiming the literary virtue of "receiving the impress of the moving age," contained characters with such names as Dedlock, Flite, Smallweed, and Krook, and explicitly (if vaguely) announced its imagina-

---

[7] *DCH,* 558; cf. pp. 12, 272, 297, 333–34, 462, 557, 592. For a modern discussion of what actualities lie behind Chadband, see Humphry House, *The Dickens World* (London: Oxford University Press, 1941), pp. 113–18.

tive approach ("I have purposely dwelt upon the romantic side of familiar things").

To return to the earlier reviews, for a point that was much discussed then and later: how up-to-date was Dickens? The *Quarterly* reviewer in 1837 maintained that Buzfuz's style of oratory had been "finally quizzed out of fashion by Lord Brougham many years ago," and that not only was Tony Weller cribbed from Washington Irving but also "the old race of coachmen were going out when Mr. Washington Irving first visited England, and were altogether gone before Mr. Dickens's time. The modern race are more addicted to tea than beer; the cumbrous many-caped great-coat is rapidly giving way to the Mackintosh" (*DCH*, 59–61). Other reviewers raised similar questions—many of which have been investigated by later scholars—about his drawing on literary models, or popular stereotypes, rather than on contemporary fact. *Pickwick* may furnish one more example, to introduce a point which only later reviewers could make: assuming that *Pickwick* did (in Thackeray's words) convey a tolerably accurate "idea of the state and ways of the people," how well could after-comers guess what the beauty had been? As an obituarist remarked:

> apart from its humour, *Pickwick* must be to the young an almost antiquarian book, containing descriptions of bygone manners and customs, of which they have no personal knowledge. Young people know nothing about the Fleet Prison; they never saw —except in Mexico or Australia—a genuine stage coachman; they do not associate a commercial traveller with a gig, but rather regard him as a gentleman who passes his days and nights in railway trains. . . . But to us oldsters *Pickwick,* quite independent of its fun, recalls the England and the London of our youth, and thus conjures up a host of delightful recollections. As for Mr. Weller the elder, I have sat by his side many a time a-top of the old Rocket or Regulator coach bound for Portsmouth. . . . All that jolly, old-fashioned, simple sort of life, described in the pages of *Pickwick* has gone by for ever. (*DCH*, 41)

And so on. Possibly this remark indicates one of the reasons for the view (which appears in many obituaries) that *Pick-*

wick was Dickens's masterpiece: such articles were written more often by middle-aged journalists than by youngsters, and *Pickwick* was valued not only for its intrinsic qualities but also nostalgically, as a reminder of the time when his obituarists were young.

Another greybeard comment, made much later, is useful in suggesting that people in the mid-nineteenth century were indeed more Dickensian than their descendants. George R. Sims, recalling the London of his youth (around 1860), wrote:

> The mid-Victorian days were the days of types. There was strongly-marked character in the various sorts and conditions of men and a sharper distinction between the classes and the masses in the matter of dress and demeanour. The early and the mid-Victorian days inspired the pen of Dickens and the pencil of Cruikshank. The author and the artist described and drew their characters from the life around them. The young men of to-day are apt to look upon the Dickens and Cruikshank types as burlesque and extravagant caricatures, but they were faithful pictures of the men and women to be met with in the everyday London life which has lost shape and form in the melting-pot of modernity. With the disappearance of the old types, our manners and customs, our ways of life, and our popular literature have undergone a marked and startling change.[8]

This paper began with a quotation from the *Daily News*: "Mr. Dickens . . . was emphatically the novelist of the age," meaning by this not only *the* novelist par excellence—(as the *Daily News* went on to say, "People who never read any other novels, read Mr. Dickens's" [*DCH*, 504])—but also the novelist who most fully depicted the age. But just what was "the Age of Dickens"? England changed enormously, of course, during his writing career, and Dickens—relatively wide-ranging and prolific though he was—wrote from a particular point of view and specialized in certain areas of the country and of society. To many contemporaries, certainly, he seemed as central and representative, besides being as conspicuous, as any author well could be.

---

[8] George R. Sims, *Glances Back* (London: Jarrolds, 1917), pp. 250–51.

The *People's Journal,* introducing a series, "The People's Portrait Gallery," in 1846, predictably made Dickens its first item, as "the unquestionably most popular man of his day" (*DCH*, 205). Two years earlier, R. H. Horne, trying to emulate William Hazlitt, had produced his book *New Spirit of the Age,* an attempt to suggest, through a series of essays on notable contemporaries, the nature of the zeitgeist: and again Dickens occupied the first, and much the longest, chapter: "Mr. Dickens is manifestly the product of his age. He is a genuine emanation from its aggregate and entire spirit." And, Horne continued, Dickens's involvement and centrality were evident, not only in his writings but also in his public activities and presence (*DCH*, 201). Certainly from overseas, and particularly from France with its very different literary tradition, Dickens looked very central, very much—perhaps to a damaging degree—the voice of what Ibsen was later to call "the compact Liberal majority," Dickens being in this respect an eminent example of what distinguished most Victorian English literature from French literature at that time. Hippolyte Taine, for instance, wrote in 1856:

Plant this talent [Dickens's] on English soil; the literary opinion of the country will direct its growth and explain its fruits. For this public opinion is its private opinion; it does not submit to it as to an external constraint, but feels it inwardly as an inner persuasion; it does not hinder, but develops it, and only repeats aloud what it said to itself in a whisper.

The counsels of this public taste are somewhat like this—

and Taine itemizes the conventional notions about love, and so on, and argues that Dickens accepts or is directed by them (*DCH*, 340–41).

As Mrs. Oliphant had said in *Blackwood's,* the year before Taine's essays, Dickens was distinctly "a *class* writer, the historian and representative of one circle in the many ranks of our social scale," and she defined this class, despite his occasional excursions outside it: "it is the air and breath of middle-class respectability which fills the books of Mr. Dickens" (*DCH*, 327). Another shot at this question, about this time, appeared in the *Rambler* (1854), and this takes us closer to defining the Dickens generation as well as the Dickens class (at least in the judgment of his contemporaries):"Charles Dickens is, in fact, pre-eminently a man of the middle of the nineteenth century. He is at once the creation and the prophet of an age which loves benevolence without religion, the domestic virtues more than the heroic, the farcical more than the comic, and the extravagant more than the tragic. [He is the] product of a restlessly observant but shallow era" (*DCH*, 294). Well, it is of course difficult to think of an age that was *not* shallow, in the opinion of its more articulate observers: but Dickens's "shallow" age can be defined more narrowly and significantly, as (for instance) was done by one of his severest critics—James Fitzjames Stephen, in his famous onslaught, "Mr. Dickens as a Politician" (*Saturday Review*, 1857):

> As every system is said to culminate, and every idea to be embodied it might have been expected *a priori* that an era of reform would find, sooner or later, its representative man. We do not know whether the restless, discontented, self-sufficient spirit which characterises so large a portion of modern speculation—especially on political and social subjects—could have had a more characteristic Avatar than it has found in Mr. Dickens. (*DCH*, 344–45)

This point was repeated by many contemporaries, with varying degrees of approval of this "era of reform" and thus of its literary embodiment. To quote just one more, Alfred Austin argued in an obituary essay that Dickens had been, in important respects, the *happy* author—happy in the sense of finding just the circumstances to nurture his genius.

> And still more happy was the genius of Dickens, being such as it was, in that he reached his majority at the precise time he did. The hour and the man arrived together. A change had come over the national dream. The world had pledged itself to a new gospel. . . . [A] host of freshly-enfranchised electors were to give us a new Parliament. . . . These, however, were but the political phenomena of a revolution which had deeper roots and more

solid aims. When the world began thus practically to assert in its rough-and-ready way that every man ought to have a chance, there naturally were not wanting advocates to plead that many men ought to have more chances than one. . . . Charles Dickens . . . was all for giving the worst men a chance, and giving it them many times over. . . . In that, he was the man of his epoch, and had the spirit-time throbbing within him. Here again was his good fortune; here again do we have him as the Happy Author—always and for ever in harmony with his conditions. Let no one underrate this circumstance. (*DCH*, 534–35)

"Happy . . . in that he reached his majority at the precise time he did": I recall G. M. Young's useful tip that, to understand a man's intellectual and ideological makeup, one should start by asking what was happening when he was twenty. This works with almost suspicious neatness for Dickens: he was twenty in the year of the first Reform Act. His contemporaries were surely right to see him as very much a voice of the hopes and disappointments of the reformist 1830s. Those later commentators who, seeking to define the Dickens period in terms of political and social history, have seen him in relation to Owenism or Marxism or the rise of the Social Democratic Federation or the trades union movement, strike me as creating irrelevancies, pursuing their own preoccupations rather than penetrating to the heart of Charles Dickens. As often, I find Humphry House closer to the truth (and to how Dickens's contemporaries saw this aspect of him), in, for instance, his remark that Dickens's literary career coincides almost exactly with the rule of the Ten-pound Householders (1832–67).[9] Manifestly Dickens cannot be summed up as a representative Ten-pound Householder: but this reference provides a better starting-point than Owen or Marx—or Blake—given that any of these references is at best but a starting-point.

Moreover, it is easier to understand the huge popularity of a novelist whose outlook was, in some essentials at least, not too far distant from the Ten-pound Householder's,

---

[9] House, p. 133.

than to explain how a more alienated or subversive novelist could appeal so widely (and no one seeing Dickens in these latter terms has made a serious attempt to offer any such explanation). Nor of course was it solely a populist appeal; as I have suggested elsewhere (*DCH*, 15), the list of eminent guests and supporters at the farewell banquet given to him in 1867, before he sailed to America, is an extraordinary demonstration, to which surely no parallel can be found in the annals of English literature, of the esteem in which he was held by the leaders of public, official, literary, and artistic life. Just before Dickens's death, George Stott in the *Contemporary Review* reverted to this perennial matter of his unchallenged popularity (it had of course been much discussed in reviews in the late 1830s, and intermittently thereafter, and especially in 1870).[10] Stott wrote:

> . . . whether our great-grandchildren do or do not read Mr. Dickens, they will all the same have to recognise that their great-grandfathers certainly did. Let them form what judgment they please on the fact, there it will be, distinct and undeniable. . . . One who had never opened a book of Mr. Dickens's would still, if he kept *au courant* with what was going on around, have to recognise him as one of the great literary facts of the age. As such he is worthy of careful investigation. To have laid hold of the mind of his time as he has done is, limit it and qualify it as we may, no slight achievement. (*DCH*, 492)

Worthy of careful investigation indeed! This is far from being the only reason for being interested in Dickens, but even if the world of his novels were a complete cloud-cuckoo-land, investigation of it would still be very rewarding from an historical point of view, for the reasons which Stott indicates: what sort of clouds and cuckoos so entranced the mid-nineteenth-century mind, and why? But obviously, "limit and qualify it as we may," his fictional world has a great deal to do, simply and directly, with the objective world of his day. Critics who lived with him in

---

[10] For some further references, see *DCH*, 634 (Index, under "popularity"), which cites nearly seventy: also my essay "The Popularity of Dickens" (in his own times), in the *Dickensian* 70 (1974), 5–20.

that world were puzzled (as commentators since have been) to devise some adequate description of his art which would do justice both to the documentary and journalistic and to the imaginative, fantastic, fairytale, and mythopoeic elements in his work—to the elements which allied him to Defoe and those which (at their highest) more resembled Shakespearean poetic drama—to this "singular union of close observation and rich fancy," as one reviewer put it (*DCH,* 364), or as G. H. Lewes more severely described it, "a mingled verisimilitude and falsity altogether unexampled" (*DCH,* 573). Many of the more humdrum reviewers, inevitably, worked on the unargued assumption that novels ought to be "like life," and praised Dickens when they found him perceptive, accurate, and wide-ranging, or criticized him when he was palpably not offering a mirror image of humanity in general or contemporary behavior in particular. And more sophisticated commentators often too easily assumed that fiction which departed from verisimilitude was (unless it could be confidently assigned to a special subgroup, such as romance) therefore the poorer—was, indeed, relegating itself to an inferior class. Walter Bagehot is an interesting instance of a critic lost between admiration and disapproval. Discussing Dickens's *"vivification* of character, or rather of characteristics," Bagehot pours out superlatives ("his marvellous power of observation," his "store of human detail ... endless and enormous," and "endless fertility in laughter-causing detail") and offers a useful description of his treatment of one important range of characters: "The boots at the inn, the pickpockets in the street, the undertaker, the Mrs. Gamp, are all of them at his disposal; he knows each trait and incident, and he invests them with a kind of perfection in detail which in reality they do not possess." This working in "the ideal" (as David Masson called it, in a notable essay [*DCH,* 256]) struck Bagehot, however, as the mark of an essentially inferior art: "Accordingly, *of necessity,* such delineations become caricatures. We do not in general contrast them with reality. . . . They are utterly beyond the pale of ordinary social intercourse."[11]

Observation and fancy: verisimilitude and falsity:—the issue was of course discussed (as these terms suggest) both by critics who highly esteemed Dickens's art and purposes and by those who deplored much in that art and who thought his presentation and assessment of society mischievously erratic. Of the many critics who attempted to grapple with it—though few brought to the task much technical agility—I would draw particular attention to the American Edwin P. Whipple, whose Dickens criticism, over three decades, impresses me as consistently intelligent: and he kept reverting to this topic, and trying to refine his sense of it. In 1849 he remarked that Dickens's was a "novel of genuine practical life"—but he was "a prose poet" too; he simplified character, and was drawn to the grotesque, but "Such caricature as this is to character what epigram is to fact. . . . The mind of the reader unconsciously limits the extravagance into which Dickens sometimes runs, and, indeed, discerns the actual features and lineaments of the character shining the more clearly through it. Such extravagance is commonly a powerful stimulant to accurate perception. . . . It is . . . caricature based on the most piercing insight into actual life . . . " (*DCH*, 238–40). Reviewing *Great Expectations* in 1861, he refers to the then-obligatory comparison between Dickens and Thackeray (Masson, in his famous contrast between the "real" in Thackeray and the "ideal" in Dickens, had provided a notable lead here):

In *Great Expectations* there is shown a power of external observation finer and deeper even than Thackeray's; and yet owing to the presence of other qualities, the general impression is not one of objective reality. The author palpably uses his observa-

---

[11] *DCH*, 394; my italics. On the critical issues implicit here, and on how discussion of them developed during this period, see Richard Stang, *The Theory of the Novel in England, 1850–1870* (London: Routledge and Kegan Paul, 1959), especially Ch. 4, and Kenneth Graham, *English Criticism of the Novel, 1865–1900* (Oxford: Oxford University Press, 1965), especially Ch. 2.

tions as materials for his creative faculties to work upon; he does not record, but invents; and he produces something which is natural only under conditions prescribed by his own mind. He shapes, disposes, penetrates, colors, and contrives everything, and the whole action is a series of events which could have occurred only in his own brain, and which it is difficult to conceive of as actually "happening." And yet in none of his other works does he evince a shrewder insight into real life, and a clearer perception and knowledge of what is called "the world." (*DCH*, 429)

In an assessment of "The Genius of Dickens" (in the *Atlantic Monthly,* May 1867), Whipple returns to this interrelationship between the "special correspondent" and the "prose poet," the observer and the transformer:

... gifted though he be with wonderfully acute powers of external observation, ... no writer stamps the character of his genius on everything he writes more plainly than he.... His observing power, when extended beyond the range of his sympathies, becomes "objective," it is true, but ceases to be creative. In his genuine productions he not only embodies all that he knows, but communicates all that he is.... Observation affords him materials; but he always modifies these materials, and often works them up into the most fantastic shapes.... To read one of his romances is to see everything through the author's eyes.[12]

Arguably, indeed, Dickens influenced his age, not only by promoting an awareness of social conditions which could and should be improved but also (and more profoundly) by altering people's whole sense of the world around them, including their mode of visual interpretation. This was asserted strongly by J. C. Jeaffreson in 1858:

We cannot walk without his leading strings, or speak without using his texts, or look out upon the world save through his eyes.

---

[12] *DCH*, 478. Around this time the *Spectator,* moved by Dickens's reminiscences of his journalistic career in a speech for the Newspaper Press Fund, published an acute essay on "The Reporter in Mr. Dickens," assessing the degree to which "in some important intellectual ... respects, ... Mr. Dickens did not cease to be a reporter even after he became an author" (27 May 1865, pp. 575–76).

Indeed it is not our world, but his, that we gaze upon. . . . In short we have so adopted, or he has so embued us with, his views of the outer world, that in moments of self-introspection we are almost frightened lest we should have been too confiding and unquestioning followers. Such in its magnitude is his influence on each one of us, in regard to the external world he has surrounded us with. (*DCH*, 380–81)

G. H. Lewes—the last of Dickens's contemporaries whom I shall quote—was more than "almost frightened" (in Jeaffreson's words) that Dickens's world had displaced the actual outside world. In his notable essay in the *Fortnightly* (1872), there is a strong sense that Dickens was almost a nightmare from which—now that he was dead and gone—one could at last awake: or, to quote a Shakespearean allusion that Lewes might have used, "But being awake, I do despise my dream":

> . . . there is considerable light shed upon his works by the action of the imagination in hallucination. . . . What seems preposterous, impossible to us, seemed to him simple fact of observation. When he imagined a street, a house, a room, a figure, he saw it not in the vague schematic way of ordinary imagination, but in the sharp definition of actual perception, all the salient details obtruding themselves on his attention. He, seeing it thus vividly, made us also see it; and believing in its reality however fantastic, he communicated something of his belief to us. He presented it in such relief that we ceased to think of it as a picture. So definite and insistent was the image, that even while knowing it was false we could not help, for a moment, being affected, as it were, by his hallucination.
>
> This glorious energy of imagination is that which Dickens had in common with all great writers. It was this which made him a creator, and made his creations universally intelligible, no matter how fantastic and unreal. His types established themselves in the public mind like personal experiences. Their falsity was unnoticed in the blaze of their illumination. . . . Against such power criticism was almost idle. (*DCH*, 571–72)

This is part of Lewes's vigorous attack on Dickens's accuracy and artistic honesty, but obviously both the strength of the attack and the terms in which it is mounted are willy-nilly a splendid tribute to the overwhelming potency of his imagination.

In conclusion, it might be useful to refer briefly to Dickens's own sense of this matter. He was not much given to self-explanation on paper (even in private letters, let alone in published prefaces or manifestoes). As he remarked in the general preface to the Cheap Edition, "It is not for an author to describe his own books. If they cannot speak for themselves, he is likely to do little service by speaking for them." It is noticeable, however, that the most frequent theme of his prefaces is the assertion, pace his critics, that such and such a character or institution in the novels is fairly and accurately presented—that he was, in a straightforward way, a truth-teller. But more than that, of course: he was not so unaware of the nature of his art as to claim not only that it was based upon the truth but that it also and always contained the whole truth and nothing but the truth.[13] What he said of *Bleak House* ("I have purposely dwelt upon the romantic side of familiar things") might have been said of other novels too. He did not often use the term "romantic," nor did he use it very precisely. The term more likely to occur in such contexts is "fanciful," as in this letter:

It does not seem to me to be enough to say of any description that it is the exact truth. The exact truth must be there; but the merit or art in the narrator, is the manner of stating the truth. As to which thing in literature, it always seems to me that there is a world to be done. And in these times, when the tendency is to be frightfully literal and catalogue-like—to make the thing, in short, a sort of sum in reduction that any miserable creature can do in that way—I have an idea (really founded on the love of what I profess), that the very holding of popular literature

---

[13] I have attempted to discuss aspects of this topic in two essays, the earlier of them premature but containing some useful material: "Queen Mab's Chariot among the Steam-Engines: Dickens and Fancy," *English Studies* 42 (1961), 78–90, and "Dickens' Self-Estimate: Some New Evidence," in *Dickens the Craftsman*, ed. Robert B. Partlow (Carbondale, Ill.: Southern Illinois University Press, 1970).

through a kind of popular dark age, may depend on such fanciful treatment.[14]

Dickens never, I think, made a Coleridgean hierarchical distinction between Imagination and Fancy, but used the terms interchangeably. He used "fanciful" again in a letter which takes up a metaphor much used in Victorian novel-criticism, and which deserves fuller discussion than it has, I think, received—the analogy of the photograph (an updated variant, of course, upon the traditional "holding up the mirror to nature"). One day in 1858, he was walking through some country unfamiliar to him, a coal-mining area. Afterwards, he wrote to W. H. Wills, his colleague on *Household Words:*

I walked from Durham to Sunderland, and made a little fanciful photograph in my mind of Pit Country, which will come well into H.W. one day. I couldn't help looking upon my mind as I was doing it, as a sort of capitally prepared and highly sensitive plate. And I said, without the least conceit (as Watkins [the photographer] might have said of a plate of his) "it really is a pleasure to work with you, you receive the impression so nicely."[15]

I entitled this paper "Special Correspondent to Posterity," and the journalistic reference suggests one useful lead into this topic. But maybe I might better have suggested the combination of elements in Dickens's art by adapting a phrase from the letter just quoted and entitling this article "The Fanciful Photographer"—keeping this complicated topic open by adding a question mark. Or a phrase might have been adapted from Edgar Johnson, "The Realistic Fairy-Tale"—for, as Professor Johnson remarks, Dickens, so early as in his first novel, had devised "a new literary form, a kind of fairytale that is at once humorous, heroic and realistic." And in his concluding discussion of Dickens's art, Professor Johnson reverts to this topic: "Only on the surface does he have affinities with naturalism; deep below,

[14] Forster, pp. 727–28.
[15] *Letters,* ed. Walter Dexter (Bloomsbury: The Nonesuch Press, 1938), III, 58.

he is vibrant with poetic undertones, pregnant with the weighted symbols of allegory, dwelling often within the dark and mysterious region of myth."[16] This, however, uses a critical vocabulary and a way of regarding prose fiction which were unavailable to Dickens's contemporaries.

---

[16] *Charles Dickens: His Tragedy and Triumph* (London: Gollancz, 1953), pp. 173–74, 1139. I am happy, albeit in a footnote, to record my debt and gratitude to Professor Johnson, and to explain a too-cryptic remark I once made in a reminiscential essay: "I first became really interested in Dickens, in quite the 'wrong' way, through reading Edgar Johnson's biography in 1953." All I meant was that, at that benighted time, I had read hardly any of Dickens's novels (and had read those in the rather querulous standoffish way then fashionable), and that it was his biography that convinced me that Dickens was a wonderfully rich and exciting author and a fascinating man. I blame myself, deprecate my teachers (but that is thirty years back), abase myself before the *manes* of Dickens, and thank Professor Johnson for directing me—belatedly but with expectation of delight—toward his work.

7 | LIGHT IN DARKNESS / Gas, Oil, and Tallow in Dickens's *Bleak House*

George H. Ford

An important feature of Victorian literature is its emphasis on the role of space, especially interior space, the roomscapes that figure so prominently in novels, poems, and autobiographies of the age. What follows does not confront that vast topic head-on. It is restricted, instead, to one spatial component, that of lighting, and to one novel, Dickens's *Bleak House*. I hope, however, that the larger general issue may be sensed behind the microcosmic specifics. My starting point, submerged now under the smaller-scale items of lamps and candles, was a statement by the late Henri Talon: "Houses are natural metaphors for their inhabitants."[1] Life

---

[1] Henri Talon, "Dombey and Son," *Dickens Studies Annual*, 1 (1970), 149. Throughout the present essay, page references (in parentheses) are to the Norton Critical Edition of *Bleak House* (New York: W. W. Norton, 1977), edited by George Ford and Sylvère Monod. Among the 470 explanatory footnotes in our edition, there are a dozen which deal with lighting, and some of these notes include information derived from the same authorities used in the present essay. I am grateful to my coeditor, Sylvère Monod, for his contributions to our joint researches into the history of lighting. I also wish to thank W. W. Norton and Company for permission to draw upon these dozen footnotes when information was relevant for the present essay.

and literature, that is, involves not only rooms with a view but views of a room, those variable spaces in which most of our lives are spent, with their accessories for eating, sleeping, talking—the "Things" (as D. H. Lawrence scornfully called them in his short story) that we surround ourselves with in trying to fill up the empty space, things that are often key tokens of what we are, or what a society is.

Critical discussions that more narrowly restrict attention to one aspect of a novel obviously run the risk of fragmentation and distortion, but for a work of the stature of *Bleak House* the risk is inconsequential; the parts reinforce one another and regroup to constitute the impressive unity of the whole. Thus, how a room is illuminated is, in this novel, not only an item of stagecraft; frequently it is a form of commentary on character and action and society.

As for stagecraft, it is evident from Dickens's letters that both as a play producer and as a public reader his concern for lighting effects was intense, indeed almost obsessive. On his play-producing tours, he frequently refers to the crucial importance of the lighting arrangements, about which he considered himself an expert, and on his reading tours, part of the success or failure of an evening seems to have depended, for him, on how the gaslight had been manipulated. In Rochester, New York, where he gave public readings (March 16, 1868), he was delighted with the "brilliant light" of the theater. "My screen and gas are set up in front of the drop-curtain," he wrote, "and the most delicate touches will tell anywhere." And it was fitting, after returning to England, that in his farewell speech following his final reading, he summed up his performance in terms of lighting: "From these garish lights I vanish now for evermore."[2]

Lights, garish and not so garish, also figure extensively in his novels, and in *Bleak House,* where so much of the action takes place at night, they are an especially prominent feature. "My object," said Conrad, "is by the power of the

---

[2] *The Speeches of Charles Dickens*, ed. K. J. Fielding (Oxford: Clarendon Press, 1960), p. 413.

written word . . . before all to make you see." Conrad's assertion has become a shopworn commonplace in discussions of fiction, but it is worth citing again here as a reminder of one of the chief aims of his predecessor.

In discussing Dickens's success in making us see, some attention has to be given to historical items. As Anthony Burton remarks: "No one with historical feeling can fail to be aware of how much has changed, not only to the eye, but to the ear and nose and stomach, since Dickens's day."[3] If we are to use our eyes—as Dickens expects of us, and imaginatively reconstruct his scenes, there are some occasions, after these 120 years, when we may be unable to visualize how a scene has been illuminated. When, for example, the Reverend Mr. Chadband delivers his sermon in the Snagsby parlor, are we to picture his big oily face shining under the gaslight (for Mr. Snagsby, we know, has gaslight downstairs in his shop), or was his face lit up by a more kindly candle? To answer such a question involves some historical reconstruction which may serve to touch up those small areas of Dickens's picture that have faded with time.

Some six different kinds of lighting then in use in mid-nineteenth-century England appear in various scenes of Dickens's novel. They provide a homely but workable way of organizing a discussion. These are: gaslight for street-lighting; indoor gaslight; lanterns; oil lamps; rushlights and candles of various varieties; and firelight.

Gaslight for Streets

One disputed point must first be briefly confronted. At what date are we to suppose the action of *Bleak House* to be occurring? The question has been variously answered. Some locate it in the late 1820s, others in the mid 1840s, for Dickens, despite his keen awareness of contemporary topics, seems to have deliberately chosen to be unspecific about dates—as D. H. Lawrence likewise chose to be un-

---

[3] Anthony Burton, *Dickensian*, 66 (September 1970), 247.

specific about the date of the action in *Women in Love*. It seems to me that the late 1830s are intended (with some wandering excursions into the 1850s as well), but for our present purposes it does not matter deeply, for at either end of the time scale London was a gaslit city—at least as far as its streets were concerned. At the later date there was simply more gas—by 1846 some 30,000 gas lamps were in use in London streets.[4]

What is more important is how this transformation wrought by gas-lighting continued to affect many of Dickens's contemporaries with a sense of wonder and awe. Rustic visitors from unlighted rural villages would be especially impressed by the dazzle, for as a report on a village at nighttime recorded: "They have no lamp on the green, and there is a fine homely rusticity in the extent to which you tumble over the pigs at night, which is highly rural."[5] Even a visitor from a country estate, such as Chesney Wold or Mr. Jarndyce's house—where, of course, no gas was available—would be impressed by the spectacle greeting him as he approached the outskirts of London at night. Despite frequent palls of fog, the sky would be lit up with a nightlong brightness never before witnessed in man's long history.[6] Esther, looking toward London from distant St. Albans, sees a "lurid glare" in the sky that prompts her to fancy "an unearthly fire, gleaming on all the unseen buildings of the city, and on all the faces of its many thousands of wondering inhabitants" (p. 380). Esther's vision of fire, like several passages in *Bleak House*, has apocalyptic dimensions that readily align it with some of the visions

---

[4] G. L. Gomme, *London in the Reign of Victoria* (London: Blackie, 1898), p. 413.
[5] *Household Words*, 8 February 1851, p. 479, and see also 19 July 1851, p. 396.
[6] See Robert Chambers, *The Book of Days* (London: W. and R. Chambers, 1864), II, 408–11. See also Tennyson's description of a country visitor seeing London in the distance from the top of a coach: "And at night along the dusky highway near and nearer drawn, / Sees in heaven the light of London flaring like a dreary dawn" ("Locksley Hall," 113–14).

discussed in Frank Kermode's *Sense of an Ending*. More commonly, however, the flames in *Bleak House* are earthly generated rather than unearthly. On the opening page we get this striking paragraph on gas-lighting: "Gas, looming through the fog in divers places in the streets, much as the sun may, from the spongey fields, be seen to loom by husbandman and ploughboy. Most of the shops lighted two hours before their time—as the gas seems to know, for it has a haggard and unwilling look." One of the many memorable features of this opening scene is that in portraying this gaslit city, the first city of light created by man, the novelist has contrived to half smother the bright lights under the cloud of an overwhelming darkness. Such darkness can be the man-made (or partially man-made) darkness of fog, or darkness itself: "Darkness rests upon Tom-all-Alone's. Dilating and dilating since the sun went down last night, it has gradually swelled until it fills every void in the place. For a time there were some dungeon lights burning . . . in Tom-all-Alone's, heavily, heavily, in the nauseous air, and winking . . . at many horrible things. But they are blotted out" (p. 551). Hillis Miller's brilliant chapter on *Bleak House* cites this passage in his discussion of entropy, and although he is primarily concerned with other manifestations of disorder than darkness, Miller does note how the narrator sees the world "as the dwelling place of a light which is rapidly, at this very moment, fading away, withdrawing to an infinite distance, and leaving the world to absolute darkness."[7] Indeed, from such passages it is not hard to see why Conrad in conceiving his worlds of darkness in *The Secret Agent* and *Heart of Darkness* retained such a deep admiration for Dickens's novel.

Yet there is a second feature of these accounts of the city of light that also calls for notice. Poets speak of "darkness visible," and although Dickens certainly provides the visible darkness too (the "great black space" of the sky as Esther

---

[7] J. Hillis Miller, *Charles Dickens: The World of His Novels* (Cambridge, Mass.: Harvard University Press, 1958), p. 212.

calls it), what is striking is that his darkness is also palpable.[8] Dickens, like Browning, has an acutely developed sense of pressure, and we are made to feel that blackness pressing upon the lights. What is also remarkable is that light, too, is made palpable as well as visible. The flames *struggle* to assert themselves against the opposing pressure, a sometimes ineffectual movement, but yet a struggle. And the figurative parallel to the efforts of the light-bearers in the moral order of the novel, such as Esther or Alan Woodcourt, scarcely requires comment.[9] The lamplighter, making his rounds at dawn to extinguish the gaslights, "strikes off the little heads of fire that have *aspired* to lessen the darkness" (p. 405).[10] Light, thus, is not only something seen but something felt, a force of energy. In treating light as energy, Dickens may have been affected by the speculations of Michael Faraday, whose lecture on "The Chemistry of a Candle" Dickens published, in modified form, in *Household Words,* August 3, 1850.[11]

From the outskirts of London we get such an overall view of the city of light, but from a closer perspective the novel offers frequent reminders of the gaslit urban mazes through which the characters make their way, and at times the focus centers on individual lamps, such as the one lighting up the entrance to the graveyard where Nemo is buried and under which Lady Dedlock dies—as can be seen in

---

[8] In describing Victorian slums, the reformer Lord Shaftesbury used a striking phrase to make a similar point: "Dirt and disrepair, such as ordinary folks can form no notion of: *darkness that may be felt; odours that may be handled* . . . hold despotic rule in these dens of despair" (italics mine); BBC "Third Programme," quoted in *Ideas and Beliefs of the Victorians* (New York: Dutton, 1966), p. 100.

[9] See, e.g., George H. Ford, "Self-Help and the Helpless in *Bleak House,*" in *From Jane Austen to Joseph Conrad,* ed. Robert C. Rathburn and Martin Steinmann (Minneapolis: University of Minnesota Press, 1958), pp. 92–105.

[10] Italics mine. The image of the aspiring flame is a common one. See, e.g., Auden's "September 1, 1939."

[11] See Ann Y. Wilkinson's valuable discussion, "*Bleak House*: From Faraday to Judgment Day," *English Literary History,* 34 (1967), 225–47.

Phiz's fine illustrations of the scenes: "Come, flame of gas burning, so sullenly above the iron gate . . . It is well that you should call to every passer-by, 'Look here!' " (p. 137).

From its introduction in 1812 throughout the years before *Bleak House* appeared, gas-lighting had come to be adopted almost universally in London streets. There were, however, some significant exceptions, as *Bleak House* accurately shows. Some slum areas would appear to have been without gaslight. I may have overlooked a reference, but so far as I can see, Tom-all-Alone's is pictured without gas lamps. The darkness here, relieved only slightly by the dungeon lights, is almost total. Oddly enough, it is at the opposite end of the social scale, the street on which Sir Leicester Dedlock has his town mansion, that installation of gas-lighting had also been long postponed. Aristocratic residents of London's West End had been firmly opposed to the innovation, and it was not until 1846 that Grosvenor Square, the last of the holdouts, reluctantly changed from oil lamps to gas.[12] Here is Dickens's version: "Complicated garnish of iron-work entwines itself over the flights of steps in this awful street; and, from these petrified bowers, extinguishers for obsolete flambeaux gasp at the upstart gas" (p. 575). Anyone familiar with West End London will readily recognize what Dickens is picturing in this stunning passage, for many of these wrought-iron structures, fronting the entrances to mansions, are still to be seen today, some 125 years after Dickens pronounced them obsolete. Into a few sentences he has compressed a whole history of street-lighting. In the comparatively dark streets of seventeenth-century London, ladies would be escorted to house doors by footmen bearing flambeaux, fiercely burning torches of pitch, which, having served their function, would then be extinguished by being rammed into a cone-shaped structure of iron mounted on the grillwork. By Dickens's time, with improved lighting, flambeaux had

---

[12] See John W. Dodds, *The Age of Paradox* (New York: Rinehart, 1952), p. 285. See also Trevor Blount, "Sir Leicester Dedlock and 'Deportment' Turveydrop," *Nineteenth Century Fiction,* 21 (1966), 151–52.

long gone out of use[13] and well might "gasp at the upstart gas" as Sir Leicester gasps at upstart Wat Tylers and Ironmasters.

Following illumination by flambeaux, and supplementing them throughout the eighteenth century, were oil lamps. At house entrances these would be suspended in an iron hoop, somewhat resembling a small basketball hoop. When gas was installed eventually, the glass lamp would be removed, but the hoop remained.

> Here and there a weak little iron hoop, through which bold boys aspire to throw their friends' caps (its only present use), retains its place among the rusty foliage, sacred to the memory of departed oil. Nay, even oil itself, yet lingering at long intervals in a little absurd glass pot, with a knob in the bottom like an oyster, blinks and sulks at newer lights every night, like its high and dry master in the House of Lords. (P. 575)

The topicality of this description can be documented by references in journals to what was called the "No Gas party."[14] At the time *Bleak House* was being conceived, *Household Words* featured a satirical article in which installation of "cheap gas" was opposed as "flying in the face of Providence." Obscure rushlight, instead of the intense brightness of gas, was recommended as "most in harmony with Nature." "If a bright light were wanted longer than we have it naturally," asserts the Dedlock-style speaker, "the sun would not leave us when it does."[15] Dickens's repre-

---

[13] On foggy streets flambeaux were occasionally still used, but not by footmen. See pictures in *Illustrated London News* (Christmas supplement, 1849), pp. 419, 432. See also George Sala ten years later: "Few and far between are the link-boys in the present 1859. The running footmen with the flambeaux have vanished these many years; and the only mementos surviving of their existence are the blackened extinguishers attached to the area railings of some old-fashioned houses about Grosvenor Square." *Gaslight and Daylight* (London: Chapman and Hall, 1859), p. 65.

[14] Dickens himself made fun of the "great No Gas party," which campaigned unsuccessfully to prevent gas from invading the seaside resort of Broadstairs. See his "Our English Watering-Place" in *Reprinted Pieces*.

[15] *Household Words*, 21 August 1852, p. 527.

sentation of rockbound attitudes is in the same vein, but much more telling.

Gaslight Indoors

Indoor gas-lighting in domestic establishments was still comparatively rare in mid-century England. Gas installations were expensive, and the very harshness of the light made it seem inferior to traditional lighting devices, with their more-pleasant, softly lit effects.[16] The prejudice against using it inside households lasted much longer than the Grosvenor Square opposition against its use for street-lighting. As late as 1878, an anonymous American published a guide to English manners and customs, with the delightful title *"Good Form" in England*. In English homes, he notes, "gas, whether it be in town or country, is not only thought unwholesome, but *not* 'good form.' "[17] Judged in these terms, Dickens himself would have seemed outside the social pale, for he had gas-lighting installed in his own house on Tavistock Square, where *Bleak House* was written.[18] Despite his own personal falling away, he does not seem to have had his characters violate good form. I think it safe to say (and Phiz's illustrations would bear this out) that in none of the domestic scenes in *Bleak House* should we visualize gas-lighting.

[16] In contrasting oil and gas lighting displays for the Great Exhibition, an editorial in *Illustrated London News* noted: "Whatever may be the demerits of gas, as contrasted with the softness and richness of effect produced by the old coloured lamps, its superior illuminating power need not be insisted upon" (19 July 1851, p. 87). See also Arthur Hayward, *The Days of Dickens* (London: Routledge, 1926), p. 14.

[17] [L. J. Ransone], *"Good Form" in England* (New York: Appleton, 1888), p. 132.

[18] Dickens's experiences with gas pipes in his Tavistock House bedroom were later recalled and put to use when he was writing *Edwin Drood*. See George H. Ford, "Dickens's Notebook and *Edwin Drood*," *Nineteenth Century Fiction*, 6 (March 1952), 277–78. On the use of gas indoors as an indication of advanced tastes, see Disraeli's novel *Coningsby* (1844), in which the hero visits the Adelphi Hotel in Manchester in 1836 and notes that "even his bedroom was lit by gas" (Ch. 24).

In commercial establishments, on the contrary, gas was extensively in use: "Twilight comes on; gas begins to start up in the shops; the lamplighter, with his ladder, runs along the margin of the pavement. A wretched evening is beginning to close in" (p. 199). Thus, Mr. Snagsby's shop, but not the rest of his house, is lit by gas. So too, as we might expect, is the police station visited by Esther, and George's shooting gallery, where the jet of raw flame, I should imagine, would have been unfurnished with a globe to soften its pulsing blaze. George Sala's *Gaslight and Daylight* (1859) has a passage that helps us to visualize this difference when he contrasts the beautiful fixtures used in a department store with the gaslight in a meat market: "The gas, no longer gleaming through ground-glass globes, or aided by polished reflectors, but flaring from primitive tubes, lights up a long vista of beef, mutton, or veal." Our first picture of George Rouncewell's assistant, Phil, with his face blackened by gunpowder, is highlighted by such flaring gas: "as he lies in the light, before a glaring white target, the black upon him shines again" (p. 271). In other shooting-gallery scenes, those in which Gridley and Jo die, Dickens makes no reference to these gas jets and concentrates instead on the figurative light towards which the dying Jo is groping his way.[19]

Gas was also used in London taverns. The Dedlock Arms, in a Lincolnshire village, is lit with candles, whereas at the Sol's Arms in the city we must picture Little Swills croaking his folderol choruses in the head-splitting barroom glare of hissing gaslight.[20]

Public hallways were another interior area in which gas

---

[19] "It's turned wery dark, sir. Is there any light a-comin?" (p. 571). Jo's reference to light gains an added dimension when Chadband's earlier speeches about him are recalled, such as his fantastic pronouncement that Jo is "devoid of the light that shines in upon some of us. What is that light? . . . It is the light of Terewth" (pp. 320–21).

[20] An article on tavern songfests indicates that the gas-lighting was considered to increase the intensity of a hangover. At one tavern where wax candles instead of gas had lit up the singers, a visitor observes that such illumination is "much pleasanter to the eye and head than gas" (*Household Words*, 17 May 1851, p. 179).

LIGHT IN DARKNESS | 193

would ordinarily provide the illumination. Dickens can accordingly make fun of the "feeble oil lanterns" in the hallway at Symond's Inn and also at Lincoln's Inn, for the lawyers of the Inns of Court, like their aristocratic clients of the West End, were among the most persistent opponents of the introduction of gas:

> It is night in Lincoln's Inn—perplexed and troublous valley of the shadow of the law, where suitors generally find but little day—and fat candles are snuffed out in offices. . . . From tiers of staircase windows, clogged lamps like the eyes of Equity, bleared Argus with a fathomless pocket for every eye and an eye upon it, dimly blink at the stars. In dirty upper casements, here and there, hazy little patches of candlelight reveal where some wise draughtsman and conveyancer yet toils for the entanglement of real estate in meshes of sheep-skin. (Pp. 391–92)

As in the passage picturing the lights in the street of the Dedlocks, Dickens here contrives once again to combine a vivid and historically accurate picture of lighting with an implicit commentary on society; the feeble, clogged lamps in a world of darkness reinforce our awareness of the ineffectuality of obsolete legal procedures to generate the light of justice. And to appreciate the poetic heightening reached in the passage, it is revealing to put beside it an account of the same scene, written at about the same time, by a lawyer who had chambers in one of the Inns of Court: "The dim lamps with which our Honourable Society (supposed to be as yet unconscious of the new discovery called Gas) make the horrors of the staircase visible, deepen the gloom which generally settles on my soul when I go home at night."[21] Perfectly respectable reportorial prose this, but strikingly different from Dickens's image-studded picture

---

[21] *Household Words*, 20 July 1850, p. 385. It is of interest that while the Inns of Court still kept to oil and candles at this date, the interior of the building occupied by the Royal College of Surgeons (referred to in *Bleak House*) was gaslit. See *Household Words*, 10 August 1850, p. 465. By 1852, however, even the courtroom featured in *Bleak House* (Ch. 65) had changed to gas. "Now, even Westminster Hall—the last place where a man would look for novelty—is lighted with it" (*Household Words*, 27 March 1852, p. 43).

in which windows have become eyes—a recurrent figure in this and others of his novels.

The concluding reference in the Dickens passage to the candlelit offices of the lawyers corresponds to scenes in other lawyers' offices in the novel. Unlike the shopkeepers, the lawyers clung to the practice of lighting their premises in the old styles. Vholes's dark office is candlelit, as is Kenge and Carboy's, where Esther, on her first visit, is startled by "its being night in the day-time, the candles burning with a white flame, and looking raw and cold" (p. 29). Mr. Tulkinghorn's street is gaslit, but his gloomy office is illuminated only by "two candles in old-fashioned silver candlesticks, that give a very insufficient light to his large room" (p. 119)—candles that on the night of his murder were "blown out suddenly, soon after being lighted" (p. 585).

Lantern Light

Lanterns appear in only a few scenes of *Bleak House* and seem to be reserved for special effects. Instead of the wide-angle lens perspectives that we obtain in such scenes as the Chesney Wold drawing room, a lantern provides, obviously, a sharp but narrow focus on a single object, as in the scene of Vholes in his carriage, or on a succession of objects. The latter is the technique of seeing which is effectively employed in two sustained scenes involving Mr. Bucket, and it is with this detective that we appropriately associate this mode of lighting, for a lantern, like Bucket's celebrated finger, is a device for probing. When conducting Snagsby on a tour into the hellish depths of Tom-all-Alone's, Bucket and the escorting policeman are equipped with bull's-eye lanterns (a device comparable to our flashlight or electric torch), which pinpoint an object momentarily in a bright circle of light before our attention is jerkily moved on to another object, from a demonlike face in the crowd of slum dwellers, to the brickmaker's child with its halo that reminds Snagsby of paintings of the Christ child (p. 279), or to Jo, who "stands amazed in the disc of light, like a ragged figure in a magic-lanthorn" (p. 280). Our sense of horror provoked by these grim scenes is intensified by the way in which they have been lighted, for although the "bull's eyes glare," as Dickens calls it, is a powerful one, its penetrations into the enveloping blackness are ephemeral and isolated, enforcing on us a sense of discontinuity and disorder. The other scene in which lantern light features importantly is in our first visit to Krook's rag-and-bottle warehouse. This hodgepodge establishment we would ordinarily associate with candles. In the first tour of inspection, however, no mention of candles is made. Instead we are conducted exclusively by the spotlight of Krook's lantern. As Esther reports: "As it was still foggy and dark, and as the shop was blinded besides by the wall of Lincoln's Inn, intercepting the light within a couple of yards, we should not have seen so much but for a lighted lantern that an old man in spectacles and a hairy cap was carrying about in the shop" (p. 49). As in the Tom-all-Alone's scene, the effect of disorder is heightened by the jumping of the lantern light from one ill-sorted object to another: "pickle bottles, wine bottles, ink bottles" (p. 48), dusty lawbooks, rusty keys, and Ada's blonde hair (I assume she must have been blonde)—each isolated item in the fantastic catalogue is further isolated by the discontinuous mode of its being seen. This part of the scene ends, fittingly, with an account of Tom Jarndyce's having blown out his brains and with Krook pointing the story by blowing out his lantern.[22]

Oil-lamp Lighting

Although scenes lit by oil lamps are much more common in *Bleak House* than the few in which lantern rays provide the focus, such lamps are not extensively referred to. In many domestic scenes we have to assume that lamplight, as well as candlelight, provides the illumination, as when

[22] Trevor Blount suggests that Krook's lantern is "perhaps meant to recall the fog-filled louvre [lantern] of Lincoln's Inn Hall in chapter I." *Dickens Studies Annual*, 1 (1970), 195.

the Mercuries, "with lamps and candles" (p. 503), follow Mr. Tulkinghorn as he makes his most dramatic entrance into the Dedlock drawing room, and again when Sir Leicester lights a bedtime candle for Volumnia "at my Lady's shaded lamp" (p. 350).

About these Dedlock lamps it should be noted that they would have burned high-quality sperm-whale oil, an illuminant which provided a clean flame and was relatively odorless. In 1850 Dickens wrote with enthusiasm about the oil lamps used in the Duke of Devonshire's private theater, which were, he said in a letter, "without smell."[23] Cheaper grades of whale oil lacked such properties and could add a distinctive odor to a room. Dickens himself, recalling in his late years his childhood visits to lamplit theaters, focuses his remembrance on the smells: "an aromatic perfume of orange-peel and lamp-oil."[24] Such lamp oil was probably the "train oil" which the clergyman, Mr. Chadband, was supposed to have a good deal of in his system (p. 200). Although from its name we might assume that this kind of oil was a lubricant for railway trains, train oil was quite unconnected with railways; it was simply a commonly used illuminant derived from inferior grades of whale oil. To appreciate what the oily presence of Mr. Chadband must have been like, it is useful to cite from the *National Encyclopaedia* of 1873, where train oil is described as a combustible fluid "of a brownish colour, rather viscid," and having "a disagreeable smell and taste."[25]

One further reference to whale blubber as the source of lamp oil also deserves notice. Late in the novel, Dickens resumes his description of the street and lights outside the Dedlock mansion in London, and this time he includes a witty allusion to the marine source of the fluid used in these obsolete outdoor lamps (the season is winter): "The day is now beginning to decline.... The gloom augments; the

---

[23] Edgar Johnson, *Charles Dickens: His Tragedy and Triumph* (New York: Simon and Schuster, 1952), II, 722, 734.
[24] Harry Stone, ed., *Uncollected Writings from Household Words* (Bloomington: Indiana University Press, 1968), I, 63.
[25] *National Encyclopaedia* (London, 1873), IX, 669.

bright gas springs up in the streets; and the pertinacious oil lamps which yet hold their ground here, with their source of life half frozen and half thawed, twinkle gaspingly, like fiery fish out of water—as they are" (pp. 698–99). One may be reminded here that Dickens began writing *Bleak House* in the same year that *Moby-Dick* was published.

Candlelight

To speak of the smell of cheap oil is not to digress from the topic of lighting effects. If we are imaginatively to reconstruct these scenes in the novel, we have to use our noses as well as our eyes—an awareness atrophied by more than half a century of electric lighting. The requirement is especially necessary in the candlelit scenes, for candles are the chief mode of interior illumination in *Bleak House*. And the variable amount of smoke and smell produced by different varieties of candles was clearly an indication of varieties of prestige, from the wax tapers of the rich to the so-called dip of the poor. As Faraday noted in 1850: "a great clumsy dip smokes more than a neat wax candle ... because the thick wick of the dip makes too much fuel in proportion to the air that gets to it."[26]

One of the most common forms of the dip referred to by Faraday was a special kind, the old-fashioned rush candle, made by dipping reeds into a coating of hot grease. Rush candles burned with a dim and flickering flame; they were frequently used, in perforated cannisters, as nightlights. The eerie effects of light and shadow on the bedroom wall produced by this device have been memorably described in *Great Expectations*.[27] A story in *Household Words* of 1850 also comments on these effects. A woman develops

[26] *Household Words*, 3 August 1850, p. 440.
[27] In Chapter 45 Pip spends a restless night in a bedroom lit by a "good old constitutional rush-light" placed in a "high tin tower, perforated with round holes," which he likens to Argus and notes that it "made a startlingly wide-awake pattern on the walls." See also *Vanity Fair*, Ch. 7.

a fear of ghosts and determines to keep a light burning all night in her bedroom, "and not a dim, flickering rush candle, but a steady wax light. She knew that her daughter wondered at the strange extravagance, but she could not bear darkness."[28] Oddly enough, rushlights are never referred to by name in *Bleak House*. In Esther's childhood the "light" that was taken away from her bedroom every night by the mean Mrs. Rachael was probably rushlight, but we are not told. Again, at the squalid cottage of the brickmakers, there is "a feeble candle in the patched window" (p. 380), which might possibly have been a rush candle fixed in its special iron bracket, but elsewhere an ordinary tallow candle, with cloth wick, seems to be what we are expected to see. When the brickmakers are at Tom-all-Alone's, their "gross candle burns pale and sickly in the polluted air" (p. 279). Likewise, the orphaned Neckett children, whose slum garret at nightfall is dimly lit by gaslight from the street, are cheered when such a candle is lit for them by their sister Charlie after her return from work.

High-quality candles made of wax, and virtually odorless, are featured, as we might expect, in the Dedlock households. After Lady Dedlock flees from home, her dark and abandoned rooms are searched by Inspector Bucket, who holds a "wax-light" (p. 671) above his head which lights up in her mirrors the reflected images of himself, with whom he carries on a dialogue. Tallow candles were another matter: "A smell as of unwholesome sheep, blending with the smell of must and dust, is referable to the nightly (and often daily) consumption of mutton fat in candles" (p. 482). This is Vholes's office, and it is likely that the "guttering" candles at Kenge and Carboy's may have produced a similar aroma during Esther's first visit to the office (p. 29). Of the tallow smells at Mrs. Jellyby's house, she comments: "Mrs. Jellyby [was] snuffing the two great office candles in tin candlesticks which made the room taste

---

[28] *Household Words*, 2 November 1850, p. 141. See also *Annual Register* (1853), Chronology, p. 140, and William T. O'Dea, *The Social History of Lighting* (London: Routledge and Paul, 1958), Ch. 9.

strongly of hot tallow (the fire had gone out, and there was nothing in the grate but ashes)" (p. 38).

It is in Krook's establishment, however, that our nostrils must be alerted for the smells of cheap tallow (among other smells as well, of course). After our first lantern-lit tour of that dark emporium, we subsequently reencounter it by candlelight. When Mr. Tulkinghorn enters the shop, on the night of Nemo's death, we learn that it "is dim enough, with a blot-headed candle or so in the windows, and an old man and a cat sitting in the back part by a fire. The old man rises and comes forward, with another blot-headed candle in his hand" (p. 123).

Armed with one of these mysterious-sounding candles,[29] fitted in an "iron candlestick," Mr. Tulkinghorn mounts the stairs to inspect the room of Krook's mysterious lodger, and the scene that follows provides a striking demonstration of how Dickens's lighting makes the reader see. As Mr. Tulkinghorn enters, his borrowed candle goes out, and what he sees of the room depends on the dim light provided by a low-burning "red coke fire," almost extinct, and by a guttering candle by the bedside of the dead man, and also by whatever light from the gaslit street penetrates through the "two gaunt holes" pierced in the window shutters. Each accessory plays its part, in turn, in enabling us to take in the roomscape. By the firelight we see the shattered and dirty furnishings; by the dying candle, the figure on the bed: "He has a yellow look in the spectral darkness of a candle that has guttered down, until the whole length of its wick (still burning) has doubled over, and left a tower of winding-sheet above it" (p. 124). When, in turn, the lodger's dying candle itself goes out, Tulkinghorn—who

---

[29] What is a blot-headed candle? I have pursued this inquiry by correspondence with historians of technology, directors of scientific museums, and candle manufacturers. No one had a satisfactory answer; in fact, one of the candle manufacturers was so baffled that he contended it must be a misprint (examination of Dickens's manuscript did not, as it happens, confirm his suspicions). From the context it seems safe to conclude that this candle was cheap, ineffective, and smelly.

has been frantically banging the inside of the door with his iron candlestick—is left "in the dark; with the gaunt eyes in the shutters staring down upon the bed." This memorable detail is reemphasized, a few minutes later, when Krook arrives with a fresh candle, and as the two men reenter the dead man's room, their light obliterates the gaslight penetrating the shutters from the street: "Thus whispering, they both go in together. As the light goes in, the great eyes in the shutters, darkening, seem to close. Not so the eyes upon the bed" (p. 125). For the rest of this scene, until the beadle arrives to arrange for the coffin, that solitary candle passes from the hands of Krook to the doctor inspecting the dead body, to Snagsby who searches the room, and back to its owner, offering a succession of candlelit panels that could have inspired Georges de La Tour, the seventeenth-century painter who made candlelight his trademark.

In her essay "Nathalie Sarraute and the Novel," Susan Sontag exclaims: "Sarraute is right . . . that the novel's traditional machinery for furnishing a scene, and describing . . . characters does not justify itself. Who really cares about the furniture of so-and-so's room or whether he lit a cigarette or wore a dark gray suit . . . ?"[30]

Readers weary of the pointless props that bulk large in scenes by lesser novelists will readily share Miss Sontag's dissatisfactions. Yet to extend one's dissatisfaction into a blanket principle of exclusion is ultimately silly and evades required discriminations. Robbe-Grillet's theory about the proper treatment of objects in fiction, which is essentially Ruskin's familiar Pathetic Fallacy argument writ large, also leads into a similar blind alley. This, for admirers of Dickens, is a relief, for if Robbe-Grillet's theories were strictly applied, there would be no room for Dickens's animistic creations; his image-studded world in which oil lamps gasp

---

[30] Susan Sontag, *Against Interpretation* (New York: Dell, 1969), p. 106. Sontag's reaction against furnishings in fiction is not a new development in criticism. Willa Cather's essay of 1922, "The Novel Démeublé," inspired by an antagonism to Balzac, is in the same vein (*On Writing* [New York: Knopf, 1949], pp. 35–43).

at the upstart gas, or holes in a shutter become glaring eyes, would be distinctly unacceptable. Bad form in fact. In any event, discrimination requires distinguishing to what use the accessory is put. When lamp or candle or lantern functions to many ends, for vision and for meaning, to banish it out-of-hand would be to forego some of the satisfactions prose fiction can provide for us.

After his effective application of lighting effects in picturing Krook's lodger and his lodgings, it would probably have been easy enough for Dickens to repeat his success with lighting in his later scene, in the same setting, on the night of Krook's death. Instead, in the second scene, although lighting plays an important role, it has here been subordinated to other effects. The awesome eyes in the shutters are no longer mentioned after Weevil takes over Nemo's room, for having passed one night under their stare, Weevil had wisely installed window curtains. As he and Guppy whisper together in the firelight during the two hours before he takes a candle downstairs to discover the whereabouts of Krook, we are called upon not so much to see as to smell and, most especially, to touch and to taste. No matter how many times one reads this scene, it is always hard to refrain afterwards from wanting to scrub one's hands (as Guppy does) and to wipe away the grease that seems to have accumulated on one's clothing. The daring mixture of wit and horror employed by Dickens in this awesome scene has been ably analyzed by Trevor Blount[31] and need not be developed further here. What does need to be noted is the way in which the principal reference to a candle stresses the atmospheric more than the visionary; the candle, trimmed or untrimmed, cannot function in this greasy air:

"There's a blessed-looking candle!" says Tony, pointing to the heavily burning taper on his table with a great cabbage head and a long winding-sheet.

---

[31] Trevor Blount, "Dickens and Mr. Krook's Spontaneous Combustion," *Dickens Studies Annual,* 1 (1970), 183–211.

"That's easily improved," Mr. Guppy observes, as he takes the snuffers in hand.

"*Is* it?" returns his friend. "Not so easily as you think. It has been smouldering like that ever since it was lighted." (p. 396)

On the visual level, what we must see here is a cheap tallow candle as it would burn in the days before self-consuming wicks. If such a wick were left untrimmed, a large, charred lump of soot, a cabbage head, could accumulate at the end of the burning wick.[32]

As a final example of candle-lighting we may turn from the smelly tallow of Krook's establishment to the world of clean-burning wax in the two households of Sir Leicester and Lady Dedlock. Once again it is the third-person narrator, rather than Esther, who provides the account, for it is in his half of the novel, rather than hers, that most of the memorable scenes involving lighting are to be found. Whether or not one goes all the way with Robert Garis's study *The Dickens Theatre*, which stresses Dickens's theatrical voice in all his work, it is certain that the third-person speaker in this novel views the world as stage producers do, and film producers as well. And of the many such scenes in *Bleak House*, perhaps the best staged (my term is not pejorative here) are those at Chesney Wold and the Dedlock house in town. Here is an account of the vast drawing room at Chesney Wold, scene of many confrontations:

> It is near bed-time. Bedroom fires blaze brightly all over the house, raising ghosts of grim furniture on wall and ceiling. Bedroom candlesticks bristle on the distant table by the door, and cousins yawn on ottomans. Cousins at the piano, cousins at the soda-water tray, cousins rising from the card-table, cousins gathered round the fire. Standing on one side of his own peculiar fire (for there are two), Sir Leicester. On the opposite side of the broad hearth, my Lady at her table. Volumnia, as one of the more privileged cousins, in a luxurious chair between them. (P. 349)

At the level of stage drama, as in the scenes of Nemo's bedroom in Krook's house, every lighting device here will

---

[32] See *Universal Dictionary of the Arts, Sciences* (Edinburgh, 1816), p. 579.

serve its purpose in later scenes. When a guest picked up one of the short-stemmed "bedroom candlesticks," it would signal his departure from the evening party,[33] an event which, in a later scene, the bored hostess, Lady Dedlock, looks forward to as she "glances wearily towards the candlesticks and heaves a noiseless sigh" (p. 350).

Our impression from the Dedlock roomscapes is of a great blaze of light: "Where the throng is thickest, where the lights are brightest, . . . Lady Dedlock is" (p. 572). And this impression of dazzling light is reinforced in the final pages of the third-person narrative by means of contrast, for in the years after Lady Dedlock's death, the lights at Chesney Wold are dwindling to darkness. There are "no rows of light sparkling by night" in the largely closed-shuttered estate; the lights have virtually given up the struggle against the darkness. Of the long drawing room we learn that "Sir Leicester holds his shrunken state . . . and reposes in his old place before my Lady's picture. Closed in by night with broad screens, and illumined only in that part, the light of the drawing-room seems gradually contracting and dwindling until it shall be no more" (p. 765). Such passages make for one of Dickens' best curtains; they serve also to qualify the somewhat cozy note of Esther's exit in her final chapter, which follows this one.

The impression of unshaded brilliance is not, however, an altogether accurate one, for even in Lady Dedlock's lifetime the darkness is ever gathering and pressing the weight of its shadow against the light. In the recurring descriptions of the Chesney Wold drawing room, with its family portraits, the author deftly introduces contrasting shadows that hint of imminent darkness even when the room is bathed in the full sunlight of daytime. These preliminaries prepare us for the tour de force of lighting to be encountered in Chapter 40, certainly one of the most impressive chapters in the novel. Here, in addition to illumination of

---

[33] The custom seems to have persisted at country houses well into the present century. D. H. Lawrence mentions the "chamber candle" he took to his bedroom when he visited Garsington in 1915.

candle and lamp, we have first an account of the light and shadow of sunset, and, later, of the light and shadow of moonlight, rendered, fittingly, in Dickens's grand manner: "At this sunset hour . . . the light . . . pours in, rich, lavish, overflowing like the summer plenty of the land." In the virtually empty house, before the arrival of guests and owners next day, the sunset light falls "on the pictured forms upon the walls." The scene and phrase may remind us of Eliot's *Waste Land* drawing room, where the firelit pictures "were told upon the walls; staring forms . . . hushing the room enclosed." Dickens's narrator is led to reflections on the dead past in a vein that mixes compassion with the sardonic:

> Then do the frozen Dedlocks thaw. Strange movements come upon their features, as the shadows of leaves play there. . . . A staring Baronet, with a truncheon, gets a dimple in his chin. Down into the bosom of a stony shepherdess there steals a fleck of light and warmth, that would have done it good, a hundred years ago. . . . A maid of honour of the court of Charles the Second, with large round eyes (and other charms to correspond), seems to bathe in glowing water, and it ripples as it glows. But the fire of the sun is dying. Even now the floor is dusky, and shadow slowly mounts the walls, bringing the Dedlocks down like age and death. And now, upon my lady's picture over the great chimney-piece, a weird shade falls. . . . Higher and darker rises shadow on the wall—now a red gloom on the ceiling—now the fire is out.[34] (P. 498)

After sunset we get further shadows as the moonlight shines into "solitary bedrooms" and into the drawing room itself, a roomscape like Madeline's bedroom in *The Eve of St. Agnes,* but with Keats's rich colors here appropriately blanched: "Now is the time for shadow, when every corner is a cavern, and every downward step a pit, when the stained glass is reflected in pale and faded hues upon the

---

[34] Janice Nadelhaft comments that this passage "evokes a world that, like the aristocratic world of *The Cherry Orchard,* is slowly dying for lack of heat and energy." "The English Malady, Corrupted Humors, and Krook's Death," *Studies in the Novel,* 1 (1969), 233.

floors" (p. 498). These preliminaries prepare us, of course, for the climactic scene of Tulkinghorn's veiled exposure of Lady Dedlock after the house has been filled with guests. Instead of the blaze of lights we might have expected, the confrontation takes place in the twilight and moonlight already described for us, and the author can dispense with his lush evocations of atmosphere and resort to a terse and jerky narrative:

> Enter Mr. Tulkinghorn, followed by Mercuries with lamps and candles.
> "No, no," says Sir Leicester, "I think not. My Lady, do you object to the twilight?"
> On the contrary, my Lady prefers it.
> "Volumnia?"
> O! nothing is so delicious to Volumnia, as to sit and talk in the dark.
> "Then take them away," says Sir Leicester. "Tulkinghorn, I beg your pardon. How do you do?" (p. 503)

By a low fire Tulkinghorn's tale is told "in the fast increasing darkness," and in the "cold pale light" of the moon Lady Dedlock can be glimpsed listening to him. At the end, when artificial light is restored, the effect is now not one of the dazzling brilliance but of an eerie distortion which has a nightmare quality: "It is past ten, when Sir Leicester begs Mr. Tulkinghorn to ring for candles. Then the stream of moonlight has swelled into a lake, and then Lady Dedlock for the first time moves, and rises, and comes forward to a table for a glass of water. Winking cousins, batlike in the candle glare, crowd round to give it" (p. 506).

This vivid scene raises an important critical question which here can only be glanced at. Robert Liddell, after praising Dickens as "supreme" among the symbolists, a novelist who "provides vast Wagnerian settings for his dramas," cites as an example one of the Chesney Wold scenes in which Lady Dedlock appears—an outdoor rather than an indoor scene. In Liddell's view, the "drama" of Lady Dedlock is "impossible" and does not engage us, and he concludes, somewhat severely: "it is more creditable to cause pity and terror by the happenings in a story, rather than by atmosphere."[35]

Of Chapter 40, the same complaint could certainly be made. It is quite true that our attention in the drawing-room scenes does not center upon the sufferings of Lady Dedlock, as Racine, let us say, would have presented them. Elements of the Racine-like drama are there, but not as the center of attention. If that is exclusively what we want, we must go to another shop. Our feelings are, nevertheless, engaged. They are engaged by what we see: an illuminated roomscape in which the play of light and shade, evoked by a great prose poet, is charged with a significance of its own, involving not so much the fate of an individual character as that of a whole society and ultimately of mankind itself. Reinforcing all this is a sense of the unreality, under changing lights, of this unsubstantial pageant as glimpsed from a Chesney Wold window: "All that prospect, which from the terrace looked so near, has moved solemnly away, and changed—not the first nor the last of beautiful things that look so near and will so change—into a distant phantom" (p. 498).

Firelight

The illuminated spectacle, then, can be relished for itself as a visual experience, but in addition it can involve us in evaluation as well as in sensory appreciation. This dual response is especially applicable for the last kind of lighting which remains to be touched on—firelight. In almost every interior scene in *Bleak House* a grate fire is mentioned, or if not mentioned, we can usually assume one to have been there—even, at times, in summer. Scenes lit by fire differ from those by gas, lantern, lamp, or candle in a way obvious enough: fire generates not only light but warmth. In this

[35] Robert Liddell, in *Charles Dickens: A Critical Anthology*, ed. Stephen Wall (Harmondsworth: Penguin, 1970), pp. 350–51. For a more sympathetic analysis see C. B. Cox, "A Dickens Landscape," *Critical Quarterly*, 2 (1960), 58–60.

double role it serves most readily to provide a measure for evaluating the moral order of the several different households and establishments of which *Bleak House* tells the stories. Fire, according to Gaston Bachelard, has served man by prompting him to thoughts of renewal rather than of destruction.[36] For Dickens, fire, the hearth fire, is even more important; for him fire betokens the possibilities of man's happiness on earth. It has been well said by Margaret Lane that the ideal household, in Dickens's writings, is one that is "warm, bright, clean."[37] Each attribute is a facet of order, while cold, darkness, and dirt—such as we encounter at Mrs. Jellyby's household, in Vholes's office, in the brickmaker's cottage, or in Krook's establishment—are related to the disorder and muddle of the dark Court of Chancery. Out of the more than twenty-four households and establishments described in *Bleak House,* perhaps only four or five meet the requirements of a warm, bright, tidy hearth. These are the London house of the Bagnets, Boythorn's country estate, the Bleak House of Esther and Jarndyce, the Bleak House of Esther and Alan Woodcourt, and the housekeeper's room of Mrs. Rouncewell. Like the lights struggling against the overwhelming darkness, each of these households has to struggle to overcome the penetrating cold, but here what might be termed warmth of spirit in affectionate human relations is more the issue than the physical warmth of fire itself. Physical cold as such is less prevalent in *Bleak House* than physical darkness. The 'prentice boy, in the opening scene, shivers on deck in the cold fog as Jo, the crossing-sweeper, will shiver in later scenes, and Miss Flite, in the genteel poverty of her garret, suffers keenly from lack of warmth. Yet it is not at the cold hearths of the poor where real chill is felt in *Bleak House;* it is, rather, in the company of characters who are spiritu-

---

[36] Gaston Bachelard, *La Psychoanalyse du Feu* (Paris: Gallimard, 1958), p. 40.
[37] Margaret Lane, "Dickens on the Hearth," in *Dickens 1970,* ed. Michael Slater (New York: Stein and Day, 1970), p. 155. On warm homes see also Lucien Pothet, "Images d'Intimité chez Dickens," *Etudes Anglaises,* 23 (1970), 136–57.

ally rather than physically frozen. Paradoxically, it is in front of their own warm hearths that such characters are sometimes shown to display their own lack of warmth, Esther's awesome aunt, for example, or Sir Leicester Dedlock. And of course there are the dreadful Smallweeds perched in front of their fire. " 'Whew!' says Mr. George. 'You are hot here. Always a fire, eh?' " (p. 264). It is remarkable how the author of *The Cricket on the Hearth* contrives to make that hot parlor of the Smallweeds into one of the chilliest roomscapes of his novel; it seems almost a parody of his celebrations, elsewhere, of the warmth of the domestic hearth.

A final example to consider is one in which fire and light play a joint role. This one is from Esther's half of the novel rather than the narrator's. I referred earlier, perhaps rather ungraciously, to Esther's somewhat cozy exit in the final chapter, and the present passage may serve to correct that impression. For we sometimes forget that Esther does have some harrowing experiences to suffer. One of these is her carriage ride in search of her lost mother. On the first night of the journey, her anxiety lends a kind of nightmare quality to what she sees that is comparable to the candlelit scene at Chesney Wold examined earlier. On the second day of the journey, at nightfall, she and Bucket stop briefly to change horses at a solitary inn: "where a landlady and her pretty daughters came to the carriage-door, entreating me to alight and refresh myself while the horses were making ready. I thought it would be uncharitable to refuse. They took me up-stairs to a warm room, and left me there" (p. 687). It has been "extremely cold" all day, but the snow was "only partially frozen." From the window of the warm room Esther looks out at a "wood of dark pine-trees." "Their branches were encumbered with snow, and it silently dropped off in wet heaps while I stood at the window. Night was setting in, and its bleakness was enhanced by the contrast of the pictured fire glowing and gleaming in the window-pane" (p. 688). As J. Hillis Miller notes, the melting snow can evoke for us the melting mood of Esther's doomed mother as she gropes her way to her death.[38] But for our purposes, the focus is on Esther's experience of the firelit hearth and on the inhospitable cold and darkness on the other side of the windows:

> They cushioned me up, on a large sofa by the fire. . . . A good endearing creature she [the landlady] was. She, and her three fair girls all so busy about me. I was to take hot soup and broiled fowl, while Mr. Bucket dried himself and dined elsewhere; but I could not do it when a snug round table was presently spread by the fireside, though I was very unwilling to disappoint them. However, I could take some toast and some hot negus; and as I really enjoyed that refreshment, it made some recompense.
>
> Punctual to the time, at the half-hour's end the carriage came rumbling under the gateway, and they took me down, warmed, refreshed, comforted by kindness, and safe (I assured them) not to faint any more. After I had got in and had taken a grateful leave of them all, the youngest daughter—a blooming girl of nineteen, who was to be the first married, they told me—got upon the carriage step, reached in, and kissed me. I have never seen her, from that hour, but I think of her to this hour as my friend.
>
> The transparent windows with the fire and light, looking so bright and warm from the cold darkness out of doors, were soon gone, and again we were crushing and churning the loose snow. (P. 688)

The passage portrays a passing episode in a journey rather than a dramatic climax, and the tone is subdued rather than high-pitched. Yet it is especially representative of the world of *Bleak House*. There are ingredients here which remind us of the early Christmas-card Dickens, of the coach ride episode in *Martin Chuzzlewit,* for example, with its chorus of jolly Yohos, or of the hearty scenes of inn-yards and of firelit inn parlors in *Pickwick Papers.* Yet in the later novel, how different! What Hemingway called, in one of his best stories, "A Clean Well-Lighted Place," finds here

---

[38] Miller, p. 203. See also the useful short essay by Susan Moth, which concludes with a discussion of this episode: "The Light / Darkness / Sight Imagery in *Bleak House,*" *Dickens Studies,* 1 (1965), 76–85.

a comparable exemplum in a world of isolation and palpable darkness. Light shines; fires burn; warmhearted people embrace—as they did in *Pickwick*. But these reassuring aspects of life's order and meaning are emphatically surrounded now by cold, by pressure of dark night, and by visions of a lonely and suffering mankind.

8 | GEORGE ELIOT'S DOUBLE LIFE / *The Mill on the Floss* as a Bildungsroman

Jerome H. Buckley

In 1855 Marian Evans convinced George Henry Lewes by a single piece in the *Westminster Review* that she was a writer of "genius."[1] Yet Lewes could scarcely have predicted from the vitriolic essay, an attack on the popular Evangelical preacher John Cumming, that she would one day prove a novelist as remarkable for her compassion as for her analytic rigor. Looking back, however, from the spring of 1860, when George Eliot completed *The Mill on the Floss,* he might have seen a foreshadowing of her approach to her own fiction in an article on the morality of *Wilhelm Meister,* which she had written at about the same time as

---

This chapter is adapted by permission from *Season of Youth: The Bildungsroman from Dickens to Golding* by Jerome Hamilton Buckley, Cambridge, Mass.: Harvard University Press. Copyright © 1974 by the President and Fellows of Harvard College.

[1] The essay, "Evangelical Teaching: Dr. Cumming," appeared in October 1855. For Lewes's comment, see J. W. Cross, *George Eliot's Life as Related in her Letters and Journals,* 3 vols. (New York, 1885), I, 384, and also the definitive modern biography by Gordon S. Haight, *George Eliot* (New York: Oxford University Press, 1968), p. 186.

her exposé of Cumming. Goethe, she had argued, took no moral side either for or against his characters; he delighted simply in "living, generous humanity—mixed and erring, and self-deluding, but saved from utter corruption by the salt of some noble impulse, some disinterested effort, some beam of good nature, even though grotesque or homely."[2]

She herself found it difficult to remain so neutral, and *The Mill on the Floss* is certainly less detached than Goethe's novel. But she strove in all her fiction to control her acerbity, to practice tolerance and understanding, and to suspend censorious judgment of the erring and the self-deluded, the homely and the unheroic. She was no longer so self-righteous in her intellectual commitments, or so assured in her rejections, as she had been in the days of her higher journalism.

While still at work on *The Mill*, she described her changed disposition: "Many things," she told a friend, "that I should have argued against ten years ago, I now feel myself too ignorant and too limited in moral sensibility to speak of with confident disapprobation: on many points where I used to delight in expressing intellectual difference, I now delight in feeling an emotional agreement."[3] Though these remarks specifically concern her altered regard for religion, even for Evangelical Christianity, the mood carries over to the whole moral life of her novel. The most intellectual novelist of her time was also the most considerate of human feelings.

Like *Wilhelm Meister*, *The Mill on the Floss* is a Bildungsroman, though neither Goethe, who established the genre

---

[2] "The Morality of *Wilhelm Meister*," reprinted from the *Leader*, July 21, 1855, in Thomas Pinney, ed., *Essays of George Eliot* (London: Routledge and Kegan Paul, 1963), p. 144. George Eliot and Lewes read *Wilhelm Meister* together in 1854 and were to read it again, aloud, in 1870; see Gordon S. Haight, ed., *The George Eliot Letters*, 7 vols. (New Haven: Yale University Press, 1954–55), II, 186 n. 3, and V, 124 (cited hereafter as *Letters*). Since Lewes was the able biographer of Goethe, George Eliot was probably more familiar with the "first" Bildungsroman than was any other English novelist attempting the genre.

[3] Letter to D'Albert Durade, *Letters*, III, 231, quoted in Haight, *George Eliot*, p. 331.

in European literature, nor George Eliot, who helped give it a characteristically English direction, ever used that label. As a Bildungsroman, it takes its place among a good many distinguished British novels of the kind—notably, *Great Expectations, The Ordeal of Richard Feverel, The Way of All Flesh, Jude the Obscure, Sons and Lovers,* and *A Portrait of the Artist as a Young Man,* all narratives of an apprenticeship to life. Though it accords childhood more attention than Goethe grants the early years of Wilhelm, it is essentially, like Goethe's book, a chronicle of adolescence, of the pains of growing up and of the trials to be faced before reaching physical maturity and some sort of integration of personality.[4] Here, as in other examples of the genre, "education" by emotional experience as much as by formal schooling is a central issue; first love and misplaced affection is a familiar theme; the finding of a career, or a work in life to do, and the necessity of money are recurrent concerns; and the questions of what constitutes the true gentleman or lady has a characteristic relevance. Like most English Bildungsromane (and many German ones, too), *The Mill* is heavily autobiographical, and the personal engagement of the novelist leads inevitably to some distortions of perspective, occasional failures in objectivity.[5] Finally, like nearly all Victorian life-novels, it was clearly influenced by

---

[4] On the Bildungsroman in England and its debt to Goethe, see Susanne Howe [Nobbe], *Wilhelm Meister and his English Kinsmen* (New York: Columbia University Press, 1930). Mrs. Nobbe, however, uses the term in a more restricted sense than I do. See also G. B. Tennyson, "The Bildungsroman in Nineteenth-Century English Literature," in *Medieval Epic to the "Epic Theater" of Brecht,* ed. Rosario P. Armato and John M. Spalek (Los Angeles: University of California Press, 1968), pp. 135–46. Professor Tennyson points out how loosely the term is used in relation to the English novel, where the distinction is seldom made between an *Entwicklungsroman* ("merely the novel of development") and a Bildungsroman ("the novel of harmonious cultivation of the whole personality") (p. 142). Certainly Maggie Tulliver's quest is less self-conscious than Wilhelm Meister's.

[5] See also my essay "Autobiography in the English Bildungsroman," in *The Interpretation of Narrative,* ed. Morton W. Bloomfield (Cambridge, Mass.: Harvard University Press, 1970), p. 95.

David Copperfield, the first major English Bildungsroman, which appeared ten years earlier.

Had its composition been delayed a few months, *The Mill on the Floss* might have immediately preceded *Great Expectations* as a serial in Dickens's *All the Year Round;* for Dickens, who was among the first to identify as a woman the writer using the pseudonym "George Eliot," was eager to have her contribute to his new weekly.[6] George Eliot, in turn, admired Dickens and appreciated his largeness of spirit, though she mistrusted his influence and wished to pursue independently her own fictional objectives. Minor characters in *The Mill*—especially Bob Jakin, with his fat mother and little wife, "Mrs. Jakin the larger and Mrs. Jakin the less," and his dog Mumps—suggest indebtedness to Dickens; and Bob's cozening of niggardly Aunt Glegg as he disposes of his yard goods has all the irrelevance and something of the charm of a Dickensian comic interlude. But, quite apart from the question of influence, George Eliot revealed a skill in depicting childhood unequaled since *David Copperfield* and, at least according to Henry James, unsurpassed anywhere in English fiction.[7] Like Dickens, she was able to enter the child's mind without adult condescension, to appreciate the "strangely perspectiveless" intensity with which a child endures his present griefs and disappointments, and to understand how—as Wordsworth insisted—every moment of childhood suffering leaves some trace which blends itself "irrecoverably with the firmer texture of our youth and manhood."[8] In this respect, as in others, *The Mill on the Floss* deserves to stand beside *Great Expectations:* Maggie Tulliver's miseries as a willful nine-year-old are no less real than Pip's traumatic terrors; her wincing from the rebukes of her aunts at dinner is comparable to Pip's discomfort across the table from Pumblechook and Mrs. Joe; her dream of joining the

---

[6] See Haight, *George Eliot,* pp. 310–11.
[7] See Henry James, "The Novels of George Eliot," *Atlantic Monthly,* 18 (1866), 489, reprinted in *A Century of George Eliot Criticism,* ed. Gordon S. Haight (Boston: Houghton Mifflin, 1965), p. 51.
[8] *Mill,* Bk. I, Ch. 7.

gypsies is as convincingly self-protective as the romance with which Pip invests the spectral dreariness of Satis House. Neither novel distorts its picture of the child's life with false idealization; yet each curiously intimates that the end of childhood is somehow an expulsion from Eden. Pip leaves his early home—and a measure of innocence—as he travels through the rising mists to London; and the world, as in *Paradise Lost,* lies all before him. When Maggie fetches her brother Tom from school to face their father's illness and bankruptcy, she departs with him into the forest of adult experience: "They had gone forth together into their new life of sorrow and they would never more see the sunshine undimmed by remembered cares. They had entered the thorny wilderness and the golden gates of their childhood had for ever closed behind them."[9]

The Mill on the Floss differs from *Great Expectations* and other English Bildungsromane in that it sets out to describe the initiation of, not one, but two principal characters. Pip goes to his ordeal alone; Maggie and Tom, together in childhood, must confront the adult world together, must choose their separate paths, and must finally be reunited in death. But desite the double focus, the autobiographical component is strong. Maggie, we gather from topical allusions, was born in 1819, and Tom, three years earlier—the precise birthdates of Marian[10] Evans and her brother Isaac; and a good many episodes and even much of the setting (though it is transferred for purposes of plot to a coastal county) apparently reflect their early life in Warwickshire. George Eliot's later sonnet sequence, "Brother and Sister," readily identifiable as personal reminiscence, describes "the twin habit of that early time" in detail that is close at almost every point to that in the novel. Brother is protective, demanding, conscious of male superiority, quick-tempered, rigid in his concept of justice; when he takes Sister fishing, he scolds her for neglecting the line but

---

[9] *Mill,* last paragraph of Bk. II; *cf. Great Expectations,* end of Ch. 19.
[10] Her original name was Mary Anne, which Miss Evans changed to Marian on coming to London. I use the latter form to avoid confusion.

warmly lauds her success in hooking a silver perch. Sister is worshipful, eager for praise, sensitive to impressions; she rambles "puppy-like" with Brother across the daisied meadows, past the gypsy camp, along the river's edge, and together they learn:

> the meanings that give words a soul,
> The fear, the love, the primal passionate store,
> Whose shaping impulses make manhood whole.

Later she will remember those hours as "seed to all my after good," much as Wordsworth recalled his boyhood as "fair seed-time" of the soul. Though schooling and the ways of the adult world end the intimacy of the children, Sister trusts that Brother, too, has gained from their relationship:

> His years with others must the sweeter be
> For those brief days he spent in loving me.[11]

Before much of *The Mill* was written, George Eliot had denied that there would be any portraits from life in it,[12] and Tom, indeed, is not literally Isaac Evans. But we see the young Marian's affection for Isaac in Maggie's love of Tom; and in Tom's rejection of Maggie after her flight with Stephen, we can surely detect Isaac's relentless respectability, prompting his repudiation of Marian when he learned of her liaison with Lewes. Similarly, Maggie is not intended as a portrait of the artist as a young woman. Yet we know enough of the young Marian Evans to recognize a close temperamental affinity and to discover many details drawn from her experience. Like Maggie, she was attracted as a child to Defoe's *History of the Devil*,[13] read widely in the Latin classics, studied Euclid and logic, and found in

---

[11] "Brother and Sister," George Eliot, *Complete Poems* (Boston, n.d.), pp. 391–97. (Cited hereafter as *Poems*.) The sonnet sequence is dated 1869.

[12] Though made about *Adam Bede*, the comment is also pertinent to *The Mill:* "There is not a single portrait in the book, nor will there be in any future book of mine" (*Letters*, III, 99).

[13] George Eliot's interest in Defoe has been explored in detail by P. G. Maheu in *La Pensée religieuse et morale de George Eliot* (Paris: Didier, 1958).

Thomas à Kempis a profound revelation. Like Maggie, she was devoted to her father and nursed him through a long illness. Though her parents bore only a slight resemblance to Mr. and Mrs. Tulliver, her attitude toward her maternal relatives, the Pearsons, clearly inspired her brilliant study of the Dodsons. Her infatuation with John Chapman may have influenced her depiction of Stephen Guest, and her friendship with François D'Albert may have suggested Maggie's interest in Philip Wakem. Maggie, of course, is physically beautiful as Marian decidedly was not. She suffers no comparable religious struggle leading to a loss of faith. Though intelligent, she is not really, like Marian, a dedicated intellectual, and she gives no indication, even in her speech, that she could ever have become a trenchant essayist or a great novelist. Even so, the similarities are sufficiently numerous and striking to convince us that the narrator in the opening chapter leaning on the bridge, looking at the child Maggie, is the author silently, sympathetically, confronting her own past self.[14]

The epigraph on the title page, which is also the epitaph of Maggie and Tom and the last line of the novel, "In their death they were not divided," underlines the fact that *The Mill on the Floss* is by design a double life, a sort of contrapuntal Bildungsroman, comparing and contrasting hero and heroine as each moves into young adulthood. Most of the tentative titles while the writing was still in progress—*The Tulliver Family, The House of Tulliver, The Tullivers,* or *Life on the Floss*—indicated that more than one protagonist was

---

[14] Maggie is not named in the Prologue (Bk. I, Ch. 1) but is identified by her bonnet and her dog, "that queer white cur with the brown ear." Later (Ch. 4) the dog is introduced as "Yap, the queer white-and-brown terrier with one ear turned back." When Maggie first enters (she has been seen through the parlor window, at the river edge), she immediately throws off her bonnet. The narrator carefully conceals her own (some critics say *his*) identity, but there is no effort to establish a persona as narrator and no reason to think of her as other than the omniscient author. Henry Auster makes an excellent case for equating the narrator and the author in his *Local Habitations: Regionalism in the Early Novels of George Eliot* (Cambridge, Mass.: Harvard University Press, 1970), pp. 171–72.

involved; and even *Sister Maggie,* the most frequently mentioned, implied a brother's judgment or point of view. On completing the manuscript, George Eliot clearly affirmed her intention; the three published volumes, she told John Blackwood, would have "the psychological unity that springs from their being the history of two closely related lives from beginning to end."[15] Accordingly, the attention given to Tom's schooling and to Tom's job, which some readers have thought excessive,[16] rests on the premise that Tom as well as Maggie merits our concern. In our estimate of the novel, we must not ignore the declared duality of purpose. We must not allow our understandable preference for Maggie to obscure the dominant theme of at least three-quarters of the book, the symbiotic relationship of sister and brother.

The Mill on the Floss pays far more heed than any earlier English Bildungsroman to the secret springs of family life, its understandings and constraints, its possessiveness and limited freedoms, its unspoken and often inarticulate loyalties. For the first time it complicates the motif of antagonism between father and son—here also between mother and daughter—by a self-conscious application of the "laws" of heredity, and in so doing it anticipates *The Way of All Flesh, Jude the Obscure,* and *Sons and Lovers,* in each of which "inherited characteristics" play a significant role. When we first meet Mr. Tulliver, he is telling Mrs. Tulliver of his plans for Tom's education and is rather ruefully comparing the boy's mental capacities with Maggie's:

"What I'm a bit afraid on is, as Tom hasn't got the right sort o' brains for a smart fellow. I doubt he's a bit slowish. He takes after your family, Bessy."

"Yes, that he does," said Mrs. Tulliver, accepting the last prop-

---

[15] *Letters,* III, 267.

[16] W. J. Harvey, for example, one of George Eliot's ablest critics, charges a "want of economy" in Bk. II, which describes Tom's school days. He considers Tom's education largely irrelevant to the "education" of Maggie, which seems to him the main theme of the novel. See Harvey, *The Art of George Eliot* (London: Chatto and Windus, 1961), p. 87.

osition entirely on its own merits; "he's wonderful for liking a deal o' salt in his broth. That was my brother's way, and my father's before him"

"It seems a bit of a pity, though," said Mr. Tulliver, "as the lad should take after the mother's side i'stead o' the little wench. That's the worst on't wi' the crossing o' breeds: you can never justly calkilate what'll come on't. The little un takes after my side, now: she's twice as 'cute as Tom. Too 'cute for a woman, I'm afraid," continued Mr. Tulliver, turning his head dubiously first on one side and then on the other.[17]

Tom proves indeed a Dodson in his sense of property and his way with money, his lack of imagination, his self-righteous deportment, and his unswerving honesty. Yet he has his father's stubborn will and vengeful temper, and he is ultimately less merciful than Aunt Glegg, who is ready to receive the disgraced Maggie, whom he has rejected. Maggie, on the other hand, though full of forgiveness and never vindictive, is decidedly a Tulliver, impulsive, generous, excitable, full-blooded, tall and awkward as a growing girl, handsome as a young woman, yet never conventionally pretty like her mother or her dainty cousin Lucy. Her first speech, as she enters disheveled and muddied from her play by the river, aligns her against the orderly Dodsons: she will not make a counterpane for Aunt Glegg, "I don't want to do anything for my Aunt Glegg—I don't like her." By the same token she feels drawn to her father's sister, the kindly, improvident, prolific Aunt Gritty. And Mr. Tulliver, for his part, is so devoted to Maggie that he shows special consideration for Gritty in the hope that Tom will one day follow his example in the practice of brotherly love. Though each character is free to make his moral choices and must be held responsible for his decisions, the disposition of each is in large part predetermined, the product of his mixed inheritance.

If Maggie must suffer as an imprudent Tulliver, Tom can be expected to control his energies and resources more efficiently, for "nobody had ever heard of a Dodson who

---

[17] *Mill*, Bk. I, Ch. 2.

had ruined himself: it was not the way of that family."[18] Better equipped than the Tullivers to face the struggle for survival, the Dodsons better exemplify the provincial ethic described in the learned first chapter of Book IV, "A Variety of Protestantism Unknown to Bossuet":

> Here, one has conventional worldly notions and habits without instruction and without polish—surely the most prosaic form of human life: proud respectability in a gig of unfashionable build: worldliness without side-dishes.... The religion of the Dodsons consisted in revering whatever was customary and respectable. ... The Dodsons were a very proud race, and their pride lay in the utter frustration of all desire to tax them with a breach of traditional duty or propriety. A wholesome pride in many respects, since it identified honor with perfect integrity, thoroughness of work, and faithfulness to admitted rules. ... A conspicuous quality in the Dodson character was its genuineness: its vices and virtues alike were phases of a proud, honest, egosim, which had a hearty dislike to whatever made against its own credit and interest....

Anticipating *Middlemarch*, which George Eliot subtitled "A Study of Provincial Life," *The Mill on the Floss* introduces the theme of provincialism to English fiction. Dickens in *David Copperfield* and Meredith in *Richard Feverel* see the city as the center of corruption and temptation, but neither attempts a close analysis of the provincial mentality that their heroes, city-bound, are leaving behind. *Great Expectations* will evoke the marshes, the village, and the country town with incomparable vividness; but the setting of *The Mill*, less detailed visually, is far more precise in terms of social and intellectual history. The temper of St. Ogg's in all its complacency and aggressive respectability emerges as distinctly as the mood of the mean-souled, avaricious Verrières in *The Red and the Black,* though George Eliot's view is calmer and more judiciously balanced than Stendhal's. Henry James was reminded of Balzac (if Balzac had been less solemn) "by the attempt to classify the Dodsons socially in a scientific manner." And E. S. Dallas in an early

[18] *Mill*, Bk. IV, Ch. 1.

and perceptive review found "the odious Dodson family, . . . these mean, prosaic people," stunningly representative of "the sort of life which thousands upon thousands of our countrymen lead." Too careful a social analyst wholly to condemn her provincials, George Eliot was distressed by Dallas's reading. "I have certainly fulfilled my intention very badly," she said, "if I have made the Dodson honesty appear 'mean and uninteresting,' or made the payment of one's debts appear a contemptible virtue. . . . I am so far from hating the Dodsons myself, that I am rather aghast to find them ticketed with such very ugly adjectives."[19] Yet the novel both labels and dramatizes the "oppressive narrowness" that conditions the lives of Tom and Maggie.

George Eliot herself was at one time a young woman fresh from the provinces, eager, as *Westminster* essayist, to establish her sophistication and her freedom from all parochialism. Yet she allows Maggie and Tom no escape from the provincial setting and only occasional transcendence of the provincial ethic. Neither ever tastes the liberation of the great city, the challenge of cultural difference, the cosmopolitan diversity of manners and opinions. But each experiences something of the city's materialism in provincial St. Ogg's, where the successful Dodsons belong and the failing Mr. Tulliver has no place. After two dreary years of schoolteaching, Maggie basks briefly in the favor of a moneyed small-town society and for the moment is almost seduced into believing that the fuller life she craves may lie in Lucy's comfortable world. After the disgrace of his father's bankruptcy, Tom dedicates himself, body and soul, to the most respected pursuit in St. Ogg's, the rapid acquisition of capital. Forgetful of the religious stuggles that molded its past, St. Ogg's is resolutely devoted to the present, the 1830s, when the industrial revolution has brought new machines and new modes of production, and the resourceful entrepreneur flourishes while the less-adaptable

---

[19] James, "The Novels of George Eliot," p. 490, and E. S. Dallas in *The Times*, May 19, 1860, p. 10, both reprinted in Haight, *Criticism*, pp. 9, 11, 52. For George Eliot's comment, see *Letters*, III, 299.

businessman flounders. St. Ogg's proves pharisaical and cruel to Maggie, but it is not the ultimate villain of the novel, for Maggie is too strong to be destroyed by the tyranny of public opinion. And it is not, as some readers have alleged, really "decadent." The flood does not come upon it as a judgment, for it survives the flood, and when the waters recede, "the wharves and warehouses on the Floss [are] busy again, with echoes of eager voices, with hopeful lading and unlading."[20]

As we might expect, St. Ogg's has only the crudest notion of what constitutes a lady or a gentleman. The one clear requirement, best met by Lucy Deane and her suitor, the provincial dandy Stephen Guest, is apparently idle affluence. Tom feels that Maggie has somehow degraded herself by serving as a teacher. "I wished my sister to be a lady," he tells her, "and I would always have taken care of you, as my father desired, until you were well married."[21] At Lucy's, Maggie is, not reluctantly, "introduced for the first time to the young lady's life";[22] yet her past suggests an intellectual restlessness not to be satisfied for long with the mere amenities of polite conversation. Tom himself has been sent to Mr. Stelling's school, where he must learn Latin and Euclid, which, as Philip Wakem informs him, belong to a general culture and are therefore a necessary "part of education of a gentleman."[23] But even in such terms, which are beyond the usual grasp of St. Ogg's, the gentlemanly ideal has little relevance to the needs or demands of the tradesman's life; and Tom's education is largely ineffectual, for Tom is no scholar and, unlike Maggie, has no real respect for books or ideas. Yet, in spite of

---

[20] *Mill,* "Conclusion." On St. Ogg's, see Auster, pp. 141–69, and U. C. Knoepflmacher, *George Eliot's Early Novels* (Berkeley: University of California Press, 1968), pp. 194–200.

[21] *Mill,* Bk. VI, Ch. 4. Tom's attitude here is no doubt close to that of Isaac Evans, who was annoyed at his sister's religious heterodoxy and afraid that it would spoil her chance of making a good match; see Haight, *George Eliot,* p. 40.

[22] *Mill,* Bk. VI, Ch. 6.

[23] *Mill,* Bk. II, Ch. 3.

himself, he acquires at Mr. Stelling's something of the deportment of a gentleman and a confident, cultivated speech, which sufficiently impresses his father.[24]

We learn nothing of Maggie's education at Miss Firniss's boarding school, where presumably she was disciplined in less intellectual, ladylike pursuits, which she must have heartily disliked. Nor are we given any details about her teaching career, apart from incidental references to the "dreary situation" and the "third-rate schoolroom, with all its jarring sounds and petty round of tasks."[25] Tom's rise in trade, on the other hand, is described as circumstantially as if he were the single protagonist of the Bildungsroman. The narrator denies that Tom is simply "the spooney type of the Industrious Apprentice," since he has "a very strong appetite for pleasure."[26] But his desire is subject to his will, and he subordinates all else to the recovery of the family fortunes. Eventually he berates Maggie, "You struggled with feelings, you say. Yes! *I* have had feelings to struggle with, but I conquered them. I have had a harder life than you have had, but I have found *my* comfort in doing my duty."[27] His work is joyless and obsessive. If he has once secretly nursed a sentimental regard for Lucy, he now has no time for love. His confession startles even his money-minded Uncle Deane: "I want to have plenty of work. There's nothing else I care about much."[28] He has made his adjustment to the materialism of St. Ogg's with almost frightening efficiency, and his initiation seems complete.

So cold, calculating, self-righteous, and unregretful does

---

[24] George Eliot attacks both the curriculum and the learning by rote at Mr. Stelling's but then, with typical fairness, adds: "Nevertheless, there was a visible improvement in Tom under this training, perhaps because he was not a boy in the abstract, existing solely to illustrate the evils of a mistaken education, but a boy made of flesh and blood, with dispositions not entirely at the mercy of circumstance" (Bk. II, Ch. 4).
[25] *Mill*, Bk. VI, Ch. 3.
[26] *Mill*, Bk. V, Ch. 2.
[27] *Mill*, Bk. VII, Ch. 1.
[28] *Mill*, Bk. VI, Ch. 5.

Tom appear, that many readers have found him repulsive, and at least one sensitive critic has declared him altogether detestable and Maggie's love for him incomprehensible, "almost like a piece of perverseness, an aberration."[29] Maggie on one occasion delivers as severe an indictment:

> "Don't suppose that I think you are right, Tom, or that I bow to your will.... You have been reproaching other people all your life—you have always been sure you yourself are right; it is because you have not a mind large enough to see that there is anything better than your own conduct and your own petty aims.... You have no pity; you have no sense of your own imperfection and your own sins. It is a sin to be hard; it is not fitting for a mortal—for a Christian. You are nothing but a Pharisee."[30]

But Maggie speaks here only on special provocation. Her affection for Tom is far stronger than her anger, and it is neither perverse nor incomprehensible. Shortly after her outburst she sees Tom in his best light, in his short moment of triumph when his long self-denial finally absolves his father's debt; and she feels that his goodness far outweighs his faults. The author makes clear from the beginning Tom's virtues as well as his vices. Though as a boy he thinks all girls "silly," Tom is "very fond of his sister" and means "always to take care of her." He is imposed upon by Mrs. Stelling when asked to mind her infant daughter, and he might be expected to hate "the little cherub," but, we are told, he is "too kind-hearted a lad for that—there [is] too much in him of the fibre that turns to true manliness, and to protecting pity for the weak." His first impulses at the time of his father's bankruptcy are right and generous; he will see that the servant Luke's loan is immediately repaid and that his uncle Moss's promissory note is destroyed. "There were subjects, you perceive," the narrator comments admiringly, "on which Tom was much quicker than on the niceties of classical construction, or the relations of a mathematical demonstration." Later, when he scolds

---

[29] Gerald Bullett, *George Eliot: her Life and Books* (New Haven: Yale University Press, 1948), pp. 194, 197.
[30] *Mill*, Bk. V, Ch. 5.

Maggie for needlessly humiliating herself, we are asked to see in his rebuke "some tenderness and bravery mingled with the worldliness and self-assertion."[31] Though he fails Maggie in her time of distress, Tom is cruelly misguided rather than essentially vicious. We should be able to understand George Eliot's insistence that she had painted Tom "with as much love and pity as Maggie."[32] And we should credit his essential quality sufficiently to believe him capable of a final moment of insight which suddenly reverses the direction of his life, a moment in which he catches the full import of Maggie's devotion: "It came with so overpowering a force—it was such a new revelation to his spirit of the depths in life that had lain beyond his vision which he had fancied so keen and clear—that he was unable to ask a question."[33]

While Tom has tried to live by self-reliance and without love, Maggie from early childhood has craved affectionate or admiring attention. "The need of being loved," we learn at the outset, is "the strongest need in poor Maggie's nature." Later, on her visit to Tom's school, Philip Wakem is struck by her dark eyes "full of unsatisfied intelligence and unsatisfied, beseeching affection." The intelligence leads her to books, but the desire to be thought quick and clever is almost as compelling as her delight in knowledge; aware as a child that she will not be praised like Lucy for daintiness or grace, she attempts, as when she discusses Defoe with Mr. Riley or geometry with Mr. Stelling, to impress with her intellectual capacity. When she reaches young adulthood, she has become a woman of great physical attraction ("this tall dark-eyed nymph with her jet-black coronet of hair"),[34] and though she claims to dislike compliments, she is grateful to Stephen Guest for making her conscious of the fact.

D. H. Lawrence would one day commend Maggie's

---

[31] *Mill*, Bk. I, Ch. 5; Bk. II, Ch. 1; Bk. III, Ch. 4; Bk. IV, Ch. 3.
[32] *Letters*, III, 299.
[33] *Mill*, Bk. VII, Ch. 5.
[34] *Mill*, Bk. I, Ch. 5; Bk. II, Ch. 5.

abundant vitality and declare that he saw in "the smooth branches of the beech trees" a reminder of her arms.[35] George Eliot might have been both pleased and alarmed by so sensual a response to her heroine, for she seems clearly, especially in the last books of the novel, to have identified with Maggie, and Maggie's beauty is apparently a belated fulfillment of the wishes of the young Marian Evans. A distinctly subjective note enters the analysis of Maggie's emotion; the novelist takes sides, and the connotative vocabulary registers her own attitude as much as her character's:

> Sometimes Maggie thought she could have been contented with absorbing fancies; if she could have had all Scott's novels and all Byron's poems! Then, perhaps, she might have found happiness enough to dull her sensibility to her actual daily life. And yet ... they were hardly what she wanted. She could make dream-worlds of her own—but no dream-world would satisfy her now. She wanted some explanation of this hard, real life: the unhappy-looking father, seated at the dull breakfast-table; the childish, bewildered mother; the little sordid tasks that filled the hours, or the more opresive emptiness of weary, joyless leisure; the need of some tender, demonstrative love; the cruel sense that Tom didn't mind what she thought or felt, and that they were no longer playfellows together; the privation of all pleasant things that had come to *her* more than to others: she wanted some key that would enable her to understand, and, in understanding, endure, the heavy weight that had fallen on her young heart.[36]

This passage immediately precedes—or introduces—the description of Maggie's discovery of Thomas à Kempis and the way of renunciation, an event we know to have been autobiographical in origin. Here and elsewhere—as Virginia Woolf and F. R. Leavis, among others, have pointed out[37]—George Eliot falters when she asks "poor Maggie"

---

[35] Lawrence, quoted by "E. T." (Jessie Chambers), in *D. H. Lawrence: A Personal Record* (London: Cass, 1965), p. 98.

[36] *Mill*, Bk. IV, Ch. 3.

[37] See Virginia Woolf, *The Common Reader* (New York: Harcourt Brace, 1953), pp. 173–74, and F. R. Leavis, *The Great Tradition* (Garden City, N.Y.: Doubleday, 1954), pp. 55–58.

to share in her "young heart" the hungers of her own adolescence. At such moments a too closely engaged sympathy may lead to the distortions of self-pity. Maggie is not to be allowed a new career as a successful writer; there will be no deliverance in human time from the "sordid tasks" of her narrow world. The child Maggie could be delineated with perspective and very little sentimentality. Pathos, delivered in affective language, somewhat blurs the later image; Maggie as a young woman necessarily escapes most of the irony that touches—and helps define—the other characters.[38]

Nevertheless, the "mature" Maggie has her immaturities, of which George Eliot is not wholly unaware. She has not outgrown her early tendency to lapse suddenly, like little Sister in the sonnet sequence, into dreamy reverie. When she is literally "borne along by the tide" with Stephen, she is at the same time being lulled into semiconsciousness by the drift of her daydreaming. Her absentmindedness encourages frequent flights from reality, and the indulgence in such "fantasy life" may, as a recent critic suggests, be the mark of a neurotic personality.[39] But Maggie's weakness in this respect is simply a product of her strength, of her quality as a human being; her fantasies arise from a sympathetic imagination that can find no adequate release in the world of the mill or St. Ogg's. Both the need to establish harmony in the present and the desire to escape to a less troubling order are apparent in her sensitive respone to music. When she was a child, a tune from Uncle Pullet's snuffbox was enough to reconcile her to angry Tom, and Christmas carolers beneath her windows could seem like angel voices in the heavens. At the time of her father's collapse she feels most keenly the loss of the family piano and the deprivation of music, and she is described as "a

---

[38] Cf. Knoepflmacher, p. 208.

[39] See Knoepflmacher, pp. 210, 212: "Tom embraces the reality of St. Ogg's; Maggie yields to the fantasy life that was her father's destruction. . . . Like Mr. Tulliver, the girl possesses a 'soul untrained for inevitable struggles': like the miller, she is deeply neurotic, incapable of accepting what Freud would call the 'reality principle.'"

creature full of eager, passionate longings for all that was beautiful and glad, thirsty for all knowledge, with an ear straining after dreamy music that died away and would not come near to her." Later, stimulated by a musical evening at Lucy's, she casts aside her self-denying austerity and confesses, "I think I should have no other mortal wants if I could always have plenty of music." Maggie's "sensibility to the supreme excitement of music," the author comments, is an aspect of "that passionate sensibility" which makes "her faults and virtues all merge in each other."[40]

Maggie, for better or for worse, is an enthusiast, whether the object of her commitment is music or philosophy. For a considerable period of her unhappy youth, it is the latter; she gives herself completely to the cult of renunciation she has learned from Thomas à Kempis. Her interest in the *Imitation of Christ,* as we know, was shared by George Eliot, even at the time of writing *The Mill,* but the fervor of her commitment is parallel only to the earlier devotion of Marian Evans to an extreme Evangelicalism.[41] Maggie sees the sacrifice of selfish pleasure as the source of true happiness, and resigned acceptance as the key to all virtue. Yet she is neither joyful nor wholly sinless in her negations. Characteristically, she throws "some exaggeration and wilfulness, some pride and impetuosity, even into her self-renunciation," with the result that she often loses "the spirit of humility by being excessive in the outward act." Her self-denial is far less mature and purposeful than the sort of self-discipline tht leads Princess Ottila, in Meredith's later Bildungsroman, *The Adventures of Harry Richmond,* acting from a sense of duty, to renounce the hero. It is rather, as Philip perceives, "a narrow asceticism" or, again, "a narrow self-delusive fanaticism," which stupefies, not quickens, the spirit, for "it is stupefaction," he explains, "to remain in ignorance—to shut up all the avenues by which the life of your fellow-men might become known to you."[42]

[40] *Mill,* Bk. III, Ch. 5; Bk. VI, Ch. 3; Bk. VI, Ch. 6.
[41] Witness the Evangelical letters of 1840 to Mr. and Mrs. Samuel Evans, in *Letters,* I, 39, 61, 73.
[42] *Mill,* Bk. IV, Ch. 3; Bk. V, Chs. 1, 3.

When Philip assails her ascetic creed, Maggie half recognizes the truth of his attack and half suspects him of advancing his own self-interest. In effect he is speaking for George Eliot, who deplored the unnecessary stifling of the intelligence. Philip indeed is the only character in the novel properly equipped to appreciate Maggie's intellectual capacities and to value the strength and delicacy of her feelings. He is also the only one who really escapes the provincialism of St. Ogg's and can bring a broad general culture to bear on his judgments of art and life. Sensitive and made more so by his handicap, tender, high-strung, occasionally petulant, Philip awakens Maggie's protective instinct, her gratitude and even her warm affection, but not her love. He is her faithful confidant, aware that he is cherished as such, yet also aware that, unlike Stephen Guest, he exerts little or no sexual attraction. The difference in Maggie's response to the two young men manifests itself, appropriately enough, in their singing at Lucy's. Philip chooses an aria by Bellini, pleading a deathless constancy, which he renders in a plaintive tenor. Maggie is "touched, not thrilled by the song." But Stephen scoffs at sweetly tenored sentiment and, by way of antidote, in a vibrant bass rolls out the cavalier lyric, "Shall I, wasting in despair, / Die because a woman's fair?" The very air of the music room pulses to the sound, and Maggie, "in spite of her resistance to the spirit of the song and to the singer, [is] taken hold of and shaken by the invisible influence— [is] borne along by a wave too strong for her."[43]

Stephen is a Victorian schoolgirl's notion of a dashing gallant. His every gesture is underlined with epithets of decorous boldness. His is "a violent well-known ring at the doorbell resounding through the house." He enters with a "bright strong presence and strong voice." He charms his female companions with "a half-ardent, half-sarcastic glance under his well-marked horizontal eyebrows. He hums a tune "in his deep 'brum-brum,' very pleasant to hear," and sings "with saucy energy." He guides a lady's

[43] *Mill*, Bk. VI, Ch. 7.

arm "with a firm grasp" and habitually smiles "down from his tall height." From the beginning many readers have thought this provincial paragon a quite unworthy mate for a young woman of Maggie's intelligence and sensibility, though few have been so severe as Swinburne, who considered him a mere "thing" to inspire "bitter disgust and sickening disdain."[44] George Eliot herself has been censured for drawing Stephen with obvious approval, as if, mature in so much less, she failed utterly to recognize his limitations, or as if such a man might once have fulfilled the dreams of Marian Evans. A few critics have insisted that the portrait is satiric, for there is indeed an unmistakable irony in his introduction: "Mr. Stephen Guest, whose diamond ring, attar of roses, and air of nonchalant leisure, at twelve o'clock in the day, are the graceful and odoriferous result of the largest oil-mill and the most extensive wharf in St. Ogg's."[45] But the irony soon yields to amused sympathy, and before long serious regard replaces the amusement. Beside either Tom or Philip, Stephen remains a shadowy two-dimensional figure, described frequently as vigorous, but charged with no inner vitality. Had he been more fully realized, he might have been the male counterpart of Rosamond Vincy in *Middlemarch*—likewise the selfish product of provincial money and an education in the superficial graces. George Eliot is able to see Rosamond in perspective and to detect a streak of "commonness" in the intelligent Dr. Lydgate, whom Rosamond ensnares. If we are not to think Maggie similarly vulgar in her tastes (and the long exposition of the novel gives us no reason or wish to do so), we must regard Stephen simply as an unsuccessful device to advance the plot. We must accept the premise of Maggie's sexual attraction to him and assume that he can indeed offer her a "great temptation"[46] to ignore the call of duty.

[44] Swinburne, in his *Note on Charlotte Brontë* (1877), reprinted in Haight, *Criticism*, p. 127.
[45] *Mill*, Bk. VI, Ch. 1.
[46] Bk. VI is entitled "The Great Temptation."

A modern reader finds it difficult to grasp the enormity of the transgression. Maggie drifts dreamily out to sea with Stephen and, bemused and bewildered, is taken aboard a Dutch freighter; but next day, wide-awake in the cold, hard light of morning, she rejects Stephen's proposal to elope and, reasoning with herself, resolves to return home. She has in fact resisted the tempter and refused to betray Lucy and Philip; and her "sin" exists only in the minds of the scandalmongers of St. Ogg's, to whom she is in all respects morally superior. But by her own standards she has been guilty of passivity, of allowing her enjoyment of the dreamy moment to subdue her free will. When Stephen first intimates that the tide has carried them too far to return and has in effect made their decision for them, Maggie protests, "You have wanted to deprive me of my choice." In the morning, when he argues that to all appearances they have already eloped, she replies firmly, "Don't try to prevail with me again. I couldn't choose yesterday." To Maggie, consent means deliberate and complete commitment. She cannot, she explains, deny all other loyalties and affections for the love of Stephen: "I have never consented to it with my whole mind. . . . It has never been my will to marry you."[47]

But when Stephen first leads her—literally—down the garden path to the rowboat "without any act of her own will," Maggie is aware only of the present. She has forgotten her "self"—or, as we are told in a curious phrase, "Memory was excluded,"—for her essential self is simply what she can remember; it is all that the past has made her. Moral choice presupposes the wakeful free will, but past experience offers precedents to guide and even to limit the choosing. "If the past is not to bind us," Maggie asks Stephen, "where can duty lie?" From her girlhood she has yearned for a sense of continuity. At the time of her father's bankruptcy she is distressed not so much by the imminence of poverty as by the thought that "the end of our lives will have nothing in it like the beginning." Later she tells Philip

---

[47] *Mill,* Bk. VI, Chs. 13, 14.

that she desires "no future that will break the ties of the past." Despite her attraction to Stephen, she knows that their life together could have "no sacredness," since to accept his proposal she would have to "let go the clue of life," her loyalty to others and her respect for her own antecedents. Though finally in disgrace, she insists on staying in St. Ogg's when she might well begin anew elsewhere, for she cannot endure the prospect of rootlessness, of being "cut off from the past." At the end, just before the floodwaters invade her room, she recoils from the temptation to ask Stephen to return; she will not once again exclude memory: "the sense of contradiction with her past self in her moments of strength and clearness," we are told, "came upon her like a pang of conscious degradation."[48]

Maggie's sensibility is distinctly Wordsworthian, and the phrasing that describes it in the last scene clearly echoes the passage in *The Prelude* that explains how "diversity of strength / Attends us, if but once we have been strong," a passage that George Eliot underlined in her own copy of the poem.[49] Maggie's natural piety, like Wordsworth's, is the force of memory that links past and present and so integrates and "educates" the personality. Piety so conceived is a major theme of *The Mill,* just as it is central to George Eliot's autobiographical sonnets, where Sister remembers her childhood with Brother and impressions which "Were but my growing self, are part of me, / My present Past, my root of piety."[50] Maggie's earliest memory, she tells Philip, is of standing beside Tom by the riverbank. Though far from blissfully happy, her childhood had an intensity which her later experience can scarcely match; and Tom is at the center of her most vivid recollections. Ultimately, Tom's approval matters more to her than Philip's affection or Stephen's love. Reconciliation with Tom, though won only in the last extremity, restores the

---

[48] *Mill,* Bk. VI, Ch. 13; Bk. VI, Ch. 14; Bk. III, Ch. 6; Bk. VI, Ch. 10; Bk. VI, Ch. 14; Bk. VII, Ch. 5.
[49] See Thomas Pinney, "George Eliot's Reading of Wordsworth: The Record," *Victorian Newsletter,* No. 24 (fall 1963), pp. 20–22.
[50] *Poems,* p. 394.

past and with it the coherence and continuity she has most ardently sought.

The end of Maggie's life and of Tom's does indeed, then, have something in it like the beginning. A pattern is complete; as the epigraph promised, in their death they are not divided. Yet the reunion, however necessary to the design of this double Bildungsroman, is effected only by completely ignoring or bypassing the moral and intellectual sources of the estrangement; and the scene is concluded with an unconvincing and sadly damaging sentimentality: "The boat reappeared—but brother and sister had gone down in an embrace never to be parted, living through again in one supreme moment the days when they had clasped their little hands in love, and roamed the daisied fields together."[51] Lewes told Blackwood, the publisher, that George Eliot's eyes grew "redder and swollener every morning" as, approaching the end of the novel, she lived through "her tragic story." But he added with deep satisfaction, "there is such a strain of poetry to relieve the tragedy that the more she cries, and the readers cry, the better say I."[52] Yet all her tears could not establish the reality of the resolution she had contrived. True tragedy must be inevitably and organically related to character and incident; the drowning of Maggie and Tom remains essentially a pathetic and gratuitous accident.

So pained was Henry James by the catastrophe that he wondered whether it was merely "a tardy expedient for the solution of Maggie's difficulties."[53] We know now that it certainly was not, since George Eliot, on first planning *The Mill,* made a careful study of murderous inundations before choosing the Trent River in Lincolnshire as a likely model for the flooding Floss. We have also her later assurance that she had looked forward to the tragic denouement "with attentive premeditation from the beginning."[54] And

---

[51] *Mill,* Bk. VII, Ch. 5.
[52] *Letters,* III, 269.
[53] James, "The Novels of George Eliot," p. 490.
[54] *Letters,* III, 374.

indeed, there are throughout the novel many references to rivers, floods, and drowning, and a good deal of water imagery and symbolism.[55] Though we are not inclined to credit the alarms of so foolish a woman, Mrs. Tulliver voices her constant fear that Tom and Maggie will be "brought in dead and drownded some way."[56] As children, Tom and Bob Jakin talk of past floods and how useful an ark will be to meet future ones. Maggie as a little girl recounts—almost prefiguratively—Defoe's tale of a witch's ordeal: "if she's drowned—and killed, you know—she's innocent, and not a witch, but only a poor silly old woman. But what good would it do her then, you know, when she was drowned? Only, I suppose, she'd go to heaven, and God would make it up to her."[57] The legend of St. Ogg, developed at some length, involves a blessing to protect his boat from the menace of the flood tides. Maggie, at sea with Stephen, dreams of being abandoned by St. Ogg and left to drown in troubled waters. Philip has also dreamed of Maggie's slipping helplessly down a waterfall; and he himself dislikes boating and teasingly warns Maggie not to "be selling her soul to that ghostly boatman who haunts the Floss—only for the sake of being drifted in a boat forever."[58] Nonetheless, despite all these carefully placed clues and intimations of tragedy, the ending, however deliberate in intention, does have the effect of a hasty expedient. The flood is a physical force outside the psychological framework of the action. It has no real relation to Maggie's dilemma;[59] it

---

[55] George Levine relates the water symbolism to George Eliot's reading of Feuerbach: "Intelligence as Deception: *The Mill on the Floss,*" *PMLA*, 80 (1965), 402–9. On the symbolism see also Knoepflmacher, pp. 164–78, and Harvey, pp. 234–36.

[56] *Mill*, Bk. I, Ch. 10; *cf.* Bk. I, Ch. 2, as Maggie's mother sees her through the window, "wanderin' up an' down by the water, like a wild thing: she'll tumble in some day," and then to Maggie, "You'll tumble in and be drownded some day, and then you'll be sorry you didn't do as mother told you."

[57] *Mill*, Bk. I, Ch. 3.

[58] *Mill*, Bk. VI, Ch. 3.

[59] Knoepflmacher (p. 220) also complains that there is "no causal connection" between Maggie's death and her flight with Stephen.

encroaches upon her melodramatically, an agent from without, just as she has resolved not to betray her past affections by calling back Stephen. Maggie is in the midst of prayer—"O God, if my life is to be long, let me live to bless and comfort'—when she is startled by a sudden cold stream beneath her feet; though she surely has not expected it, she is, we are told, "not bewildered for an instant"[60]—she knows it is the flood. The ironies here are more frightening than the novelist could have foreseen. It is not clear whether uncontrolled nature, an actual, grim deus ex machina, is intended to mock the prayer or to fulfil it. The title of the last book, "The Final Rescue," suggests that death alone will provide release and transendence. Yet even if we accept the flood as a possible means of reconciling Tom and Maggie, their deaths may still seem but a cruel accident. Until the last half-page of the narrative, another sort of rescue would have been conceivable; the large boat passing by might have offered assistance instead of mere warnings of disaster.

George Eliot herself confessed that the conclusion of *The Mill on the Floss* seemed to her unduly compressed and precipitant. But it is unlikely that a more leisurely pace would have made the "tragedy" more convincing. Any tragic ending would probably remain as unsatisfactory as the revised happy ending of *Great Expectations*—but for a quite different reason. Dickens feels sufficiently detached from his hero—whom he nevertheless resembles—to offer him the sort of future most of his readers might wish him to have. George Eliot has identified herself too closely, too emotionally, with Maggie to know precisely what to do with her. She cannot grant Maggie a second life like her own in London, an escape in intellectual journalism, without compromising the natural piety that binds the girl to the past. She is apparently reliving through Maggie her own early sense of responsibility and her reluctance to break family ties. Yet she cannot imagine Maggie's finding the meaningful career in St. Ogg's that she herself could not find in

---

[60] *Mill*, Bk. VII, Ch. 5.

Warwickshire. On the other hand, if we have seen in the first chapter of the novel the narrator looking back on her childhood, meeting the eyes of her younger self as Maggie, we surely cannot credit Maggie's death. Like *Sons and Lovers* and Joyce's *Portrait,* Bildungsromane subjectively engaged in a similar way, *The Mill on the Floss* describes the beginning of a life necessarily still incomplete; and its interest and power lie in the unfolding of that life rather than in the arbitrary end imposed upon it.

9 | WEAVE A CIRCLE / Baron Kirkup and His Greatest Friends

D. A. Robertson, Jr.

Their ghosts still stand, as I said before,
  Watching each fresco flaked and rasped,
Blocked up, knocked out, or whitewashed o'er.
  —"Old Pictures in Florence"

Phantoms and dust, the mere echoes of echoes.
  —The Aspern Papers

For nearly half of the last century, anyone in Florence could have directed us to the apartments of Seymour Kirkup—southwest corner of the Ponte Vecchio, by the Borgo San Jacopo, in the old hospital of the Templars, *1° piano*.[1] Even now, yes, we recognize that name; for Sey-

---

[1] For access to materials, and for permission to quote from unpublished letters, I am indebted to Professor W. B. Pope; to Emily Driscoll (formerly of New York), and Winifred A. Myers (London), and Leo S. Olschki (Florence); and to the cognizant authorities of the following institutions: Library of Congress; Houghton Library, Harvard University; British Library; Royal Academy; Keats Memorial Library, Hampstead; Bodleian Library, Oxford; Keats-Shelley Memorial House, Rome; Instituto per la Storia del Risorgimento, Rome; Biblioteca Nazionale Centrale di Firenze.
  Lionel Cust, writing on S. K. for the *DNB*, sought (and apparently obtained) some data from Teodoro Cioni and from Paolina Morandi.

mour Kirkup appears and reappears in the letters and memoirs of greatly distinguished friends who regarded him with a mixture of affection and wonder. Hawthorne, we are told, put him into "The Dolliver Romance" and "Dr. Grimshawe's Secret." More often than not, the *Barone* looks old—seventy or more.

Within the apartments, we pass through the kitchen into a great chamber cluttered with bookcases, pictures, and curious objects—a carved chest once owned by Machiavelli, a ghastly portrait of Savonarola, a lifelike mask of Dante, a painting by Kirkup of naked spirits whirled along in the *bufera infernal,* a crystal ball, a faded puppet show. Out of the litter of manuscripts and early printed books a shriveled sprite materializes: slovenly in dress, but still the English gentleman, "with rather more embroidery of courtesy than belongs to an Englishman"; very deaf, but a willing talker, with memories of Blake and Haydon, tales of the Anglo-Florentines, news of Swinburne and the young Rossettis; wifeless, but with a pretty child of somewhat mysterious parentage frisking about him like a butterfly; an artist-turned-mage, pale, delicately made, his hair and long beard silky white, his nose high and thin, his eyes glittering under brows arched as if in unrelievable astonishment.[2]

Evocations of Kirkup in youth have been rarer; but there are evidences—as there are not for the Duke Prospero of Milan or for the Chevalier of Pensieri-Vani—that the remarkable baron was once a boy. He began life unremarkably in 1788, the eldest child of a London jeweler and diamond merchant; but he developed quite early two tastes that distinguished him: one for proximity to interesting

---

[2] See particularly A. H. Layard, *Autobiography and Letters,* ed. W. N. Bruce (New York: Scribners, 1903), I, 28–33; Nathaniel Hawthorne, *Passages from the French and Italian Note-Books* (Boston: Wayside Edition, 1899), pp. 386–91 (12 August 1858); Francis Power Cobbe, *Italics: Brief Notes on Politics, People, and Places in Italy, in 1864,* 2d ed. (London: Trubner, 1864), pp. 394–96; and Charles Eliot Norton to James Russell Lowell, 24 February 1870, in Norton, *Letters,* ed. Sara Norton and M. A. DeWolfe Howe (Boston: Houghton Mifflin, 1913), I, 373–77.

personages, preferably not Tories; the other for Art. After rather more than a year of study under John Flaxman, the young man gained admission in 1809 to the Antique School of the Royal Academy; and in 1811 he won a medal for a drawing of Raphael's Apollo on Parnassus—"I remember poor old Fuseli used to say it was impossible: "The twelfth of an inch changed between the nose and lip, and the God is lost."[3] Incomparable teachers, in those days: "Fuseli, Flaxman, and Turner! What men!" Kirkup knew Lawrence, too, and was in his confidence: "It was he made me paint portraits, which I never intended."[4] In 1815, if Canova had not come to London, Kirkup would have had the Academy's gold medal for painting: "They refused the medal after making us paint for it because in their economy they saved it and £100, along with it, in order to spend it in a grand dinner to Canova! Poor Etty reminded me of it but a short time before his death. I was considered the victim, sure of the prize."[5]

Among the fellow students was Charles Eastlake, later President of the Royal Academy and Director of the National Gallery, a lifelong friend.[6] Eastlake's first master outside the Royal Academy had been Haydon, an admirable painter, in Kirkup's judgment, with extraordinary knowledge of the human figure—the greatest designer in Europe, "as I ascertained when I went to Paris, and made the acquaintance of David and all his school"—but a man ruined by vanity.[7] "Too religious," moreover, "and too much

[3] S. K. to Layard, 31 March 1859 (British Library: Add. MSS. 38,986).
[4] S. K. to A. C. Swinburne, 4 September [1870], in Edmund Gosse, "Swinburne and Kirkup," *London Mercury*, 3 (December 1920), 165; S. K. to Layard, 19 February 1861 (British Library, Add. MSS. 38,987).
[5] S. K. to H. C. Barlow, 18 March 1857, in Barlow, *On the Vernon Dante* (London: Williams and Norgate, 1870), p. 49 n. Cf. W. T. Whitley, *Art in England, 1800–1820* (New York: Macmillan, 1928), pp. 251–52.
[6] This essay stems from work on *Sir Charles Eastlake and the Victorian Art World* (Princeton, N.J.: Princeton University Press, 1978).
[7] S. K. to W. M. Rossetti, 2 March 1869, in *Rossetti Papers*, ed. W. M. Rossetti (New York: Scribners, 1903), p. 427, and S. K. to Swinburne, 4 September [1870], in Gosse, "Swinburne and Kirkup," p. 165. Haydon thought S. K. "a refined, delicate creature" and "a comfort always,

of a Tory for me." William Blake, even when people were questioning his sanity, made better sense and lived a happier life. Kirkup first met him through Butts of the War Office, father of another young art student:[8] "Yes, I knew Blake well, and liked him, and respected him. . . . I used to think him mad then, but I think now he was quite sound. There never was an honester man than he, or one who lived in finer poverty,—poor but strictly simple in his habits. I remember his wife, who was a very nice good woman, once said to me, 'Oh I have very little of Mr. Blake's company, he passes all his life in Paradise.'" It made for trouble, of course, that Blake "could only give his word for the truth of his visions."[9]

In 1816 Kirkup showed signs of pulmonary weakness and left England, planning to live six months in Italy. In fact, he stayed the next eight years at Rome. Not that he much liked foreigners. Among the Roman women, to be sure, were "really some divine creatures"; but the married were promiscuous, and the unmarried "too closely secured by their kinsmen, the Church, and the laws."[10] Italian men were excitable and incompetent at their jobs. In April 1817, when Kirkup was sailing down the coast for Naples with Eastlake, who had come to Italy at the same time, the vessel ran into violent winds and high seas, struck on a bar near Terracina, and heeled over; and the so-called mariners,

---

though he is a devil of a Radical." See Benjamin Robert Haydon, *Diary*, ed. W. B. Pope (Cambridge, Mass.: Harvard University Press, 1963), V, 172, 195.

[8] Norton to Lowell, 24 February 1870, in Norton, *Letters*, I, 373–77. Swinburne, having begun his *William Blake* (1868), visited Florence in 1864 (as Gosse explained), "with a double aim, if possible to see Landor and to talk to Kirkup about Blake." His introduction to Landor was arranged by R. M. Milnes (Lord Houghton). On Milnes and S. K. (who had met first in the thirties), see S. K. to Swinburne, 30 November 1865, in Gosse, "Swinburne and Kirkup," p. 162; S. K. to W. M. Rossetti, 19 January 1866, in *Rossetti Papers*, p. 171; and S. K. to Houghton, 25 March and 18 December 1870, in T. Wemyss Reid, *Life, Letters, and Friendships of Richard Monckton Milnes, Lord Houghton* (London: Cassell, 1890), II, 222–23, 249–50.

[9] S. K. to W. M. Rossetti, 19 January 1866, in *Rossetti Papers*, p. 171.

[10] S. K. to Haydon, 18 October 1818 (Ms. collection of W. B. Pope).

instead of lowering the sails promptly, mouthed invocations to the Madonna del Mercato.[11] One of them tore off his clothes, and Kirkup paled. As for the Germans at Rome, the Nazarene painters, he saw nothing in their works but "ugliness, tameness, and deformity boasted of with the most deplorable ignorance and conceit."[12]

Happily, there was a good-sized English colony, presided over by the Duchess of Devonshire and the Countess of Westmorland. "English society," said Kirkup to Haydon, "never appears so valuable as abroad." In 1819 he helped to welcome Lawrence, who had been commissioned to paint the pope and his secretary of state; he met Catherwood, who later traveled in Central America and drew the Mayan remains, and Nicholas Wiseman, not yet an agent of Papal Aggression but "only an Irish Friar"; he subscribed, with a dozen compatriots, to establish an English academy where members could draw in the evening from living models.[13] Among the other sharers in this enterprise were Eastlake, the sculptor John Gibson, and Joseph Severn.

Severn, with his friend Keats, had arrived at Rome in November 1820, bearing a letter to Kirkup from Charles Armitage Brown.[14] Keats lived only until February 1821; he was buried on the twenty-sixth. Kirkup lay in bed with a fever that day, unable to attend the funeral, but showed in the ensuing weeks kindnesses that Severn could never forget.[15] To the disconsolate Severn—at the easel in

---

[11] Lady Eastlake's "Memoir of Sir Charles Lock Eastlake," in his *Contributions to the Literature of the Fine Arts*, 2d ser. (1870), p. 66.
[12] S. K. to Lady Westmorland, 20 February 1867 (author's collection).
[13] V. W. von Hagen, *Frederick Catherwood Arch^t* (New York: Oxford University Press, 1950), pp. 14–20; S. K. to Layard, 31 October 1871 (British Library: Add. MSS. 38, 987); Eastlake to Lawrence, 6 May 1823 (Royal Academy: Lawrence Letter-Books, vol. IV).
[14] Gosse, "Swinburne and Kirkup," p. 157. According to Lady Birkenhead (*Against Oblivion*, New York: Macmillan, [1944], p. 146, and *Illustrious Friends*, New York: Reynal, [1965], p. 70), Severn was introduced to S. K. by William Ewing, the sculptor.
[15] S. K. to Severn, 4 April 1868, in William Sharp, "Joseph Severn and his Correspondents," *Atlantic Monthly*, 68 (December 1891), 747–48.

Eastlake's studio, trying to get on with a *Death of Alcibiades*—Kirkup presented a splendid paint box; and Kirkup introduced him to Lady Westmorland (whose ward ultimately became Mrs. Severn), invited him and the other members of the English academy to a Christmas dinner with music and plum pudding, and provided at all seasons good talk "over the *true thing in Art*."[16] Severn wrote of him:

His noble mind, his learning, his taste, and his good heart remind me of Keats. Every one here seem[s] to love him, and have something good to say of him. . . . He has a small fortune and is studying historical painting. He is a fine musician. This good little fellow (for he is just the same size as Keats) has done me most essential service. . . . I should tell he has even purchased a Piano Forte for my playing on. He accompanys me on the Violin or Guittern.[17]

When word came that Shelley had been lost in the Bay of Spezzia, Kirkup may well have remembered with a shudder his own experience off Terracina. At the interment of Shelley's ashes on 2 January 1823, he joined the little band of mourners; and thereafter he claimed Edward Trelawny, Shelley's greatest friend, as his own—"not only my best friend but the best I ever heard of": "So you remember Trelawny. He is a magnificent, magnanimous fellow and friend; but perhaps too much of a republican for you—not for me; and he is the sincerest of men, and the great enemy of priestcraft."[18] Kirkup painted Trelawny in the garb of an Albanian corsair, and he gave Trelawny a priceless ar-

---

See also Sharp, *Life and Letters of Joseph Severn* (New York: Scribners, 1892), pp. 103–5.

[16] Severn to his sister Maria, 26 December 1821 (Keats Memorial Library, Hampstead), and Severn to S. K., 20 August 1833 (Keats-Shelley Memorial House, Rome).

[17] Severn to William Haslam, 5 May 1821, in *The Keats Circle,* ed. Hyder Edward Rollins (Cambridge, Mass.: Harvard University Press, 1948), I, 239–40.

[18] Severn to Brown, 21 January 1823, in Sharp, *Life,* pp. 123–24; S. K. to W. M. Rossetti, 19 January and 6 March 1867, in *Rossetti Papers,* pp. 248, 254. Further references to Trelawny occur in *Rossetti Papers,* pp. 426, 449, 480; S. K. to W. M. Rossetti, 2 March, 14 July, and 30 October 1869.

ticle of furniture—Shelley's sofa-bedstead. "I have slept for months on it," said Kirkup, "in hopes of seeing Shelley's ghost."[19]

In 1824 Kirkup's efforts to paint a Magdalene and a Juliet were frustrated by a severe illness which required the attendance of the highly skilled James Clark, later Physician in Ordinary to the Queen:[20]

"I never saw any living being so far gone. . . . I lived *entirely* on asses' milk and a bit of bread three times a day; and after a fortnight the milk began to disagree with me, and he substituted Iceland moss. . . ." "We feel angry," said Brown of the patient, "that he cannot make his body as powerful as his mind."[21] By late summer, however, he had recovered enough strength for a short visit to Florence— which city, as his Roman friends quickly and regretfully perceived, altogether captivated him.[22] In the event, this visit lasted forty-eight years.

Almost at once, through Brown, Kirkup met another of his greatest friends—Landor, who "had the reputation of being a violent man, and no doubt was so."[23] Indeed, Kirkup himself heard Landor vehemently dispute points of history with Francis Hare and points of connoisseurship

---

[19] S. K. to W. M. Rossetti, 24 April 1870, in *Rossetti Papers*, p. 531 (and editorial notes by W. M. Rossetti, pp. 501, 530). See also Trelawny to W. M. Rossetti, quoting S. K., in *Letters of Edward John Trelawny*, ed. H. Buxton Forman (London: Oxford University Press, 1910), pp. 260–61. Trelawny gave the sofa to W. M. R., from whom it passed to Mrs. Rossetti Angeli.

[20] S. K. to W. M. Rossetti, 23 March 1867, in *Rossetti Papers*, p. 255.

[21] "Actors and Artists at Rome," a letter to Leigh Hunt, published as No. 16 of "The Wishing-Cap," *Examiner*, 4 October 1824, p. 627.

[22] Brown to Severn, 8 September 1824, in *Letters of Charles Armitage Brown*, ed. Jack Stillinger (Cambridge, Mass.: Harvard University Press, 1966), p. 189; Severn to the Rev. Col. Robert Finch, 4 October 1824, quoted in Joanna Richardson, *The Everlasting Spell* (London: Cape, 1963), p. 59.

[23] S. K., as quoted by John Forster, in *Walter Savage Landor* (London: Chapman and Hall, 1869), II, 204–6. See also pp. 200 and 236–37. On Landor and S. K. talking together of painting and of politics, 5 September 1830, see *Henry Crabb Robinson on Books and Their Writers*, ed. Edith J. Morley (London: Dent, 1938), I, 384–85.

with George Wallis; saw Landor knock the hat from the head of a marchese, his landlord in the Palazzo Medici; had once, as Landor's second, to extricate his principal from a duel with an attaché of the French legation; and knew Landor to have been offended by servants who, seeing his very shabby attire, took him for a beggar. In course of time, as a loyal friend, Kirkup learned a great deal about Landor's problems, familial as well as financial. But he profoundly admired Landor's powers of language; delighted in his passion, unlearned though it was, for painting; respected his courtesy to the lordly but laughable Dillon, author of *Rosaline de Vere* and *Sir Richard Maltravers;* and, in short, liked to think of his leonine friend as embodying the traits of an English gentleman of the old school—eccentric and impatient, especially to foreigners, but"chivalresque."

Early in 1825 William Hazlitt appeared at Florence, with his second wife. He expressed a desire to call upon Landor; "and he walked up to his house one winter's morning in nankeen shorts and white stockings; was made much of by the royal animal; and often returned."[24] One day he told Landor, Brown, and Kirkup how evidence for his divorce had been arranged, "to save Mrs. H.'s honour." The incompatible pair had gone up to Edinburgh, and Hazlitt had enlisted the services of "a not very respectable female confederate" and put her into his bed, and then Mrs. H. had walked in with two gentlemen as witnesses. "She turned to them, and said: 'Gentlemen, do you know who that person is in that bed along with that woman?' 'Yes, madam,' they politely replied, ''tis Mr. William Hazlitt.' On which, sir, she made me a curtsey, and they went out of the room, and left me and my companion *in statu quo.*"[25]

Kirkup discouraged gossip about his own quasi-marital affairs. By this time, however, he had snared, or had been snared, clearly enough: "He and Madama," Brown reported, in September 1824, "dined with me in my Nun-

---

[24] Forster, *Walter Savage Landor,* II, 201.
[25] Ibid.,II, 207–8.

nery."²⁶ But who can say whether Madama was Kirkup's first inamorata or the successor to some divine but unknown Roman? If the first, she can have held his affections only briefly; if not, this must have been the same charming Maria that filled his thoughts a few months later and seems beyond question to have been counted by knowing friends as the *second* "Mrs. K."

This affair with Maria was not to be spoken of, please, in England. Trouble with the police. Brown, who came to share Kirkup's quarters in the Piazza del Duomo, and who was himself endeavoring to persuade a girl of eighteen or twenty, Euphemia by name, to give up her intention to teach embroidery in a convent and to become rather his housekeeper or the governess to his little son Carlino, observed the complications with sympathy: Maria's blackguardly *genitore* and damnable sister, who had a magistrate as her *amico;* the police, acting "with something, as appears, like personal animosity"; a treacherous lawyer, "at least as fat gutted as Falstaff, and with a fistula in one of his leering eyes."²⁷ In November 1825, when the contrary forces seemed to be yielding, Kirkup bought a hearthrug—prematurely, alas. He found it expedient to spend the greater part of 1826 away from Florence, first at Venice and later at Parma with his painter-friend George Hayter.²⁸

But on New Year's Day 1827 Kirkup returned, and "he and his" spread the hearthrug, as Brown rejoiced: "We've gained the victory at last,—tantara-ra, ra-tarra,—tantarrir-rirra!!! Here he is, the police all graciousness, the 'genitore' a greater blackguard than ever, Marina in our house as 'aja del bambino di Signor Carlo Brown,' and we sit

---

²⁶ Brown to Severn, 8 September 1824, in *Letters of Charles Armitage Brown,* p. 189.
²⁷ Brown to Leigh Hunt, 24 September, 20 October, and 24 November 1825, in Brown, *Letters,* pp. 224, 231–33, 236.
²⁸ Brown to Finch, 12 January 1826, and Brown to Hunt, 29 May and 29 October 1826, in Brown, *Letters,* pp. 241, 255, 262. Cf. Elizabeth Nitchie, *The Reverend Colonel Finch* (New York: Columbia University Press, 1940), pp. 89–90.

down five...."²⁹ For about two years the domestic arrangements continued without serious disruption. Then Brown left the Piazzo del Duomo, because his bedroom was unhealthy; and Kirkup fell desperately ill. Once he had made progress toward survival, Maria departed. "Kirkup is perfectly recovered; and, moreover, is again a widower, Marina being married to an actor, who bears a good character, is young, and picks up a pretty penny by playing Stentorello. What a lucky fellow Kirkup is to get rid so well of two incumbrances."³⁰ No such luck for George Hayter—whose mistress had taken an ounce of arsenic, reconsidered, swallowed castor oil to get rid of the poison, and promptly died.³¹ And Hayter wondered why society cut him adrift!

It did not reject Kirkup, and Kirkup did not turn misogynist. He settled now in the spacious apartments by the Ponte Vecchio, with windows over the Arno; and he seemed, at least to some of his not quite domesticated friends, a confirmed believer in the suitably attended hearth and home. Gossiping at Cheltenham in 1835 with Thomas Campbell, the sculptor, Trelawny scoffed at the unlikely story that Kirkup "had foresworn the society of Ladykind."³² To Kirkup, for a while, he entrusted his own little Zella, the niece of Odysseus; and he assured Claire Clairmont that Kirkup managed children far better than "any woman I ever got hold of...." Instead of taking Zella from him, I am thinking of sending him a little red Indian thing, a thorough bred—from the western wilderness of America, her dam a squaw of the Chippeway nation—Wa-em-boesh—grand-daughter of Black Hawk."³³ Had he

²⁹ Brown to Hunt, [19 February 1827?], in Brown, *Letters,* p. 266.
³⁰ Brown to Hunt, 28 November 1829, in Brown, *Letters,* pp. 288–91.
³¹ Ibid. See also the entry for 24 October 1827 in *The Journal of the Hon. Henry Edward Fox,* ed. Earl of Ilchester (London: Butterworth, 1923), p. 235. Hayter painted for the Queen and received a knighthood in 1842, but he never gained election to the Royal Academy.
³² Trelawny to S. K., 26 August [1835] (Houghton Library, Harvard, bMS Am 1631).
³³ Trelawny to Claire Clairmont, 14 May 1836, in Trelawny, *Letters,* pp. 201–2.

rounded her up and packed her off immediately, another *aja* might still have been at Kirkup's, to lend a hand with the child care; for in 1837 Brown wrote to Hunt: "I heard from Kirkup lately,—he was very well. Last year he married off his third Mrs. K. to a Florentine Marquis,—a Medici!"[34]

Kirkup the painter, said Leigh Hunt, was "poor enough, I fear, neither in purse nor accomplishment, to cultivate his profession as he ought."[35] He painted at scenes from *Othello* and *The Merchant of Venice;* actually finished a *Cassio* for the Royal Academy exhibition of 1833; and attempted a portrait of Rose Aylmer's half sister as Juliet, but could not induce her to look sentimental enough.[36] At his best, exerting himself, he had portrayed a number of beautiful and well-placed ladies whose sons in later years became his friends: Lady William Russell, "whose bloom could, after dancing, dare the dawn"; the part-Spanish mother of the Layard boy, who liked to potter about in the cluttered studio; Lady Jane Ashburnham, who married a seadog named Swinburne and bore in 1837 a little son named Algernon.[37]

But in the mid-thirties Kirkup went deaf and gave up portrait painting as a profession: "I could not hear what my sitters said to me and I could not talk to them, and they used to drop asleep,—and then I cold not go into society and get people to come and buy my pictures. . . ."[38] The affliction resulted from a willingness to collaborate with an aristocratically exigent Dantean. Lord Vernon, then under forty, wanted illustrations for the great work that would

---

[34] Brown to Hunt, 10 June 1837, in Brown, *Letters,* p. 344.

[35] Leigh Hunt, *Lord Byron and Some of His Contemporaries* (London: Colburn, 1828), p. 495.

[36] Brown to Hunt, 1 June 1830, in Brown, *Letters,* p. 319; R. H. Super, *Walter Savage Landor* (New York: New York University Press, 1954), p. 250. In *The Lions of Florence* (1847), p. 37, "An Artist" wrote that S. K. had lately finished a *Juliet* for the Duke of Devonshire.

[37] Arthur Russell to Lady Westmorland, 4 December 1866 (author's collection)—and Byron's "Beppo"; Layard, *Autobiography and Letters,* I, 10, 28; Swinburne to S. K., 11 August [1865], in *The Swinburne Letters,* ed. Cecil Y. Lang (New Haven: Yale University Press, 1959), I, 128.

[38] Norton to Lowell, 24 February 1870, in Norton, *Letters,* I, 373.

finally appear as the Vernon Dante (1858–65); and Kirkup, though reluctant to draw subjects already treated by his master Flaxman, agreed to help by collecting old views and portraits. "Hm, hm, it was old Lord Vernon made me deaf; it was indeed! I was doing some work with him, and it was very cold winter weather, and he always insisted on wearing his silk stockings and living in a hot house, and one night I went home in the snow and a *tramontana* blowing. I pulled up my collar, but there was a crack that let in the air, and the next morning I woke up stone deaf."[39]

Kirkup caught the Dantophilia too and began to read and collect everything he could lay hands on. Talking with Florentine professors, he concluded that all the best work on Dante must be going on elsewhere. A friend of Eastlake's mentioned an expatriate teaching in London, Gabriele Rossetti by name: "Do but read him," said Ingram, "and you will know more of Dante than all the Italians, from Milan to Naples."[40] Kirkup read *Lo Spirito Antipapale*, engaged in correspondence with the author, and became his staunch ally. Rossetti, therefore, was among the first to hear of Kirkup's marvelous good fortune in obtaining from the sculptor Lorenzo Bartolini a quite convincingly lifelike portrait-mask of Dante, superior to the bust owned by the Marchese Torrigiani.[41] There was reason, perhaps, to admit doubts about the mask. All Bartolini had asked in exchange was a purebred King Charles spaniel. Kirkup, however, took to describing the treasure as "cast from nature. . . . The veins in the temples, the lines and wrinkles, the pressure of the mould on the bending nose, the un-

---

[39] Ibid. See also S. K. to W. M. Rossetti, 14 July 1869, in *Rossetti Papers*, pp. 448–49.
[40] S. K. to Gabriele Rossetti, 12 January 1840 (Istituto per la Storia del Risorgimento, Rome: Busta 276).
[41] S. K. to Gabriele Rossetti, 5 May 1840, ibid. Other letters of S. K. on the subject will be found in R. T. Holbrook, *Portraits of Dante* (Boston: Medici Society, 1921). Some time after February 1842, S. K. acquired a related mask, which had been used by the sculptor Stefano Ricci in modeling the Dante monument for Santa Croce.

equal half closing of the eyes, are all proofs of its authenticity."[42]

Yet greater excitement arose soon after. Somewhere on a wall of the old chapel in the Bargello, hidden from sight by whitewash, there was said to be a portrait of Dante by Giotto. It had been mentioned by several writers, including Vasari, and noted by Domenico Moreni in his edition (1828) of Filelfo's *Vita Dantis*. An ineffectual attempt to discover it had been made by the Keeper of Drawings in the Royal Galleries. To say for sure who made the first move to renew the search would be exceedingly difficult— Seymour Kirkup, or Eastlake's friend Giovanni Aubrey Bezzi, a Piedmontese who had spent years in England as an exile, or Richard Henry Wilde, a Dublin-born American with a driving interest in the great Italian poets. These three, anyhow, undertook at their own expense to employ a restorer, Antonio Marini, to uncover the walls.[43] Bezzi skillfully managed negotiations with the Florentine authorities, and Marini set to work. Since the chapel had been divided in two, it had six walls. After Marini had cleared three, without success, the government assumed responsibility.

On 21 July 1840, removing whitewash from the fifth

---

[42] S. K. to Lady Westmorland, 11 January 1867 (author's collection). F. J. Mather, Jr., *The Portraits of Dante* (Princeton: Princeton University Press, 1921), p. 36, n. 9: "Perhaps the most discreditable chapter in Dante scholarship is the credulous acceptance of the Death-mask by such scholars as Cavalcaselle, Norton, Paur, Maria Rossetti and others."

[43] The fullest account of the operation, and of the ensuing disputes, is in Holbrook, *Portraits of Dante*, particularly Ch. 9 ("Giotto's Dante: The Discovery"). On Bezzi, see also *Il Risorgimento Italiano*, II: *Gli Uomini Politici*, I (1941), in *Enciclopedia Biographica e Bibliographica "Italiana,"* Ser. 42. On Wilde, see C. C. Jones, Jr., *The Life, Literary Labors, and Neglected Grave of Richard Henry Wilde* ([Augusta, Ga.?], 1885), and E. L. Tucker, *Richard Henry Wilde* (Athens, Ga.: University of Georgia Press, 1966). Wilde's MS "Life and Times of Dante" is now in the Library of Congress. S. K. was one of the five whom Wilde thanked for assistance.

wall, Marini found Dante. " *'L'abbiamo, il nostro poeta!'* was the universal cry," wrote Lord Lindsay, "and for days afterwards the Bargello was thronged with a continuous succession of pilgrim visitors."[44] Bezzi and Wilde had left Florence, but Kirkup hurried to see that face:[45] "The poet looks about 28—very handsome—*un Apollo colle fattezze di Dante*. The expression and character are worthy of the subject, and much beyond what I expected from Giotto. Raphael might own it with honor. Add to which it is not the mask of a corpse of 56—a ruin—but a fine, noble image of the Hero of Campaldino, the Lover of Beatrice." And to think that Marini had botched it! The wretch had pulled out a nail and left a large hole where the eye had been: "What a pity, said I. *Era un chiodo*, he replied. How could he tell? He had drawn it out instead of cutting it, and had brought away a bit of the wall, about 3 inches by 2, which went on crumbling away by the wiseacres putting their fingers in, *Oh, c'e una buga!*"[46] Imbeciles!

At first, the Jacks-in-office would not allow Kirkup to make a copy—"*Sono tanto gelosi.*" Considering himself to have been a *magna pars* in the enterprise, he pocketed some colors and his copy of the *Convivio*, entered the chapel with the ordinary pilgrim visitors, held the book inside his wide felt hat, and began to draw. The guard protested, twice, but then accepted a pecuniary inducement to leave the gentleman alone, locked in, during the dinner hour.[47] Thus, surreptitiously, Kirkup was enabled not only to finish his drawing in the *Convivio* but also to take "a tracing on thin paper, so as to obtain the exact outline and precise

---

[44] Lord Lindsay, *Sketches of the History of Christian Art* (London: Murray, 1847), II, 174.

[45] S. K. to Gabriele Rossetti, 12 September 1840, in W. M. Rossetti, *Gabriele Rossetti* (London: Sands, 1901), pp. 144–47.

[46] S. K. to H. C. Barlow, 9 February 1857, printed in the *Athenaeum*, 4 July 1857, and quoted in Holbrook, *Portraits of Dante*, 84, from the MS at University College, London. See also Barlow, *On the Vernon Dante*, pp. 35–37.

[47] S. K. to Mrs. Gillum, 1873, quoted in Holbrook, *Portraits of Dante*, pp. 89–90.

size." These, in fact, were the most reliable records of the Giotto portrait as it looked before the unprincipled Marini "restored" the eye and daubed over the face: "It is now 15 years older, a mean pinched expression, and an effeminate character compared to what it was. . . . I mean to take my time and perhaps some day I may restore Dante to himself a second time. I had the principal part in the late discovery."[48] The drawings Kirkup sent to Rossetti inspired a watercolor by the Professor's son Dante Gabriel, *Giotto Painting the Portrait of Dante*.[49] On another drawing, for Lord Vernon, the Arundel Society based its well-known colored print (1859).

Throughout the forties, the discovery, its consequences, and related studies filled most of Kirkup's existence. He delved in *Il Mistero dell' Amor Platonico* and *La Beatrice di Dante,* accepted Rossetti's identification of Beatrice as Filosofia, and saluted the professor as "an extraordinary unraveller."[50] To Carlo Eastlake (whom he readily pardoned for having listened to Bezzi's self-interested account of the discovery), he sent extracts from a Florentine manuscript bearing upon the Portinari family's business interests in Flanders.[51] Completely the bookworm now, he painted only rarely—"generally when I want some MS. or relique beyond my purse." Around him accumulated piles of dusty manuscripts and thousands of old books—Dante, Petrarch,

---

[48] S. K. to Gabriele Rossetti, 14 September 1841, in *Gabriele Rossetti,* pp. 147–50. Cf. F. T. Kugler, *The Schools of Painting in Italy,* ed. C. L. Eastlake, 2d ed. (London: Murray, 1851), p. 126, n. 3; and J. A. Crowe and G. B. Cavalcaselle, *A New History of Painting in Italy* (London: Murray, 1864), I, 260–70.

[49] Reproduced in H. C. Marillier, *Dante Gabriel Rossetti* (London: Bell, 1899), opposite p. 40.

[50] S. K. to Gabriele Rossetti, 5 February 1843, in *Gabriele Rossetti,* pp. 150–54.

[51] S. K. to Haydon, 18 June 1843 (W. B. Pope's collection), and S. K. to Capt. Francis Brooke, 23 December 1847 (Winifred Myers, Catalogue No. 6, spring 1967); Eastlake to S. K., 6 April 1849 (author's collection). Cf. Eastlake's *Materials for a History of Oil Painting* (London: Longman, 1847) I, x and II (1869), 9–10 n.

Boccaccio, Cecco d'Ascoli, Albertus Magnus. . . . "They are my family and companions," Kirkup wrote to Haydon in 1844. "I have two beautiful spaniels, and that's all." Society bored him. He seldom went out; but he agreed to breakfast at the Café Doney with Hiram Powers and young Watts the painter, and in 1847 he expressed some curiosity about a newcomer to the English colony—"There is a Mrs. Browning here, a Miss Barret [sic] that was, a Great Grecian and poetess, I hear."[52]

An artist and antiquarian who cared so much about the portrait of Dante by Giotto naturally took part during the fifties in enthusiastic reappraisal of the "Primitives." Kirkup hoped to uncover lost Masaccios in the Carmine, examined judiciously the specimens of early painting acquired by his American friend Jarves, and suggested quite glorious attributions—Cimabue, Giottesque if not Giotto, Ghirlandaio—for the old pictures found among heaps of trash in a corn shop by his greatest new friend, Robert Browning: "I am glad you know Mr. Browning. I have found him a sincere friend. He is both a philosopher and a poet, and would have been a sculptor if he had continued his modelling."[53] Kirkup turned out also in what seemed to be the best interest of an aging and tormented artist in still another medium: "I saved Rossini's life . . . strychnine!"[54] But Kirkup was now developing a more ob-

---

[52] Ronald Chapman, *The Laurel and the Thorn* (London: Faber, 1945), p. 30; S. K. to Haydon, 4 January 1842 and 23 March 1844 (W. B. Pope's collection); and S. K. to Brooke, 25 May 1847 (Myers, Catalogue No. 6).

[53] S. K. to Layard, 15 May 1860 (British Library: Add. MSS. 38,986); Francis Steegmuller, *The Two Lives of James Jackson Jarves* (New Haven: Yale University Press, 1951), p. 193 n. 43; Mrs. Browning to Mrs. Jameson, 4 May [1850], in Elizabeth Barrett Browning, *Letters*, ed. F. G. Kenyon (London: Smith, Elder, 1897), I, 448; S. K. to Lady Westmorland, 11 January 1867 (author's collection). Note Browning's "Pacchiarotto," II: "My Kirkup!"

[54] S. K. to W. M. Rossetti, 14 July 1869, in *Rossetti Papers*, p. 449. The year, by S. K.'s reckoning, would have been 1854. Francis Toye, *Rossini* (London: Heinemann, 1934), pp. 201–3, says nothing of S. K. but makes it clear that at Florence in 1854 Rossini, suffering acutely from

sessive interest in mediums of that other sort, less distinctly related to the arts as commonly defined: he picked up, as quickly as any of the Anglo-Florentines, American reports of table turnings and spirit rappings.

The occult had fascinated him for years. "I have a vast collection," he had told Haydon in 1842, "of occult Science especially." Seeking a cure for his deafness, he read about Vital Magnetism in Dr. G. P. Billot's *Recherches psychologiques* (1839) and came, by the way, upon persuasive arguments "in favour of the existence of good spirits."[55] What miraculous luck, then, to find a medium living under his own roof! This was the remarkably beautiful Regina Ronti, one of his housekeeper's daughters, consumptive but under the protection of an angel named Isacco. In a mesmeric sleep she could take messages from the other world and retransmit them either by rapping or by involuntary writing. Through her, Kirkup learned from the late Czar Alexander I that he had been poisoned.[56] And on 29 November 1854 Regina saw Dante in the room, looking old, just like the mask; and Kirkup seized his first chance to ask questions: "He confirmed Rossetti, who is either unknown or decried by the priests and jesuits. I was in great favour and learned *much* from him. No imposture or illusion possible...."[57]

Alas, Regina wasted away; and on 30 October 1856, only nineteen years of age, she joined the company of the spirits. Layard happened to call: "There, laid out on the floor, on a black velvet pall, and surrounded by lighted tapers and flowers, lay the body of Regina, dressed in her holiday

---

neurasthenia, "would upbraid himself for his lack of courage in not committing suicide."

[55] S. K. to Haydon, 12 June 1842 (W. B. Pope's collection); S. K. to W. M. Rossetti, 19 January and 27 February 1866, in *Rossetti Papers*, pp. 171–72, 176–79.

[56] Hawthorne, *Passages*, pp. 388–89. At reports that Alexander did not die in 1825, but lived on till 1870 as a hermit named Fomich at Tomsk, S. K. must have smiled.

[57] S. K. to Swinburne, 30 November 1865, in Gosse, "Swinburne and Kirkup," p. 161. See also S. K. to W. M. Rossetti, 24 April 1866 and 19 January 1867, in *Rossetti Papers*, pp. 183, 248.

garments, a cross upon her breast, her beautiful features still unchanged."[58]

Earlier in 1854, she had given birth to a daughter.[59] From Hawthorne's paragraphs about little Imogen, written on 12 August 1858, the day after his call upon Kirkup in the company of Isa Blagden and Annette Bracken, Mrs. Hawthorne discreetly excised a number of sentences in preparing the *French and Italian Note-Books* for publication. In the passages here quoted from Hawthorne's manuscript, the published bits are italicized:

The necromancer set a great value upon Regina; nor were their communications, as it appears, exclusively spiritual; for, by and by, the medium produced this little girl, whom she declared, upon her death-bed, kissing the cross, to be the child of Mr. Kirkup. The poor old man seems to have had doubts respecting this paternity; indeed, if I interpret the thing aright, he did not quite know that he had done anything to bring the matter about. Nevertheless, he could not withstand the solemnity of Regina's declaration on the crucifix; *and when the mother died, he received the poor baby into his heart, and now believes it to be absolutely his own—* as perhaps it is. . . .

It seems that Regina had another lover and a sister who was very disreputable. The child was born some time before her death (of consumption) but she never imputed the paternity to Mr. Kirkup till she lay on her death-bed, when, naturally, she was considering how to provide for the future of the little girl; and, I suppose, Catholic and Italian morality would think a false oath even on the crucifix a venial crime, the object being to secure the welfare of an orphan child. Mr. Kirkup is a very credulous man, and would be likely to believe the story all the more readily, the more improbable it was. *It rather adds than otherwise to the romance of the affair—the idea that this pretty little elf has no right whatever in the asylum which she has found.*[60]

[58] Layard, *Autobiography and Letters*, I, 32–33.
[59] According to S. K., who usually got ages right, Imogen was twelve in January 1867 and fourteen in May 1868. S. K. to W. M. Rossetti, 19 January 1867 and 18 May 1868, in *Rossetti Papers*, pp. 248, 355.
[60] Quoted by permission from Hawthorne's MS. Journal, VI, 70–71 and 74–75 (Pierpont Morgan Library, New York). Cf. Hawthorne, *Passages*, pp. 389, 391; and Julian Hawthorne, *Hawthorne and his Circle* (New York: Harper, 1903), pp. 345–48. Some of the wording in the

Certainly, though he sometimes wrote of Imogen (or "Bibi") as adopted, Kirkup always treated her as his own. No doubt she enjoyed also the attentions of her grandmother and her aunt, for there is ample reason to suppose that they continued to manage the household. Kirkup assured Lady Westmorland that Bibi displayed great mediumistic gifts, even as an infant "too young for deception."[61]

When Regina came back, with other spirits in attendance, Kirkup felt well-nigh convinced that somehow, though he lacked such powerful gifts himself, he stimulated them in others who were close to him. He witnessed four miraculously rapid cures of cholera and one of an enormous dropsy.[62] Mysteriously, articles vanished from a room in his tower; and a very heavy table rose so high from the floor that Colonel Bowen, a tall man, could pass right under it.[63] Miss Ironsides, gazing into one of Kirkup's crystal balls, drew the angel and child she saw there.[64] Yet more noteworthy, because "a novelty," was the apparition of a living person—a nun resident on the far side of Florence, in a convent of the strictest order, where only the confessor and the physician were allowed to enter. The spirits brought her to the tower in a magnetic trance: "Two persons have seen her, and my medium returns her visits (to near the Porta Pinti). It may be all a dream or an invention but I am preparing a test which will put it beyond human art or imagination. She has requested a portrait and when I have done it I will place it with the window open and the

---

italicized sentences underwent change before publication—*e.g.,* "another lover" became "a lover."

[61] S. K. to Lady Westmorland, 11 January 1867 (author's collection).
[62] S. K. to W. M. Rossetti, 19 January 1866, in *Rossetti Papers*, p. 172.
[63] Browning, Jarves, and T. A. Trollope investigated the disappearances. Mrs. Browning to her sister Arabel, winter of 1857, cited in Katherine H. Porter, *Through a Glass Darkly* (Lawrence: University of Kansas Press, 1958), pp. 53–54. On the levitation, see G. Damiani, "Spiritualism in Italy," in *The Year Book of Spiritualism* (1871), p. 142 n.
[64] S. K. to Severn, 18 August 1861, in Sharp, *Life and Letters of Joseph Severn,* p. 267. Cf. Mrs. Browning to her sister Henrietta, 10 January 1857, in *Letters to Her Sister, 1846–1859,* ed. Leonard Huxley (New York: Dutton, 1930), p. 265.

door double-locked. . . . The spirits are to take the portrait to her, frame and all."⁶⁵ Was she (I wonder) Olimpia, ex-nun and somnambule, who later served as maid to little Imogen?

Against fraud and hallucination, Kirkup insisted, one had to be constantly on guard; but the dear man, as Mrs. Browning conceded, really was "not philosophical in his modes of carrying on experiment." Her forthright husband, fond though he was of Kirkup, called him a "silly old goose."⁶⁶ Landor, listening to guff about the spirits, laughed so loudly that even poor deaf Kirkup could hear; Layard saw him as the dupe "of some designing persons"; T. A. Trollope described him as the besotted victim of "a clever, worthless hussy"; Swinburne feared that the "dear old muddled brain" might get *"quite* cracked."⁶⁷ Kirkup must have known that these sincerely affectionate friends would never abandon him, whatever their views of Spiritualism; but he wrote to Sludge the Medium, who had promised him a photograph, "I have no such friend as you."⁶⁸ He found some other sympathizers in a new Florentine society which met twice a week and issued a periodical, *Gli Annali dello Spiritismo in Italia*.

In May 1865 Florence celebrated Dante's 600th birthday,

---

⁶⁵ S. K. to Layard, 19 February 1861 (British Library: Add. MSS. 38,987).

⁶⁶ Mrs. Browning to her sister Henrietta, 12 February 1855, in *Letters to Her Sister,* p. 212; Robert Browning in conversation, July 1876, as quoted in Gosse, "Swinburne and Kirkup," p. 159. For a story told by Browning to Val Prinsep, see Mrs. Sutherland Orr, *Life and Letters of Robert Browning,* 2d ed. (London: Smith, Elder, 1891), pp. 219–20: "The woman and her family made a good thing of poor Kirkup's spiritualism."

⁶⁷ Landor as reported by Mrs. Browning to Miss E. F. Haworth, 16 June 1860 [postmark], in E. B. Browning, *Letters* (London: Smith, Elder, 1897), II, 395; Layard, I, 30; Thomas A. Trollope, *What I Remember,* 2d ed. (London: Bentley, 1887), I, 386; Swinburne to W. M. Rossetti, 31 March [1869], and to his mother, 2 November [1874], in his *Letters,* ed. Lang, II, 11, 351.

⁶⁸ S. K. to D. D. Home, 16 January 1863, in Jean Burton, *Heyday of a Wizard* (London: Harrap, 1948), pp. 150–51; S. K. to Layard, 19 February 1861 (British Library: Add. MSS. 38,987).

and the minister of public instruction conveyed to Kirkup a royal certificate of knighthood in the Order of SS. Maurizio e Lazzaro.[69] Inadvertently, it was said, Victor Emmanuel spoke of the recipient as *Barone* rather than *Cavaliere;* and ever after, since the king could do no wrong, the deracinated English Radical graciously accepted the loftier title. Surmising that the honor recognized his part in the recovery of the Giotto portrait, he felt obligated at first to Layard, who had arranged for publication of the Arundel Society's print; but soon, as he informed young Swinburne, who had come to see him in 1864, he began to perceive that thanks were due to another. Dante himself appeared to Bibi on 12 October 1865, while she slept: "My opinion is that he has influenced the mind of the minister who recommended me to King Emmanuel, but that is only opinion—I have no proof, but it is all so unaccountable that I see no other clue to the mystery, or the coincidence, or what not."[70] The Baron had to endure only a few months of uncertainty. On 7 January 1866 the spirits passed to Bibi and Olimpia the message "that it was Dante who had influenced the Minister." On April 15 corroboration came through from Dante.

Thereafter he came often, as a familiar in the household, usually with a spirit party of five: Regina, Isacco, Olimpia's sister Marietta, an unidentifiable Giovanni, and Count Ladislas Ginnasi, quite recently deceased, a handsome cousin of Teresa Guiccioli.[71] Sometimes, when the men had to

---

[69] S. K. to Layard, 24 August 1865 (British Library: Add. MSS. 38, 991); S. K. to W. M. Rossetti, 19 January 1867, in *Rossetti Papers,* pp. 248–49; S. K. to Severn, 4 April 1868, in Sharp's article for the *Atlantic,* 68 (December 1891) 747–48. Cf. Browning to Isa Blagden, 19 October 1865, in *Dearest Isa,* ed. E. C. McAleer (Austin: University of Texas Press, 1951), pp. 226–27. Concerning S. K.'s title, Holbrook, *Portraits of Dante,* p. 210, cites Alessandro D'Ancono, "Il vero ritratto Giottesco di Dante," in *La Lettura,* March 1901. See further, S. K. to W. M. Rossetti, 15 January 1870, in *Rossetti Papers,* p. 509: "Wonders will never cease! The King has now given me the Order of the Corona d'Italia."
[70] S. K. to Swinburne, 30 November 1865, in Gosse, "Swinburne and Kirkup," p. 161.
[71] On Ginnasi's psychic powers in *this* life, see Orr, *Life and Letters,* pp. 219–20.

be away, looking after Garibaldi, only Regina and Marietta would come; but Kirkup, though always disappointed in his hope to *see* Dante, had marvelous opportunities to question him:

Did you help your son Jacopo to find the Cantos of the *Paradiso* missing at your death?—*Si.*
Is anything hidden in your house in Piazza San Martino?—*Non.*
Can you find or direct us to any piece of your handwriting, however small?—*Cerchero, e ti diro Giovedi.*[72]

Thursday never came. The shape of his head, then, *sans* cap? Would he outline it if Kirkup sketched the features and left the paper in a double-locked room with a window sixty feet above the Arno? Reluctantly, yes. The sketch disappeared on 23 May 1866; it was returned fifty days later with the head faintly delineated—signed "Dante Allighieri." In 1868, for Bibi, Dante performed an even greater feat.[73] To replace her pet rabbit, which had died, he spirited into a closed room of the tower a living lamb, which he had transported in three minutes from a *bosco* at Rosara near Pisa.

For human playmate, Bibi had Paolina Carboni, whose father Pasquale was said to have been an English viceconsul at Rome. Browning could remember glimpsing the child at Kirkup's door, "simply clad in the scantiest and raggedest of all chemises,—*rien que cela!*"[74] In 1871, at eighteen, she came on a long visit from Leghorn; and her dead sister Annina materialized clearly enough for a spirit photograph.[75] It was at this time that *gli spiriti* advised the

---

[72] S. K. to W. M. Rossetti, 19 January 1867, in *Rossetti Papers,* p. 249.
[73] S. K. to W. M. Rossetti, 26 April and 18 May 1868, in *Rossetti Papers,* pp. 351–55.
[74] Browning to Isa Blagden, 25 April 1871, in *Dearest Isa,* p. 358. The letter, as printed, makes references to an unidentifiable "Poldina." *Paolina,* I feel sure.
[75] S. K., "Letter to the Editor," 14 July 1871, in *Human Nature,* 5 (1871) 472–74.

Baron to sell his possessions and move to Leghorn.[76] Important news for bibliophiles! Norton already knew that he wanted some of those books and manuscripts: "I have, ghoul-like, inspired a worthy book-seller here with a zeal to get them that I may, if I survive, have some of them! This is horrible,—but one does not want the old women in the kitchen to burn them."[77] The library was dispersed at Sotheby's in December 1871.[78] A fifteenth-century illuminated manuscript of *Launcelot du Lac* ("Unique and most Splendid") reached £400, and Cardinal Bembo's manuscript of Petrarch's *Rime* ("most Exquisite and Charming") made £93; but the early printed books sold for very little— "all such woefully bad copies," said Norton's man, who spent just £7.13.6. Altogether, the 4,194 lots fetched only £2,555.

In 1872, thus remunerated, Kirkup left Florence for Leghorn. There, as it turned out, Bibi had a suitor; she married this Teodoro Cioni, bore two children, and died at twenty-five. And what had become of Kirkup? Did he still have the mask of Dante? Norton wanted it for Shady Hill:

I have not heard of old Seymour Kirkup's death, and take it for granted he is lingering on in squalor and spiritualism. . . . He would not be at all shocked at an immediate proposition to him to part with his mask, and I would give any reasonable sum for it. It would be a treasure worth having in America. . . . If you should see old Kirkup, and you can make him hear what you say, pray give him my remembrances,—I can hardly send my respects to such a dirty old villain.[79]

[76] Cf. Trollope, *What I Remember*, I, 389.
[77] Norton to J. R. Lowell, 24 February 1870. See also Kermit Vanderbilt, *Charles Eliot Norton* (Cambridge, Mass.: Belknap Press, 1959), p. 144.
[78] Norton left two copies of the sale catalog to Harvard. One is marked. In the other are letters to Norton from F. S. Ellis and Thomas Boone. The latter acted for Norton at the sale. Cf. D. G. Rossetti to his brother William, [6 March 1871] in *Dante Gabriel Rossetti: His Family-Letters*, ed. W. M. Rossetti (Boston: Roberts, 1895), II, 229.
[79] Norton to Lowell, 19 January 1874, in Norton, *Letters*, II, 31.

The Baron still lived. Indeed, on 16 February 1875, at the age of eighty-seven, he married Paolina Carboni. They resided in Leghorn at 4 Via Scali del Ponte Nuovo till finally, on 3 January 1880, the pallid little sprite slipped out of this world.

If Paolina likewise endured to ninety-two, as Signora Morandi of Bologna she might have heard some youngsters shouting in the summer of 1944 that the Germans, in retreat from Florence, had destroyed the southern approach to the Ponte Vecchio. By that act of demolition, Kirkup's tower got blown to kingdom come.

10 | STRETHER'S CHAD NEWSOME / A Reading of James's *The Ambassadors*

Gordon S. Haight

Chad Newsome, the center of all the action in Henry James's *The Ambassadors*, is the character readers know least about. He makes an even less vivid impression than his mother, who never appears in the novel. Following his father's death, Chad had been expected to take over the family business at Woollett, Massachusetts. But before settling down in the prosperous company, manufacturing the unnamed "little object," (pp. 48–49)[1] Chad at the age of twenty-two had come to Paris for a little diversion. After knocking about for six months with the riffraff of the American bars, he reported that he was going in "for economy and the real thing" on the Left Bank, where "the best French and many other things" were to be found (p. 67). He took lodgings up the Montagne Sainte-Geneviève with a group of "clever fellows," young painters, sculptors, architects, and medical students. Almost every evening he dined with "a band of earnest workers under one of the great artists, who had taken him right in"; there was even

---

[1] Quotations are taken from *The Ambassadors* by Henry James, *The New York Edition* (New York: Scribners, 1907–17), Vols. 21–22. Page numbers follow the quotations in the text.

a suggestion that he might enroll in some atelier to study painting (p. 67).

Within a few months, however, the curtain dropped between Paris and Woollett. Through the "intensity of silence" (p. 80), his family could only guess that his pursuit of the best French had shifted to involvement with one ferociously "interested" little woman after another. The last of these deplorable persons, "base, venal—out of the streets" (p. 45), had transported him back to the Right Bank, where in an expensive apartment on the Boulevard Malesherbes the "wretched boy" (p. 45) (as Strether called him, though he was now twenty-eight) had been living with her for more than three years. He had ignored all his mother's appeals to return home. Threats to cut off his allowance were futile because he possessed a substantial inheritance from his grandfather. At length Mrs. Newsome had dispatched her old friend Strether, her fiancé, to free Chad from the toils of the wicked woman and to bring him back to Woollett. There he would take his proper place in the business and, probably, marry nice young Mamie Pocock. "Mamie will save him!" (p. 57).

When Strether arrived, Chad was away from Paris, having left little Bilham, an American artist friend, in his apartment. Strether was amazed to find it a charming place, full of beautiful and valuable things that reflected a discriminating taste. Chad was at Cannes, a place where decent men never went with the kind of lady Woollett was assuming; at Cannes, Strether was told, "it's all people you know"—and if Chad knew such people, so much the better for him (p. 85). There was no trace of any vulgar woman who had him "in her toils." His friends to whom Bilham introduced Strether were all delightful, cultivated people. When Chad first appeared, arriving late to take Bilham's place at the Comédie Française, Strether mistook him for some distinguished stranger who had got into the wrong box. The rough, awkward boy he remembered at Woollett stood before him, handsome, smooth and polished, his thick black hair streaked with gray (p. 94), his voice toned, his accent established—an accomplished man of the world

(p. 100). Strether had faced "every contingency but that Chad should not *be* Chad" (p. 92). The transformation of the entire man seemed to him "a miracle almost monstrous" (p. 109).

By now we have been drawn so closely into Strether's consciousness that we too accept the miracle. Only by a careful rereading of the whole novel can we discern that the real Chad is a very different man from the glamorous youth Strether's romantic imagination has created. No one else in the novel sees Strether's Chad; the truth, as we piece it together from others' comments, varies widely from *his* view. In retrospect we realize that Chad was actually ready to go home when Strether arrived. But he was finding it awkward to break away from his mistress, and he meant to use Strether's embassy to help end the liaison, which after three years was beginning to pall.

This fact underlies Chad's calm acceptance of Strether's first blunt ultimatum—to make him break with everything and take him straight home. Chad treats the question as tacitly concluded. He sympathizes with the "horrors" Woollett has imagined:

"Well, I've no doubt," said Chad, "you've come near enough. The details, as you say, don't matter. It *has* been generally the case that I've let myself go. But I'm coming round—I'm not so bad now." With which they walked on again to Strether's hotel.

"Do you mean," the latter asked as they approached the door, "that there isn't any woman with you now?"

"But pray what has that to do with it?"

"Why it's the whole question."

"Of my going home?" Chad was clearly surprised. "Oh not much! Do you think that when I want to go any one will have any power—"

"To keep you"—Strether took him straight up—"from carrying out your wish? Well, our idea has been that somebody has hitherto—or a good many persons perhaps—kept you pretty well from 'wanting.' " (P. 103)

Woollett's suspicions don't matter if Chad is not entangled now.

"I never *was* that—let me insist. I always had my own way." With which he pursued: "And I have it at present."

"Then what are you here for? What has kept you," Strether asked, "if you *have* been able to leave?"

It made Chad, after a stare, throw himself back. "Do you think one's kept only by women?" His surprise and his verbal emphasis rang out so clear in the still street that Strether winced till he remembered the safety of their English speech. "Is that," the young man demanded, "what they think at Woollett? . . . I must say then you show a low mind!" (P. 104)

With preternatural intelligence, Strether's new friend, Maria Gostrey, had from her brief first glimpse of Chad deduced a woman behind the brilliant transformation, a woman "too good to admit!" and has cautioned Strether to "judge her only in Chad."

"Don't make up your mind. There are all sorts of things. You haven't seen him all."

This on his side Strether recognised; but his acuteness none the less showed him the danger. "Yes, but if the more I see the better he seems?"

Well, she found something. "That may be—but his disavowal of her isn't, all the same, pure consideration. There's a hitch." She made it out. "It's the effort to sink her."

Strether winced at the image. "To 'sink'—?"

"Well, I mean there's a struggle, and a part of it is just what he hides. Take time—that's the only way not to make some mistake that you'll regret. Then you'll see. He does really want to shake her off."

Our friend had by this time so got into the vision that he almost gasped. "After all she had done for him?"

Miss Gostrey gave him a look which broke the next moment into a wonderful smile. "He's not so good as you think!" (P. 111)

But Bilham had given him a milder opinion. When Strether asked, "*Is* there some woman? Of whom he's afraid of course I mean—or who does with him what she likes?" Bilham replied, without answering the question: "Chad's a rare case! He's awfully changed."

"Then you see it too?"

"The way he has improved? Oh yes—I think every one must

see it. But I'm not sure," said little Bilham, "that I didn't like him about as well in his other state."

"Then this *is* really a new state altogether?"

"Well," the young man after a moment returned, "I'm not sure he was really meant by nature to be quite so good. . . . I believe he really wants to go back and take up a career. He's capable of one, you know, that will improve and enlarge him still more. . . . I seem to see it as much the best thing for him. You see he's not happy."

"*Do* I?"—Strether stared. "I've been supposing I see just the opposite—an extraordinary case of the equilibrium arrived at and assured."

"Oh there's a lot behind it. . . . He ought to get married. *That* would do it. And he wants to."

"Wants to marry her?"

Again little Bilham waited, and, with a sense that he had information, Strether scarce knew what was coming. "He wants to be free. He isn't used, you see," the young man explained in his lucid way, "to being so good."

Strether hesitated. "Then I may take it from you that he *is* good."

His companion matched his pause, but making it up with a quiet fulness. "*Do* take it from me."

"Well then why isn't he free? . . . Why isn't he free if he's good?"

Little Bilham looked him full in the face, "Because it's a virtuous attachment." (P. 116)

The "virtuous attachment" proves to be a certain Madame de Vionnet, who with her daughter has just returned to Paris. Chad presented Strether to them the next Sunday at a party in the garden of the famous sculptor Gloriani. There Bilham pointed out some of the celebrities—ambassadors, bankers, generals, cabinet ministers, artists, actors. At Gloriani's parties there were always awfully nice women, "in particular the right *femmes du monde* (p. 127). There are lots of people with collections, Bilham added. "You'll be secured!" (p. 128).

"Have Madame de Vionnet and her daughter arrived?"

"I haven't seen them yet, but Miss Gostrey has come. She's in the pavilion looking at objects. One can see *she's* a collector," little Bilham added without offence.

"Oh yes, she's a collector, and I knew she was to come. Is Madame de Vionnet a collector?" Strether went on.

"Rather, I believe; almost celebrated." The young man met, on it, a little, his friend's eyes. "I happen to know—from Chad, whom I saw last night—that they've come back; but only yesterday. He wasn't sure—up to the last." (P. 128)

While walking over to the party with Strether, Chad had not mentioned them. Bilham, pressed to say whether they are the "virtuous attachment," replies: "I can only tell you that's what they pass for" (p. 129).

Strether had a pause. "The husband's dead?"
  "Dear no. Alive."
  "Oh!" said Strether. After which, as his companion laughed: "How then can it be so good?"
  "You'll see for yourself. One does see."
  "Chad's in love with the daughter?"
  "That's what I mean."
Strether wondered. "Then where's the difficulty?"
  "Why, aren't you and I—with our grander bolder ideas?"
  "Oh mine—!" Strether said rather strangely. But then as if to attenuate: "You mean they won't hear of Woollett?"
  Little Bilham smiled. "Isn't that just what you must see about?" (P. 129).

When Miss Barrace, who has lived all her life in Paris, comes up to them, Bilham's remark that Strether was about "to pounce" on Madame de Vionnet evokes her "Madame de Vionnet? Oh, oh, oh!" (p. 129) in wonderful crescendo with the opinion: "You are wonderful, you people, for not feeling those things—by which I mean impossibilities" (p. 130).

At this point Chad, easy and more wonderful than ever, comes to take Strether to Madame de Vionnet. But as they start towards the house, she comes out to meet them, "a young woman" (she was thirty-eight), very blonde, dressed in a light transparent black with long sleeves covering many gold bracelets. Chad is "excellently free and light" about the presentation: "Here you are then, face to face at last;

you're made for each other—*vous allez voir;* and I bless your union." And he slips off to find Jeanne: "Ah, but you know, he must see *her*" (p. 133). With the mother, Strether's conversation is brief:

"I've heard a great deal about you," she said.

"Well, about *you*, Madame de Vionnet, I've heard, I'm bound to say, almost nothing."

"Hasn't Miss Gostrey said a good word for me?"

"I didn't even know of her knowing you."

"Well, now she'll tell you all. I'm so glad you're in relation with her." (P. 134)

The interchange is interrupted by two gentlemen and a lady addressed as "Duchesse," who sweep Madame de Vionnet away. A moment later Strether sees her across the garden in animated conversation with Gloriani.

Chad now reappears with Jeanne de Vionnet. The hackneyed diction in which Strether clothes his first impression of her is James's way of defining the level of Strether's self-delusion: Chad

had plucked this blossom; he had kept it overnight in water; and at last as he held it up to wonder he did enjoy his effect. That was why Strether had felt at first the breath of calculation—and why moreover, as he now knew, his look at the girl would be, for the young man, a sign of the latter's success. What young man had ever paraded about that way, without a reason, a maiden in her flower? . . . Chad however had just excellently spoken. "This is a good little friend of mine who knows all about you and has moreover a message for you. And this, my dear"—he had turned to the child herself—"is the best man in the world, who has it in his power to do a great deal for us and whom I want you to like and revere as nearly as possible as much as I do." (Pp. 139–40)

Jeanne's little speech, delivered with her hands clasped "as if in some small learnt prayer," expresses Mamma's hope that Strether would come to see them very soon. "She has something important to say to you" (p. 140). Then Chad takes her away, promising to return. But he doesn't.

He comes instead early the next morning to make certain that Strether will call on Madame de Vionnet. Denying that an engagement to marry Jeanne is his "hitch," he insists that he is staying in Paris as long as possible to give Strether a chance to know her mother.

> "She's herself my hitch, hang it—if you must really have it all out. But in a sense," he hastened in the most wonderful manner to add, "that you'll quite make out for yourself. She's too good a friend, confound her. Too good, I mean, for me to leave without—without—" It was his first hesitation.
> "Without what?"
> "Well, without my arranging somehow or other the damnable terms of my sacrifice."
> "It *will* be a sacrifice then?"
> "It will be the greatest loss I ever suffered. I owe her so much." (P. 148)

By this Strether understands that Chad was "indebted for alterations, and she was thereby in a position to have sent in her bill for expenses incurred in reconstruction" (p. 149). If Strether consents to know Madame de Vionnet, Chad gives his word of honor that he will surrender himself to return to Woollett.

That afternoon they call on her in her charming apartment in the Rue de Bellechasse—a name rich in Jamesian overtones. Within a dozen minutes Chad, "with a look at his watch and then another at their hostess, says genially, gaily, 'I've an engagement, and I know you won't complain if I leave him with you. He'll interest you immensely; and as for her,' he declares to Strether, 'I assure you, if you're at all nervous, she's perfectly safe'" (p. 151). It was not a very graceful exit for a man of the world. Madame de Vionnet, sitting perfectly still, launched into her explanation, which was her own idea, not at all "what Mr. Newsome had in mind" (p. 154). Chad's idea was "simply what a man's idea always is—to put every effort off on the woman."

> "The 'woman'—?" Strether slowly echoed.
> "The woman he likes—and just in proportion as he likes her. In proportion too—for shifting the trouble—as she likes *him*."

Strether followed it; then with an abruptness of his own: "How much do you like Chad?"

"Just as much as *that*—to take all, with you, on myself." But she got at once again away from this. "I've been trembling as if we were to stand or fall by what you may think of me; and I'm even now," she went on wonderfully, "drawing a long breath—and, yes, truly taking a great courage—from the hope that I don't in fact strike you as impossible." (P. 155)

She wanted Strether to tell Mrs. Newsome "about *us*..... Tell her I've been good for him. Don't you think I have?" (Pp. 157–58). Forced to admit that the change she has wrought in Chad is wonderful, Strether leaves with the vague promise, "I'll save you if I can" (p. 159).

The fleeting, perfunctory role Chad plays in these scenes contributes to our shadowy view of him. A further example occurs at the dinner party he gave ten days later. There Madame de Vionnet, resplendent in a collar of large old emeralds worn with a silvery-gray dress, her bare arms and shoulders white and beautiful, acts as hostess openly enough to betray her domesticated relation even to the bemused Strether. He discusses her with Miss Barrace.

"She strikes you to-night as particularly magnificent?"

"Surely. Almost as I've never seen her. Doesn't she you? Why it's *for* you."

He persisted in his candour. " 'For' me—?"

"Oh, oh, oh!" cried Miss Barrace, who persisted in the opposite of that quality.

"Well," he acutely admitted, "she *is* different. She's gay."

"She's gay!" Miss Barrace laughed. "And she has beautiful shoulders—though there's nothing different in that."

"No," said Strether, "one was sure of her shoulders. It isn't her shoulders."

His companion, with renewed mirth and the finest sense, between the puffs of her cigarette, of the drollery of things, appeared to find their conversation highly delightful. "Yes, it isn't her shoulders."

"What then is it?" Strether earnestly enquired.

"Why, it's *she*—simply. It's her mood. It's her charm." (P. 164)

Asked if she would ever divorce:

Miss Barrace looked at him through all her tortoise-shell. "Why should she?"

It wasn't what he had asked for, he signified; but he met it well enough. "To marry Chad."

"Why should she marry Chad?"

"Because I'm convinced she's very fond of him. She has done wonders for him."

"Well, then, how could she do more?" . . .

Strether considered a moment this proposition. "You mean it's so beautiful for our friends simply to go on so?"

But whatever he said made her laugh. "Beautiful." (Pp. 164–65)

Bilham, sitting apart with him after dinner, gives Strether a history of Chad's affair, which he had watched for three years.

"He wasn't so bad before it as I seem to have made out that you think. . . . Still, you know," the young man in all fairness developed, "there was room for her, and that's where she came in. She saw her chance and took it. That's what strikes me as having been so fine. But of course," he wound up, "he liked her first."

"Naturally," said Strether.

"I mean that they first met somehow and somewhere—I believe in some American house—and she, without in the least then intending it, made her impression. Then with time and opportunity he made his; and after *that* she was as bad as he."

"Strether vaguely took it up. "As 'bad'?"

"She began, that is, to care—to care very much. Alone, and in her horrid position, she found it, when once she had started, an interest. It was, it is, an interest; and it did—it continues to do—a lot for herself as well. So she still cares. She cares in fact," said little Bilham thoughtfully, "more." . . .

"More, you mean, than he?"

On which his companion looked round at him, and now for an instant their eyes met. "More than he?" he repeated.

Little Bilham, for as long, hung fire. "Will you never tell any one?"

Strether thought. "Whom should I tell?"

"Why I supposed you reported regularly—"

"To people at home?"—Strether took him up. "Well, I won't tell them this."

The young man at last looked away. "Then she does now care more than he." (Pp. 194–95)

They can't marry, for Monsieur de Vionnet "may live for ever."

"A woman—" said Bilham, "a particular woman may stand that strain. But can a man?" . . .

"Not without a very high ideal of conduct. But that's just what we're attributing to Chad." (Pp. 176–77)

Strether passes over Bilham's remark that "Chad ought to marry" with the comfortable assurance that "When it's for each other that people give things up they don't miss them. . . . Let them face the future together!" If Chad should give her up and go back to a business career, as he had lately told Bilham he wanted to, "he ought to be ashamed of himself" (p. 177).

In this extraordinary reversal Chad's plan to use Strether to extricate himself has backfired. When a cable from Mrs. Newsome directs Strether to "Come back by the first ship," Chad declared, "I've really been ready this month. I've only been waiting for you" (p. 192). As for Madame de Vionnet,

"Ah *her* wanting me not to go has nothing to do with it! It's only because she's afraid—afraid of the way that, over there, I may get caught. But her fear's groundless."

He had met again his companion's sufficiently searching look. "Are you tired of her?"

Chad gave him in reply to this, with a movement of the head, the strangest slow smile he had ever had from him. "Never."

It had immediately, on Strether's imagination, so deep and soft an effect that our friend could only for the moment keep it before him. "Never?"

"Never," Chad obligingly and serenely repeated. (P. 195)

He proposes to go home for a month or two, leaving Strether in Paris. "Madame de Vionnet," smiles Chad, "would look after you in the interval" (p. 197). But Strether, intent on "saving" her, will stay only if Chad does.

Sarah Pocock, Chad's sister, and her husband soon

arrive to supplant the faithless ambassador. Sarah betrays not the smallest sign of seeing that her brother is not the same old Chad; and when Strether finally puts the direct question as to her appreciating his "fortunate development," "Fortunate?" she echoes again. "I call it hideous" (p. 296). Madame de Vionnet had come to call on her the morning after she landed, and though her famous charm failed to thaw Sarah's icy rigor, she turned it on Jim Pocock with considerable success, "more wonderful than ever" (p. 281). At her invitation he goes to the Rue de Bellechasse—alone—for tea. Had it been workable, she might even have gone to Switzerland with the Pococks—"for Jim and symmetry" (p. 308). She appeared at the station with Chad to see them off.

Though Madame de Vionnet had never gone about with Chad in public, there were times when she used to see him every day. While the Pococks were in Paris, she saw less of him than ever, not wanting to worry him. Still Chad had not neglected her interests: he had found a husband for her little Jeanne, a suitable young man named de Montbron, and had concluded all the tough practical negotiations for a French marriage. Though James does not say so, these had obviously included a substantial dowry for Jeanne, Chad's "definite and final acknowledgement" (p. 257) to Madame de Vionnet, the last payment on her "bill for alterations" (p. 149). He had "settled the terms of his sacrifice," and was now more than ready to go home. "I was ready six weeks ago," he declared (p. 303).

But he was not to escape from her so easily. A few days after the Pococks' departure Madame de Vionnet took Chad to the little rustic retreat they had in the country. There, quite by accident, Strether, strolling about alone, encountered them rowing on the river. The fiction of the "virtuous attachment" created by his fervid imagination was irreparably shattered. "There had been simply a *lie* in the charming affair" (p. 329). Chad of course, put the whole burden of explanation on her. He "habitually left things to others," always letting people have their way "when he felt that it would somehow turn his wheel for him" (p. 337). He copped out. For a whole week he was not to be found. Neither Strether nor Madame de Vionnet had any word of him. In tears, afraid for her life, "old and abject and hideous" (p. 343), she sees no hope of holding Chad. Strether agrees to make one last appeal.

At midnight, on the eighth day, he discovered Chad smoking on his balcony overlooking the Boulevard Malesherbes and walked up the three flights to his apartment. Chad received him cordially as ever. "I've been to England," he said. "One must sometimes get off" (p. 355). Strether had come to say good-bye—and something more:

"You'll be a brute, you know—you'll be guilty of the last infamy—if you ever forsake her. . . ."

"Oh, rather!—if I should do anything of *that* sort. . . ."

"I want it," said Strether, "to be my last word of all to you. I can't say more, you know; and I don't see how I can do more, in every way, than I've done."

Chad took this, almost artlessly, as a direct allusion. "You've seen her?"

"Oh yes—to say good-bye. And if I had doubted the truth of what I tell you—"

"She'd have cleared up your doubt?" Chad understood— "rather"—again! It even kept him briefly silent. But he made that up. "She must have been wonderful."

"She *was,*" Strether candidly admitted—all of which practically told as a reference to the conditions created by the accident of the previous week.

They appeared for a little to be looking back at it; and that came out still more in what Chad next said. "I don't know what you've really thought, all along; I never did know—for anything, with you, seemed to be possible. But of course—of course—" Without confusion, quite with nothing but indulgence, he broke down, he pulled up. "After all, you understand. I spoke to you originally only as I *had* to speak. There's only one way—isn't there?—about such things. However," he smiled with a final philosophy, "I see it's all right." (Pp. 354–55)

Showing no embarrassment, Chad explained that at their meeting in the country he had been disturbed only *for* Strether, and had gone to London to let him down more gently. Strether repeated his solemn appeal to Chad to stay:

"You'd not only be, as I say, a brute; you'd be . . . a criminal of the deepest dye."

Chad gave a sharper look, as if to gauge a possible suspicion. "I don't know what should make you think I'm tired of her."

Strether didn't quite know either, and such impressions, for the imaginative mind, were always too fine, too floating, to produce on the spot their warrant. There was none the less for him, in the very manner of his host's allusion to satiety as a thinkable motive, a slight breath of the ominous. "I feel how much more she can do for you. She hasn't done it all yet. Stay with her at least till she has."

"And leave her *then?*"

Chad had kept smiling, but its effect in Strether was a shade of dryness. "Don't leave her *before*. When you've got all that can be got—I don't say," he added a trifle grimly, "that will be the proper time. But as, for you, from such a woman, there will always be something to be got, my remark's not a wrong to her." Chad let him go on, showing every decent deference, showing perhaps also a candid curiosity for this sharper accent. "I remember you, you know, as you were."

"An awful ass, wasn't I?"

The response was as prompt as if he had pressed a spring; it had a ready abundance at which he even winced; so that he took a moment to meet it. "You certainly then wouldn't have seemed worth all you've let me in for. You've defined yourself better. Your value has quintupled."

"Well then, wouldn't that be enough—?"

Chad had risked it jocosely, but Strether remained blank. "Enough?"

"If one *should* wish to live on one's accumulations?" After which, however, as his friend appeared cold to the joke, the young man as easily dropped it. "Of course I really never forget, night or day, what I owe her. I owe her everything. I give you my word of honour," he frankly rang out, "that I'm not a bit tired of her." Strether at this only gave him a stare: the way youth could express itself was again and again a wonder. He meant no harm, though he might after all be capable of much; yet he spoke of being "tired" of her almost as he might have spoken of being tired of roast mutton for dinner. "She has never for a moment yet bored me—never been wanting, as the cleverest women sometimes are, in tact. She has never talked about her tact—as even they too sometimes talk; but she has always had it.

She has never had it more"—he handsomely made the point—
"than just lately." And he scrupulously went further. "She has
never been anything I could call a burden."

Strether for a moment said nothing; then he spoke gravely,
with his shade of dryness deepened. "Oh if you didn't do her
justice—!"

"I *should* be a beast, eh?" (Pp. 356–57)

As Chad walked back with him to the hotel, Strether
learned that in London he had been getting some news of
the art of advertising, the great new force. "It really does
the thing, you know."

"Affects, you mean, the sale of the object advertised?"

"Yes—but affects it extraordinarily; really beyond what one
had supposed. I mean of course when it's done as one makes
out that, in our roaring age, it *can* be done. I've been finding out
a little; though it doubtless doesn't amount to much more than
what you originally, so awfully vividly—and all, very nearly, that
first night—put before me. It's an art like another, and infinite
like all the arts." He went on as if for the joke of it—almost as if
his friend's face amused him. "In the hands, naturally, of a master. The right man must take hold. With the right man to work
it *c'est un monde.*"

Strether had watched him quite as if, there on the pavement,
without a pretext, he had begun to dance a fancy step. "Is what
you're thinking of that you yourself, in the case you have in
mind, would be the right man?"

Chad had thrown back his light coat and thrust each of his
thumbs into an armhole of his waistcoat; in which position his
fingers played up and down. "Why, what is he but what you
yourself, as I say, took me for when you first came out?" (P. 359)

This is our last view of Chad. The open ending leaves us
free to project his future as we like. A careful scrutiny of
the Chad seen through other eyes than those of the romantic Strether makes it hard to believe that Madame de
Vionnet will play a part in it. More than anyone, she had
always "felt him to have the makings of an immense man
of business." As he stands there under the streetlamp, Chad
brings to mind the figure of his shrewd father, Abel New-

some. Gathering the hints dropped by his friends, we can easily predict that Chad will join the Pococks on their return to Woollett, where the new art of advertising applied to the still-unnamed little object will soon make the whole place hum.

11 | CHARACTER IN THE NOVEL / A "Real Illusion"

J. Hillis Miller

That a primary function of novels is to present "characters" is a regnant assumption in much criticism of fiction, especially perhaps in English and American criticism. Examples are the work on the novel of F. R. Leavis, such a book as W. J. Harvey's *Character and the Novel* (1965), the influential studies of the novel by Barbara Hardy, and the brilliant discussions of the topic by Martin Price. The list could be extended indefinitely. It would of course include critical reflections by those who have some doubts about traditional notions of character and traditional ways of representing it, for example, Virginia Woolf's well-known attack on Edwardian realism, "Mr. Bennett and Mrs. Brown."

In fact the assumption that the thing to talk about when discussing a novel is the characters is so deeply ingrained in our culture that it is exceedingly difficult to get students to talk or to write about anything else. For reasons which are both cultural and literary, that is, for reasons which derive from the "real" expectations of people in their living together and at the same time from their expectations about this particular form of literature, most readers of novels pass through the language of works of fiction as though it were a transparent glass and begin talking about the characters in the story as if they were real people, seen perhaps through that glass and perhaps distorted by it, but not "created" by it.

Such readers or critics talk about the characters in a novel in the same way that the narrator of that novel characteristically talks about them, that is, as if they had an independent psychological existence. Usually there is a change from the past to the present tense: "Dorothea Brooke convinces herself that marrying Casaubon would be like marrying Milton . . . etc., etc." The language of the critic extends the language of the narrator. It mimes that language and yields to the illusion generated by the narrator, filling in gaps in the narrator's analysis, extrapolating from it, paraphrasing it. This is the "How-many-children-had-Lady-Macbeth?" fallacy blithely made the basis of an entire mode of the criticism of fiction. Such criticism is an odd form of depersonalization. The critic has caught a trick of the language of the text, as one catches a disease. He has been contaminated by the language he reads. He speaks unwittingly as though he were one of the invented characters in the novel, the narrator. Far from being more a means of engagement in the "real world" than a discussion of technique or of the language of the novel, such criticism is a spontaneous evasion into impalpable fictionalities. It makes of the critic himself a fiction, the player of a role.

To change the metaphor of the transparent glass, one might say that it is as unnatural an act to pay attention to the language of a work of fiction (though an unnatural act which, to be sure, many people have learned these days), as to study the threads of a tapestry rather than look at the blazoned picture it represents. This figure, however, like all visual or spatial figures for the mode of existence of a work of fiction, is misleading. A work of fiction is that curious kind of tapestry in which the fact that its picture is made of threads is woven into the picture. This fact is one of the things it is a picture "of," perhaps the essential thing it is of. A work of fiction always in one way or another allegorizes problems of language in terms of the characters and their interactions. This allegorizing is explicitly called attention to in many details of the language of any given novel. The picture in the tapestry points to its own threads and to their modes of weaving.

Nevertheless, for the readers who belong to the tradition in which these novels were written, "realistic fiction" has as perhaps its most salient characteristic the ability to create the powerful phantasms of personalities. The reader feels he knows Elizabeth Bennet, Dorothea Brooke, Plantagenet Palliser, Michael Henchard, or Joe Christmas in the same way he knows his friends or relatives. Perhaps he knows them even better. One of the powerful attractions of the reading of novels (when this activity was a central feature of our culture, which is probably no longer the case), was the way this seemed to give an even more intimate access to the mind and heart of another person than the reader could ever feel himself to have in "real life." Nevertheless, the feeling that one is encountering a "character," a "person," "another self," is demonstrably an illusion, both in the novel and in real life. It is as much an illusion as the other basic concepts of Occidental metaphysics, with which it is inextricably connected. Moreover, if realistic novels have been a puissant reinforcement for the last four hundred years of the illusion of selfhood, they have at the same time constantly and explicitly deconstructed that illusion. They have shown it to be the result of a misinterpretation, the misreading of signs.

There is no novel, however, that is "really a novel," from *Don Quixote* to *Ulysses, The Waves,* or even *L'Innomable,* which does not create in two ways the powerful illusion of characters. One is the illusion of the character of the narrator. The narrator seems to be a man (or woman) speaking to men (or women). There is an almost irresistible temptation to think of the narrative voice as that of the author himself. The second illusion is that of the characters in the story. They seem to be men and women like ourselves. This positing of two forms of character is a distinguishing feature of novels as such, or perhaps of narrative as such, since who would deny these illusions, *mutatis mutandis,* to fairy tales, to Norse sagas, or to *The Odyssey?*

The *mutatis mutandis* is the law of parsimony in the creation of artistic illusion by conventional means. Ernst Gombrich has made this familiar in his magisterial challenge to the idea of photographic realism, "Meditations on a Hobby Horse." The illusion of character is produced differently within each culture or each "period" of a culture. It may be produced by the most economical means, since it is reinforced by powerful conventions and presuppositions about character within the public for whom a given novel is intended. As two sticks and a bit of yarn will do as a gallant steed for a child, so a few words lightly sketched out at the beginning of a novel create magically, for the readers within its tradition, the strong impression of two characters: that of the protagonist, that of the storyteller. In the case of a first-person novel, the two are of course the same. Often, it is worth noting, the magic gesture depends unostentatiously on some figure of speech, as in the initial presentations of Pip in *Great Expectations,* of Dorothea Brooke in *Middlemarch,* and of Jim in *Lord Jim:*

I called myself Pip.

"How very beautiful these gems are!" said Dorothea.

He was an inch, perhaps two, under six feet, powerfully built, and he advanced straight at you with a slight stoop of the shoulders, head forward, and a fixed from-under stare which made you think of a charging bull.

In the first case the figure is that of "pip" as seed. The second presents in the image of the gems the first parabolic emblem in *Middlemarch.* The third, in the image of the bull, creates, for me at least, the distinct impression of a personality, an outline which the rest of the novel does no more than fill in a little.

What is arbitrary, conventional, and parsimonious about this procedure may be experienced by reading a novel in a somewhat different tradition from one's own. There is something slightly odd and almost unconvincing, for an English or American reader, about the presentation of character in French, German, or Russian novels, for example in *Jacques le fataliste* or *La Chartreuse de Parme,* in *Die*

Wahlverwandschaften, or in *Crime and Punishment,* in spite of the ability such a reader has to yield to the "real illusion" (Walter Pater's phrase) of characters in them. He does this by training and by a slight effort of depersonification, a slight alienation from his own culture such as courses in "The European Novel" are designed to provide. Until the reader gets used to the new conventions, however, these slightly alien novels show, for him, their conventions. He sees the two sticks and the bit of yarn behind the noble charger. Cinema seems perhaps the most "realistic" of narrative forms. Is it not photographs of actual people? Nevertheless, a film is, anthropologists have discovered, difficult for "primitive" peoples to interpret until they have had appropriate training. They cannot make anything out of the images on the screen or are distracted by all sorts of peripheral details which would scarcely be noticed by a Western moviegoer.

The function of novels within the community of its readers may then by hypothesis be said to be circular. Each culture and each period of that culture has its own complex presuppositions about selfhood. An example would be the relatively fixed notion of selfhood in England, perhaps reinforced by certain aspects of Protestantism, as against the relatively fluid feeling for character in France. These presuppositions are in each community of readers, during the period of the reign of the novel as a major genre, reinforced and partly created by novels. The reader goes to a novel to be reassured, to encounter characters "like himself." He reads the novel according to his presuppositions about selfhood, so that, confronted by the characters on the page, which have the magic power to generate the illusion of character, he is like the child with his hobbyhorse, not like the "savage" at the cinema. On the other hand, once that interpretation has been made—once he has yielded to the real illusion of knowing Pip, Lord Jim, Elizabeth Bennet, or Dorothea Brooke, following their lives through as he follows the text through, knowing them better and better, knowing them intimately from within—he turns the line around and interprets his neighbors and himself according to the models he has encountered in novels. He peoples the world with Willoughbys, Claras, and Dorotheas. In this way nature imitates art. England after 1836 begins to be filled with Dickensian characters, even with people who feel themselves to be Dickensian characters.

The novel, then, has a powerful, perhaps indispensable, social function during its reign. It sustains and creates the fictions of character and the characteristic lifelines of characters. These form one of the fundamental cohesive forces keeping each community of readers together. A community may be defined as a group of people who live by the same fictions, the same simplifications, the same hypostatized figures posited as substances. The novel helps to make and sustain such communities.

This function of novels seems clear enough, but what is the function of the contrary aspect of each work of fiction, its putting in question of the notions of character on which its benign power to maintain society depends? This disintegrating would seem to be not only antisocial but even autodestructive, since it demolishes the illusion of character on which the novel's power and function depend. This autodeconstruction reduces the readers of a given novel to the state of the child who has outgrown his toy and sees the sticks and yarn behind the hobbyhorse. Why is this dissolution of its own fundamental fiction as constant a feature of realistic fiction as the creation of the fiction of character in the first place?

I suggest that the function is apotropaic. It is a throwing away of what is already thrown away in order to save it. It is a destroying of the already destroyed in order to preserve the illusion that it is still intact. All men and women living within a culture accepting a certain notion of character have an uneasy feeling that their belief in character, even their belief in their own characters, may be confidence in an illusion. The function of the self-deconstructive aspect of novels would then be to assuage this covert suspicion by expressing it overtly, in a safe region of fiction. Character is then triumphantly reaffirmed in the face of its putting in question, even if that reaffirmation may be no more than the persistence of that deconstructing voice, the voice of the narrator who says "I am I," and goes on saying "I am I" even when he has demonstrated that there is no "I," or the persistence of the character who says, "I have and am no I."

My hypothesis, then: the novel as the perpetual tying and untying of the knot of selfhood for the purpose, in the psychic economy of the individual and of the community, of affirming the fiction of character by putting it fictionally in question and so short-circuiting a doubt which, left free to act in the real social world, might destroy both self and community. Belief in the subject, in character, is thereby precariously maintained by the novel over the abyss of its dismantling. Is not the positing of the subject necessary to the positing of its fictionality, in a perpetual torsion of naysaying and yea-saying, of naysaying which cannot be said without the yea-saying its saying unsays? The novel demonstrates, in a "safe" realm where nothing serious is at stake, the possibility of maintaining the fiction of selfhood in the teeth of a recognition that it is a fictive projection, an "interpretation" not a fact, and so always open to being dissolved by a contrary interpretation—for example, that of the multiplicity or the nonentity of the ego. The novel is an instrument, a production of its society which has a certain function within the psychic economy of that society. It is not a mimetic copy of something which could do perfectly well without the copy. Nor is it the creation of a supplementary alternative "world" with no relation other than that of accurate mirroring to the real social world.

The apotropaic function, however—warding off the loss by enacting it safely and recovering what was lost in simulated or fetichistic form, beyond its loss—is performed better if it is covert. It should be performed over and over every time *Robinson Crusoe, Great Expectations, Middlemarch,* or *To the Lighthouse* is read, but it should not be recognized as such. The function of the fiercely maintained and yet manifestly absurd theory of mimetic representation—the single exclusive official theory of fiction during all the period of the heyday of the realistic novel, held by authors, critics, and readers alike, and still imperturbably, or almost imperturbably, assumed by many critics and readers today—is to serve as a screen. This screen allows the hidden, repressed function of the novel to be effectively performed. The importance of that function, and the need to keep it secret, even though the novels themselves everywhere betray the secret, is indicated by the energy, both intellectual and moral, with which the mirror theory of the novel is maintained. It is also indicated by the energy of indignation, again both intellectual and moral, with which the alternative theory is denied. The alternative theory is said to be an inappropriate application of "modern" theories to texts which are innocent of everything but a desire to mirror accurately the social and psychological "realities" of their times for the highly moral purpose of teaching us to know our neighbors better and to love them as they are. Chapter 17 of George Eliot's *Adam Bede* is of course the *locus classicus* for this theory in the Victorian novel, though few readers seem to have noticed how she pulls the rug out from under her own theory, both in the conceptual analysis toward the end of that chapter and in her practice of realism in the novel itself.

The texts of "classical realism" in the novel know better, however. It is only necessary to read those novels carefully, though this is extremely difficult to do, since the energy of repression is strong. As much commentary on these novels demonstrates, the passages deconstructing the notion of character in *Middlemarch,* say, or in *Daniel Deronda* (to cite archetypes of realistic fiction in the Victorian period) are commonly passed over in silence as if they were not there. The presuppositions in favor of "character" in the mind of the critic are so strong that he imposes an interpretation based on those presuppositions willy-nilly, like a network over the text. Any strong community will rightly resist strongly, and name as dissolute, the dissolution of the fictions it lives by, even the revelation of the covert function, as supports of the community, of those entities which it names "works of fiction." As Friedrich Nietzsche says, "to be able to read off a text as a text without interposing an interpretation is the last-developed form of 'inner experience'—perhaps one that is hardly possible" (*The Will to Power*, Section 479). If it is hardly possible, it may not even be desirable. In fact, a reading of George Eliot's novels (to continue with that example) which follows out those passages undoing the notion of character is no less an interpretation than the one which accepts the characters and talks of them as real people. Both are also equally based on judgments of moral utility, though different ones in each case. The "deconstructive" reading of George Eliot is by no means that "hardly possible" reading off a text as a text without interposing an interpretation that Nietzsche names. What would a text without interpretation be? A set of absurd signs not seen as signs but only as material marks without significance. The text of a novel like *Adam Bede* or *Middlemarch* contains the possibility, in the words on the page, both of the "realistic" reading and of the contrary "deconstructive" one, but both are interpretations cast over the text. The relation between these two interpretations is not that of simple opposition. It is a paradoxical inherence of each in the other. It is a relation of dependence in which each posits the other as the presupposition of its own operation but at the same time makes that presupposition impossible exclusively to presuppose. If my hypothesis about the double function of realistic fiction, as an affirmation of character and as a putting in question of character, is correct, readings of such novels should perhaps try to do justice to both aspects of their presentation of character. Like any hypothesis, the one I have presented here would need to be tested on an appropriate number of examples. That remains to be done.

CHECKLIST OF THE PRINTED
WORKS OF EDGAR JOHNSON

CONTRIBUTORS

INDEX

CHECKLIST OF THE PRINTED WORKS OF EDGAR JOHNSON

Books

Unweave a Rainbow: A Sentimental Fantasy. Garden City, N.Y.: Doubleday, Doran, 1931. Reissued, New York: Macmillan, 1956.

One Mighty Torrent: The Drama of Biography. New York: Stackpole, 1937. Reissued, New York: Macmillan, 1956.

The Praying Mantis. A Novel. New York: Stackpole; London, Cassell, 1937.

A Treasury of Biography. New York: Howell, Soskin, 1940.

A Treasury of Satire. New York: Simon and Schuster, 1945.

Charles Dickens: His Tragedy and Triumph. 2 vols. New York: Simon and Schuster; London: Gollancz, 1952. Reissued, Boston: Little, Brown, 1964; London: Hamish Hamilton, 1970. Book-of-the-Month Club main selection; Readers' Subscription selection.

Dickens to Miss Burdett-Coutts. Letters selected and edited from the collection in the Pierpont Morgan library, with a critical and biographical introduction. London: Jonathan Cape, 1952. Published in America as *The Heart of Charles Dickens.* New York: Duell, Sloan, and Pearce, 1952.

Charles Dickens: Past, Present, and Future. A symposium with George Ford, J. Hillis Miller, and Sylvère Monod at the Dickens Fellowship Conference, Boston, 1961. Boston: Charles Dickens Conference Center, 1962.

The Dickens Theatrical Reader. Edited with a prologue and notes in collaboration with Eleanor Johnson. Boston: Little, Brown; London: Gollancz, 1964.

Sir Walter Scott in the Fales Collection. New York University Libraries: Bibliographical Series No. 4. New York: New York University Libraries, 1968.

Sir Walter Scott: The Great Unknown. 2 vols. New York: Macmillan; London: Hamish Hamilton, 1970. American Heritage Prize for Biography. Readers' Subscription selection.

Charles Dickens: His Tragedy and Triumph. Revised edition in one volume of the original two-volume edition. New York: Viking; London: Penguin, 1977. Book-of-the-Month Club alternate selection. Readers' Subscription selection.

Articles

"Some Real and Imaginary Obligations of Criticism." *Washington University Studies,* 12 (1925), 233–53.

"Is Criticism Pedantry?" *Contempo,* 1 (August 21, 1931), 1, 4.

"American Mosaic." *New Republic,* 90 (1937), 115–16.

"Henry Adams: The Last Liberal." *Science and Society,* 1 (1937), 362–78.

"American Biography and the Modern World." *North American Review,* 245 (1938), 364–80.

"Contemporary Biography and the Modern Spirit." In *Byrdcliffe Afternoons.* Ed. Martin Schultze. Woodstock, N.Y.: Overlook Press, 1939, pp. 53–66.

"Hate in Aldous Huxley." *University Review,* 4 (1940), 221–35.

"George Bernard Shaw: Argument and Casuistry in Satire." *Accent,* 1 (1941), 67–75.

"Thorstein Veblen: Man from Mars." *New Republic,* 105 (1941), 121–23.

"The Garden of Scepticism." *Eliot Magazine,* 4 November 1942, pp. 10, 16.
"Satiric Irony." *Accent,* 4 (1944), 159–63.
"Dickens and the Bluenose Legislator." *American Scholar,* 17 (1948), 450–58.
"Dickens Clashes with his Publisher, I." *Dickensian,* 46 (1949), 10–17.
"Dickens Clashes with his Publisher, II." *Dickensian,* 46 (1950), 76–84.
"Dickens, Fagin, and Mr. Riah: The Intention of the Novelist." *Commentary,* 9 (1950), 47–51.
"Farewell the Separate Peace: The Rejections of Ernest Hemingway." In *Ernest Hemingway: The Man and His Work.* Ed. John K. M. McCaffery. Cleveland: World Publishing, 1950. First published in *Sewanee Review,* 48 (1940), 289–300.
"*The Christmas Carol* and the Economic Man." *American Scholar,* 21 (1950–51), 91–98.
"*Bleak House:* The Anatomy of Society." *Nineteenth-Century Fiction,* 7 (1952), 73–89. Also published as Part Eight, Chapter 2, pp. 762–82, of *Charles Dickens: His Tragedy and Triumph* (1952).
"Dickens and Shaw." *Shaw Bulletin,* 1 (1953), 1–7.
"The Paradox of Dickens." *Dickensian,* 50 (1954), 149–58.
Introduction and Bibliographical Note to Charles Dickens, *A Christmas Carol.* A facsimile of the first edition. New York: Columbia University Press, 1956. Reissued, Ann Arbor: University Microfilms, 1967.
"The Dilemma of Hamlet," in *Great Moral Dilemmas in Literature, Past and Present.* Ed. Robert Morrison McIver. New York: Institute for Religious and Social Studies, 1956, pp. 99–111.
"Stevenson: *Travels with a Donkey.*" *Invitation to Learning Reader No. 19,* 5 (1956), 354–60. With Lyman Bryson and Pierre Szanick.
"Dickens: *Great Expectations.*" *Invitation to Learning Reader No. 21,* 6 (1956), 28–33. With Lyman Bryson and Charles Frankel.

"The Garrick Club Affair." *PMLA,* 71 (March 1956), 256–59.

Introduction to Sir Walter Scott, *Rob Roy.* Boston: Houghton Mifflin, 1956.

Introduction to Edward George Bulwer-Lytton, *The Last Days of Pompeii.* New York: printed for members of the Limited Editions Club at the Officina Bondoni, Verona, 1956; New York: Heritage Press, 1957.

Introduction to Charles Dickens, *Oliver Twist.* New York: Pocket Books, 1957.

Introduction to Charles Dickens, *A Tale of Two Cities.* New York: Pocket Books, 1957.

"Dickens and Shaw: Critics of Society." *Virginia Quarterly Review,* 33 (1957), 66–79.

"The Case for the 'Useless' in American Education." *City College Alumnus,* November 1959, pp. 7–10.

Afterword to Charles Dickens, *David Copperfield.* New York: New American Library, 1962.

"Dickens and His Critics." *Saturday Review,* 45 (10 February 1962), 31, 69.

Introduction to Charles Dickens, *Dombey and Son.* New York: Dell, 1963.

Afterword to Charles Dickens, *A Tale of Two Cities.* New York: New American Library, 1963.

Introduction to Charles Dickens, *The Pickwick Papers.* New York: Dell, 1964.

Afterword to Sir Walter Scott, *Waverley.* New York: New American Library, 1964.

Introduction to Charles Dickens, *Bleak House.* New York: Dell, 1965.

Introduction to Charles Dickens, *Martin Chuzzlewit.* New York: Dell, 1965.

"Dickens and the Spirit of the Age." *Bibliotheca Bucnellensis,* NS 4 (1966), 1–13.

"Dickens: The Dark Pilgrimage." In *Charles Dickens, 1812–1870: A Centenary Volume.* Ed. E. W. F. Tomlin. New York: Simon and Schuster, 1969, pp. 41–63.

"Sceptered Kings and Laureled Conquerors: Scott in London and Paris." *Nineteenth Century Fiction,* 7 (1969),

299–320. Also published in similar form as Part Five, Chapter 10, pp. 488–504, in *Sir Walter Scott: The Great Unknown* (1970).

"Scott and the Corners of Time." In *Scott Bicentenary Essays.* Ed. Alan Bell. Edinburgh and London: Scottish Academic Press, 1973, pp. 18–37. Also published in condensed form in *Virginia Quarterly Review,* 49 (1973), 46–62.

"Dickens as an Anti-Chauvinist." In *Nineteenth Century Literary Perspective.* Ed. Clyde de L. Ryals. Durham, N.C.: Duke University Press, 1974.

Edgar Johnson has published verse in *Contempo, New Democracy, New English Weekly,* New York *Evening Post,* New York *Herald-Tribune Books,* and *Saturday Review.*

Edgar Johnson has published more than two hundred reviews. These have appeared in *City College Alumnus, City College Campus, Contempo, Contemporary Verse, English Language Notes, Hunter College Bulletin, Journal of Philosophy, Kenyon Review, New Books, New Masses, New Republic,* New York *Herald-Tribune Books,* New York *Evening Post,* New York *Sun,* New York *Teacher,* New York *Times Book Review,* St. Louis *Post-Dispatch, Saturday Review, Science and Society, Victorian Studies,* and *Virginia Quarterly Review.*

CONTRIBUTORS

JEROME H. BUCKLEY is Gurney Professor of English at Harvard University. Among his books are *The Victorian Temper*, 1951, and *Tennyson: The Growth of a Poet*, 1960. His contribution to the present volume is adapted from his *Season of Youth: The Bildungsroman from Dickens to Golding*, 1974.

PHILIP COLLINS, Professor of English at the University of Leicester, is the author of *Dickens and Crime*, 1962, and *Dickens and Education*, and editor of *A Dickens Bibliography*, 1970, and *Dickens: The Critical Heritage*, 1971.

DAVID DAICHES is Professor Emeritus of the University of Sussex. His many books include *The Novel and the Modern World*, rev. ed. 1960, *Some Late Victorian Attitudes*, 1969, and *A Critical History of English Literature*, 2 vols., 2d ed., 1970.

LEON EDEL is Citizens Professor Emeritus, University of Hawaii. His distinguished biography of Henry James was published in four volumes between 1953 and 1972. Other books include *The Psychological Novel*, 1955, *Literary Biography*, 1957, and *Bloomsbury: A House of Lions*, 1979.

GEORGE H. FORD, Professor of English at the University of Rochester, is the author of *Dickens and His Readers*, 1955, editor of Dickens's *Bleak House*, *David Copperfield*, and *Hard Times*, and one of the editors of *The Norton Anthology of English Literature* and of *Victorian Fiction*.

GORDON S. HAIGHT, Professor Emeritus of English at Yale University, is author of *George Eliot: A Biography*, 1968, and editor of the Yale edition of *The George Eliot Letters*, 1954–55, 1978.

FRANCIS RUSSELL HART is Professor of English at the University of Massachusetts and author of *Scott's Novels: The Plotting of Historic Survival*, 1966, *Lockhart as a Romantic Biographer*, 1971, and *The Scottish Novel: From Smollett to Spark*, 1978.

J. HILLIS MILLER is Professor and Chairman of the Department of English at Yale University. His works include *Charles Dickens: The World of His Novels*, 1958, and *The Form of Victorian Fiction*, 1968.

JOHN HENRY RALEIGH is Professor of English at the University of California at Berkeley. Among his books are *Matthew Arnold and American Culture*, 1957, and *Time, Place, and Idea: Essays on the Novel*, 1968.

DAVID ALLAN ROBERTSON, Jr., is McIntosh Professor of English at Barnard College, Columbia University. He is the author of *Sir Charles Eastlake and the Victorian Art World*, 1978.

Contributors

LIONEL STEVENSON, late Professor of English at Duke University, wrote, among other books, *The Ordeal of George Meredith*, 1953, and *The English Novel*, 1960. He was editor of *Victorian Fiction: A Guide to Research*, 1964.

THE EDITORS: Samuel I. Mintz is Professor of English at the City College of New York and the City University Graduate Center. He is a specialist in the history of ideas and the author of *The Hunting of Leviathan*, 1962. Alice Chandler is President of the State University of New York at New Paltz. She is the author of *A Dream of Order: The Medieval Ideal in Nineteenth-Century English Literature*, 1970. Christopher Mulvey is senior lecturer in English and director of American Studies at King Alfred College, Winchester. His study of trans-Atlantic travel impressions in the nineteenth century will be published by Cambridge University Press.

INDEX

Adams, Henry, 163
Adventures of Harry Richmond, The (Meredith), 228
Alemán, Mateo, 17
Allen, Walter, 98
Aristotle, 66, 68
Arnold, Matthew, 4, 139, 149
Auden, W. H., 3, 4, 5
Austen, Jane, 100, 115, 127
  Mansfield Park, 107, 126, 127
  Northanger Abbey, 100
Austin, Alfred, 173
Aytoun, William Edmondstoune, 161

Bachelard, Gaston, 207
Bagehot, Walter, 158, 166, 176
Balzac, Honoré de, 220
Bezzi, Giovanni Aubrey, 249, 250, 251
Bildungsroman, 18, 22, 26, 39
  defined, 212–14
  George Eliot and, 211–36 *passim*
Billington, James, 61, 73
Blake, William, 238, 240
Bloom, Harold, 9
Blount, Trevor, 201
Boswell, James, 5, 7
Brenninkmeyer, Ingrid, 91
Brown, Charles Armitage, 241, 243, 244–45, 247
Browning, Elizabeth Barrett, 252, 256
Browning, Robert, 134, 135–37, 142, 146, 156, 188, 252, 256, 258
Brummell, George Bryan ("Beau"), 84, 93, 94, 125, 128

Bulwer Lytton, Edward George, 86, 92, 93, 108, 118, 123, 127, 129, 132, 146, 147
  Pelham, 106, 129–33
Burke, Edmund, 101
Burney, Fanny, 86, 92, 111, 113, 115, 118
  Camilla, 102–6, 113
  Cecelia, 100–102, 113
  Evelina, 95–100
Burton, Anthony, 185
Butler, Samuel, 39
Byron, George Gordon, Lord, 1, 2, 57, 62, 92, 122, 130, 133
Byronism, 130–31, 153

Canova, Antonio, 239
Catherine the Great, 53, 54, 60, 73
Catherwood, Frederick, 241
Cervantes, Miguel de, 37
Chaadaev, Peter, 50, 53, 71
Character and the Novel (Harvey), 277
Chartreuse de Parme, La (Stendhal), 280
Chaucer, Geoffrey, 7
Citizen of the World, The (Goldsmith), 139
Clarissa (Richardson), 139
Cleland, John, 38
Clough, Arthur Hugh, 134
Cobbett, William, 88, 94
Coleridge, Samuel Taylor, 167
Condorcet, Jean A. N. C., 7
Confessions of a Justified Sinner (Hogg), 142
Conrad, Joseph, 184–85, 187
Conway, Moncure, 163
Crabbe, George, 167

Craft of Fiction, The (Lubbock), 5
Crime and Punishment (Dostoyevsky), 281
Cromwell, Oliver, 60, 67
Cruse, Amy, 129
Cumming, John, 211

Dallas, E. S., 220–21
Dante, 23, 248, 249–52, 253, 256, 257–58
Defoe, Daniel, 11, 17, 37, 137–38, 139, 176, 216, 225, 235
DeQuincey, Thomas, 133, 144
Dickens, Charles, 4, 11, 31, 38, 47, 78, 144, 235
    debt to Smollett, 32, 42
    Bleak House, 158, 169, 180
        significance of lighting in, 183–210 *passim*
    Cricket on the Hearth, The, 208
    David Copperfield, 214, 220
    Great Expectations, 26, 33, 177, 197, 214–15, 220, 235, 280, 283
    Little Dorritt, 163
    Martin Chuzzlewit, 209
    Nicholas Nickleby, 165, 166
    Oliver Twist, 165, 167, 168, 169
    Our Mutual Friend, 44, 164
    Pickwick Papers, 25, 28, 38, 158, 160, 163, 165, 170–71, 209, 210
Disraeli, Benjamin, 86, 92, 93, 118, 123, 129
    Vivian Grey, 106, 129–33
Don Quixote, 12, 279
Dramatic mololoque
    in Browning, 136–37, 142, 156
    origins of, 134–37
    in Thackeray, 142–56

Eastlake, Sir Charles, 239, 240, 241, 242, 251
Edgeworth, Maria, 86, 92, 106, 118, 123
    Absentee, The, 110–12
    Belinda, 106–9, 111
    Patronage, 109–10, 123
Eliot, George, 3, 284, 285
    Adam Bede, 284, 285
    "Brother and Sister" (sonnet sequence), 215–16, 227, 232
    Daniel Deronda, 284
    Middlemarch, 220, 230, 280, 283, 284, 285
    Mill on the Floss, as a Bildungsroman, 211–36 *passim*
Eliot, T. S., 4, 204

Fable of the Bees (Mandeville), 84
Faraday, Michael, 188, 197
Fashion, novel of, 84–133 *passim*
    defined by novelists, 85–86
    defined by social theorists, 84–86, 90–92
Ferrier, Susan, 86, 92, 112, 118, 123
    Destiny, 112
    Inheritance, The, 115–17, 118, 127
    Marriage, 113–15, 117
Fielding, Henry, 11, 153
    Jonathan Wild, 12, 140, 153
    Joseph Andrews, 140
    Tom Jones, 32
Flaxman, John, 239, 248
Fontenelle, Bernard le Bovier de, 7
Ford, Richard, 167
Forster, John, 161, 166
Freud, Sigmund, 7, 8
Fry, Roger, 2, 7
Fuseli, Henry, 239

Garis, Robert, 202
Gibbon, Edward, 52
Gibson, John, 241
Gil Blas (Lesage), 37
Giotto, 249, 250, 251, 252, 257
Goethe, Johann Wolfgang von, 69, 115, 212
Gogol, Nikolai, 61–62, 78
Golden, Morris, 11
Goldsmith, Oliver, 140
Gombrich, Ernst, 280
Gorki, Maxim, 61
Gothic novel, 92, 130
Gulliver's Travels (Swift), 138, 140
Guzmán de Alfarache (Alemán), 17, 40

Hallam, Henry, 52
Hardy, Barbara, 277
Harvey, W. J., 277

INDEX | 299

Hawthorne, Nathaniel, 163, 238, 254
Haydon, Benjamin Robert, 238, 239, 241, 252, 253
Hayter, George, 245, 246
Hazlitt, William, 133, 172, 244
Heart of Darkness (Conrad), 187
Hegel, Georg Wilhelm Friedrich, 67
Hemingway, Ernest, 209
Herzen, Aleksandr, 50, 60
History of the Devil (Defoe), 216
History of the Russian State (Karamzin), 49–50
Hobsbawm, E. J., 89
Hogg, James, 142
Home, Henry, Lord Kames, 18
Hook, Theodore, 86, 118, 143
 Gilbert Gurney, 120–21
 Sayings and Doings, 118
Horace, 123
Horne, R. H., 172
House, Humphry, 174
Hugo, Victor, 67
Hume, David, 52
Hunt, Leigh, 247

Ibsen, Henrik, 172
L'Innomable (Beckett), 279
Inset histories, 32, 38
Irving, Washington, 161, 170

Jack, Ian, 127
Jacques le fataliste (Diderot), 280
James, Henry, 1, 2, 4, 5
 on Dickens, 163–64
 on George Eliot, 214, 220, 233
 Ambassadors, The 261–76 *passim*
Jarves, James Jackson, 252
Jeaffreson, J. C. 178–79
Johnson, Edgar, 4, 181–82
Johnson, Dr. Samuel, 5, 8
Joyce, James, 5
Jude the Obscure (Hardy), 213–18

Kafka, Franz, 5
Karamzin, Nikolai, 50, 51, 60, 62, 71
Keats, John, 204, 241, 242
Kermode, Frank, 187
Kipling, Rudyard, 148

Kirkup, Seymour, 237–60 *passim*
Knapp, Lewis, 11
König, René, 84, 90, 91, 92

Lamb, William, 2d Viscount Melbourne, 168
Landor, Walter Savage, 243–44, 256
Lamb, Charles, 144
Lane, Margaret, 207
Lawrence, D. H., 184, 185, 225
Lawrence, Sir Thomas, 239, 241
Layard, A. H., 253, 256, 257
Leavis, F. R., 11, 226, 277
Lewes, G. H., 162, 166, 176, 179, 211, 216, 233
Liddell, Robert, 205
Lister, Thomas Henry, 86, 118, 123, 127, 129, 165
 Arlington, 127–29
 Granby, 124–27
 Herbert Lacy, 93, 127
Literary Biography (Edel), 6
Lockhart, J. G., 133
Lord Jim (Conrad), 280

Mackenzie, Henry, 18
Mandeville, Bernard, 84
Martineau, Harriet, 161
Martz, Louis, 98
Marx, Karl, 174
Masson, David, 176, 177
McCarthy, Justin, 159
Memoirs of a Woman of Pleasure (Cleland), 38
Meredith, George, 134
Michelet, Jules, 1, 6, 52
Mill, John Stuart, 169
Miller, J. Hillis, 187, 208
Milton, John, 67
Moby-Dick (Melville), 197
Moers, Ellen, 126
Moll Flanders (Defoe), 17, 24, 41, 138
Morazé, Charles, 86, 87
Morris, Mowbray, 159
Morris, William, 134

Nabokov, Vladimir, 3, 4
New Criticism, 9

Nietzsche, Friedrich, 284–85
Norton, Charles Eliot, 259
Nouveau roman, 5

Oliphant, Margaret, 172
Ordeal of Richard Feverel (Meredith), 213, 220
Orsay, Count Alfred d', 128
Owen Robert, 174

Paradise Lost, 215
Parker, A. A., 17, 24, 25
Parkman, Francis, 163
Parreaux, André, 93
Pater, Walter, 281
Peter the Great, 52, 53, 54, 83
Picaresque novel, 17, 40
Plautus, 148
Plumb, J. H., 86, 88, 90
Plutarch, 6
Pogodin, Mikhail, 50, 53, 54
Portrait of the Artist as a Young Man (Joyce), 213, 236
Prelude, The (Wordsworth), 107, 232
Price, Martin, 277
Proust, Marcel, 3, 5
Pugachev, Emalian, 54, 55, 56, 57–61, 73–75, 77–83 *passim*
Pushkin, Aleksandr, 48–83 *passim*
  on history and historiography, 50, 52–54
  influenced by Scott, 48–49, 62, 68
  Angelo, 64
  Boris Gudonov, 51, 63
  Bronze Horseman, The, 55, 58–59
  Captain's Daughter, The 48, 55, 61, 63, 65, 72, 73–80, 83
  Dubrovsky, 72–73, 83
  History of the Pugachev Rebellion, 55, 59
  Negro of Peter the Great, The, 55, 72–73, 83
  "Of Walter Scott's Novels," 69
  Poltava, 51
  Songs About Stenka Razin, 56
  Table Talk, 58
Pygmalion (Shaw), 39

Ray, Gordon, 4
Razin, Stenka, 55, 56, 58, 61, 80, 83

Red and the Black, The (Stendhal), 220
Renwick, W. L., 106
Richardson, Samuel, 11, 139, 140
Rise of the Novel, The (Watt), 11
Robbe-Grillet, Alain, 200
Robinson Crusoe (Defoe), 138, 283
Rosa, M. W., 121
Rossetti, Dante Gabriel, 134, 251
Rossetti, Gabriele, 248, 251
Rossini, Gioacchino, 252
Rousseau, Jean Jacques, 108, 115, 122
Rudé, George, 88
Ruskin, John, 200

Sackville-West, Edward, 3
Sainte-Beuve, Charles Augustin, 3
Sala, George, 192
Sand, George, 83
Sapir, Edward, 90
Sartor Resartus (Carlyle), 130
Scott, Walter, 11, 31, 47, 48–83 *passim*, 141
  Bride of Lammermoor, The, 65
  Fortunes of Nigel, The, 32
  Heart of Midlothian, The, 63, 64
  Ivanhoe, 72, 81
  Rob Roy, 79, 142
  Waverley, 72, 73–77, 79
  Woodstock, 67
Secret Agent, The (Conrad), 187
Sense of an Ending (Kermode), 187
Sensibility, cult of, 18, 32, 46–47
Sentimental Journey (Sterne), 46
Severn, Joseph, 241, 242
Shakespeare, William, 4, 7, 28, 37, 43, 64–65, 69, 160, 176, 179
Shaw, George Bernard, 39
Shelley, Percy Bysshe, 133, 242, 243
"Silver Fork" novelists, 106, 121
Sims, George R., 171
Smollett, Tobias, 11–47 *passim*, 141
  Adventures of an Atom, 46
  Ferdinand Count Fathom, 12, 40–46
  Humphry Clinker, 11, 15, 18–21, 30, 141
  Peregrine Pickle, 12, 17, 24, 32–37
    as source of Shaw's *Pygmalion*, 39–40

Smollett, Tobias (*cont.*)
   Regicide, The, 29
   Roderick Random, 12, 17, 18, 23–24, 26–28, 30, 32
   Sir Launcelot Greaves, 12, 15, 21–22
   Travels in France and Italy, 46
Smollett and the Scottish School (Golden), 11
Sons and Lovers (Lawrence), 213, 218, 236
Sontag, Susan, 200
Stendhal, 220
Stephen, James Fitzjames, 173
Sterne, Laurence, 141
Stott, George, 175
Strachey, Lytton, 2, 6
Swinburne, Algernon Charles, 134, 230, 238, 247, 256
Swift, Jonathan, 37, 139

Tacitus, 52
Taine, Hippolyte, 172
Talon, Henri, 183
Tennyson, Alfred, Lord, 134, 135
Thackeray, William Makepeace, 4, 47, 123, 158, 170, 177
   dramatic monologues in, 142–56 *passim*
   Adventures of Philip, 155
   Barry Lyndon, 12, 153–54, 155
   "Epistles to the Literati," 147
   "FitzBoodle" stories, 149–50
   Henry Esmond, 155
   Memoirs of Mr. C. J. Yellowplush, 145–47
   Newcomes, The, 155
   Pendennis, 155–56
   "Ramsbottom Letters," 143
   Some Passages in the Life of Major Gahagan, 148–49

"Titmarsh" papers and tales, 150–52
Vanity Fair, 24, 119, 154–55
Thomas à Kempis, 217, 226, 228
To the Lighthouse (Virginia Woolf), 283
Tolstoy, Leo, 67, 75
Ton, 84, 102, 104, 110, 116, 131; *see also* Fashion, novel of
Trelawny, Edward, 242, 246
Tristram Shandy (Sterne), 33, 140
Trollope, Anthony, 123

Ulysses (Joyce), 279

Vaughan, Henry, 31
Vernon, Lord, 247–48, 251
Vicar of Wakefield, The (Goldsmith), 140
Victoria (Queen of England), 168
Vigny, Alfred de, 67
Voltaire, 51, 130

Ward, R. P., 86, 92, 118, 123, 129
   DeVere; or, The Man of Independence, 123–24
   Tremaine, 106, 108, 121–23
Waste Land, The (Eliot), 204
Waves, The (Virginia Woolf), 279
Way of All Flesh, The (Butler), 39, 213, 218
Whipple, Edwin P., 177–78
Wilde, Richard Henry, 249, 250
Wilhelm Meister (Goethe), 211
Women in Love (Lawrence), 185
Woolf, Virginia, 1–2, 3, 7, 226, 277
Wordsworth, William, 133, 167, 214, 216, 232

Yeats, William Butler, 2–3
Young, G. M., 174

DATE DUE			

WITHDRAWN from the Alma College Library

DEMCO 38-297